D0071706

CREATIVE

REHOMING

FOR DOGS

JACQUELINE O'NEIL

ILLUSTRATIONS BY DEBRA K. WAGNER

HOWELL
BOOK HOUSE
NEW YORK

Howell Book House
A Simon & Schuster Macmillan Company
1633 Broadway
New York, NY 10019

MACMILLAN is a registered trademark of Macmillan, Inc.

Library of Congress Cataloging-in-Publication Data:
O'Neil, Jacqueline.
    Second start: creative rehoming for dogs / Jacqueline O'Neil: illustrations
by Debra K. Wagner.
        p. cm.
    ISBN 0-87605-729-6
    1. Dogs.   I. Title.
SF427.057   1997
636.7'088'7--dc21   96-38045
                                          CIP

99 98 97 8 7 6 5 4 3 2

Interpretation of the printing code: the rightmost number of the first series of
numbers is the year of the book's printing; the rightmost number of the second series of numbers is the number of the book's printing. For example, a
printing code of 97-1 shows that the first printing occurred in 1997.

Printed in the United States of America

Design by Heather Kern

DEDICATION

■

To my cousins,
Barbara and Aaron Furman.
Thanks for being there for me
when I needed a second start.

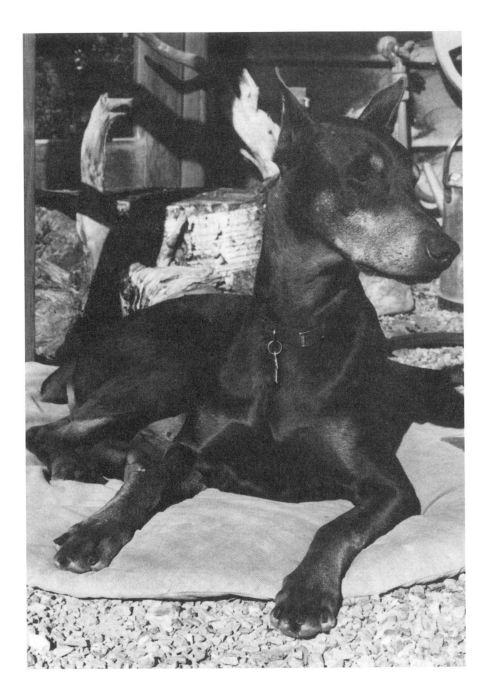

TABLE OF CONTENTS

■

ACKNOWLEDGMENTS

Illustrator Debra K. Wagner gave my pages personality, and photographer Paulette Braun, of Pets by Paulette, gave them beauty and charm. Thank you, talented friends.

Judy Marden, Dave Wedum, and Gee Weaver furthered my education about rescued and fostered dogs and allowed me to quote them. Thank you, caring friends.

Dr. Mary Bruch, psychologist, contributed a section on transitions and their effect on pet ownership. Thank you, intellectual friend.

My editor Seymour Weiss suggested the subject of this book. I tried to do your idea justice, my creative friend, and I'm sure that after your excellent editing we'll both be proud of it.

My husband Tom O'Neil took several of the photographs for this book, put up with my moods when the computer acted up, and kept smiling. Thanks, darlin'.

PART ONE

LOOKING FOR LOVE

Older dogs still love to play. P.J., an eight-year-old Golden Retriever, retrieves a stick at a gallop.

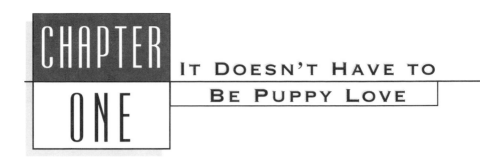

CHAPTER ONE

IT DOESN'T HAVE TO BE PUPPY LOVE

Bentley has come a long way since he was found tied to a tree beside an abandoned house in Joliet, Illinois. Chip and Janet Warrick adopted the starving Mastiff and quickly discovered he had a great smile and a jolly nature in spite of his past. Through a bit of babying and a nutritious diet, the Warricks added ninety pounds to Bentley's big, bony frame and he now weighs a formidable 210.

Last year the Warricks' neighborhood voted Bentley "Dog of the Year." "He's everybody's best friend," says Chip Warrick. "He loves his daily walk and visits all his young friends along the way. Our own three grandchildren are crazy about him and the feeling is mutual.

Once neglected and practically dead from starvation, gentle Bentley, a Mastiff, was voted "Dog of the Year" by his neighborhood.

Since they are two, four, and six, Bentley has to put up with a lot of aggravation but he seems to look forward to it."

The Warricks' success with Bentley is repeated thousands of times every year by people who realize the advantages of acquiring an adult dog. But what about puppies? Isn't it a shame to miss all the cute stages?

Yes, puppies are precious. Some are softer than a stuffed teddy; others have winsome ringlets framing their charming faces; and all of them feel wonderfully warm in your arms. Puppies are vivacious and fun-loving and indulge in antics guaranteed to elicit your love and laughter. In fact, puppies have a lot in common with human babies. While lovely to look at and delightful to hold, they need constant supervision and frequent feeding. They also eat sloppily, go potty often, teethe on whatever they can reach, and sleep a lot (but not on your schedule). Curious and bright, puppies learn quickly, as long as their owners are consistent and take the time to teach them. Are they worth it? Of course they are—provided you keep a regular schedule, have plenty of patience, and enough time for long-term training.

So before falling in puppy love, ask yourself if you, or someone in your family, will be available to look after a puppy every time it needs food, a potty break, or general supervision. Without constant supervision, your puppy may teethe on the furniture, soil the rug, or even lap up something poisonous. Sure your puppy will eventually grow up to be a clean, sensible dog. But only if you keep it on a regular schedule and teach it good house manners and social graces.

Are you fated to be dog-deprived because of your work schedule? Or because you don't relish the time-consuming task of raising a puppy? No way! You don't have to go dogless just because you can't make it home every three or four hours. If you have time to enjoy a dog, but can't (or don't want to) meet a puppy's demanding schedule, there is a solution. Skip the frequent feeding and teething stages. Open your heart and home to an adult dog.

ADVANTAGES OF AN ADULT DOG

Many adult dogs are already housebroken and limit their chewing to their own toys. Such dogs are extremely desirable as they will need only a little guidance to transfer their good habits to your home. Mature dogs also have bigger bladders and longer attention spans than puppies. So even if the grown dog of your choice isn't housebroken, it will probably learn house manners much quicker than a puppy would.

You can learn a great deal about an adult dog's personality before deciding whether to take it home. Plus, you won't have to guess about its mature size, appearance, and how much grooming it needs. Another bonus of adult dogs is that they often become family guardians within a few weeks of entering a new home, while puppies seldom bark a warning until they are between seven and fourteen months old.

As you will see, both dynamite dogs and destitute dogs are available if you know where to find them, and both of them need a second start. Dynamite dogs have beautiful bodies, shiny coats, great dispositions, and previous training. They are lovely, affectionate animals you can enjoy and take pride in from the first day you bring one home. Destitute dogs, on the other hand, are survivors. They've been through tough times and it shows. Their coats are matted and dry, their bodies emaciated, even scarred. In many cases, their lives depend upon someone giving them a second start right away. If you choose a destitute dog, the period of adjustment will be longer. Your dog will need time to learn to trust again, and its body may not glow with health for many months. But when it does (and it will), you'll feel the special pride of not just having saved a life, but of having re-created one!

Wait a minute! Aren't dogs supposed to be beloved family members? So if an adult dog is available, doesn't that mean it has a serious behavior or health problem, something that keeps it from being a good companion?

WHERE ADULT DOGS COME FROM

Mature dogs lose their homes for a wide variety of reasons, and many of those reasons are not the animal's fault. Some disappointed their owners by not growing up with the superior conformation (appearance) necessary to win dog shows. Others won a championship title, were used by a fine kennel to breed the next generation of champions, and are now ready for retirement to a private home. Corporate moves, divorces, terminal illnesses, allergies, and the owner's death are all reasons why perfectly nice dogs need a second start. Another reason is unrealistic expectations. Some people fail to do any research before getting a dog and purchase the wrong breed for their lifestyle. Yet that same dog might be the ideal match for another person. For example, a terrier that belonged to the vice president of a garden club lost its home because it persisted in digging around its owner's prize roses. A rural family gave it a second start. Today it plays tirelessly with the children and pleases the parents by digging up and killing the gophers that damage their pasture. The digging instinct that was so objectionable in the dog's first home is highly prized in its second and permanent home.

Of course, not every adult dog needing a second start is an ideal companion just waiting to brighten your life. Some are in mourning for a beloved owner who died or abandoned them, and will need a few months of one-way affection before they bond with a new owner. Others have behavior problems their previous owners couldn't or wouldn't tolerate—problems that can be cured through simple, consistent training. In fact, objectionable behavior sometimes disappears as if by magic when a dog moves to a different environment. Of course some behaviors, like the terrier's instinctive digging, don't change, but are either neutral or desirable in the new home.

Sadly, some dogs' problems result from neglect, or even abuse. Such dogs need a special person as their new owner—someone with the patience to understand the dog's initial fear and distrust, take it one day at a time, and not get their feelings hurt when they encounter minor setbacks.

A few dogs have behavior problems that are beyond rehabilitation. Their previous owners couldn't handle them and neither should you. Don't worry. This isn't one of those "the dog is always right and the owner is always to blame" books. Some dogs, like some people, are impossible. This book will tell you how to recognize and avoid the few truly bad ones—those that bring nothing to a relationship but havoc and heartache.

Sometimes dogs with physical defects are given up for adoption by owners who can't afford the price of treatment. Some of these dogs would live long, active lives following a routine surgical procedure. Others will stay healthy for years provided they get daily medication. Are they worth the effort? It depends on the dog and the situation. Chapter 3 will help you find the right dog for your personality and lifestyle, a search surprisingly similar to finding the ideal human mate. When the right one comes along and you know it, it's prudent to overlook minor imperfections. Besides, too much perfection, in dogs or in people, can be downright boring!

So where do adult dogs come from? They come from show dog kennels and they come from "death row" at the pound. They come from purebred rescue groups and they come from service dog organizations. They come from field trailers, hunters, and "free to good home" ads in the newspaper. They come from college kids who graduate and move to the city to begin careers, and they come from the death beds of the terminally ill. Some have had years of top-notch training. Others were never even taught their names. Some are so beautiful strangers on the street ask permission to pet them. Others are so wretched you wonder if they will ever look better. Some are young adults, barely past puppyhood. Others are long past their prime. Some are registered purebreds. It's impossible to guess the ancestry of others. What do so many diverse dogs have in common? All of them need a second start, and most of them will make wonderful companions.

BUT WHAT IF . . . ?

Acquiring a dog is a major emotional investment, so you may be asking yourself, "What if the Warricks were just especially lucky, and an adult dog brings me nothing but heartache? For example, will I have lots of veterinary bills with a mature dog? What if I fall for an older dog, only to have it die in a few short years?"

When it comes to long-term health, there are no guarantees, not for puppies, adult dogs, or even people. In truth, an adult dog that has been well cared for during its life often has fewer health problems than a young puppy, and is usually through with messy puppy problems such as diarrhea and vomiting. And while it's true that older dogs can develop heart trouble or kidney disorders, puppies can get their share of serious problems too. The bottom line is healthy middle-aged dogs are at no special risk, but you should expect higher veterinary bills during the first year if you adopt a destitute dog. It may be several months until such a dog is completely healthy.

While most adult dogs in need of a second start are relatively young (usually between one and five years of age), life span is certainly a consideration if your search for the perfect dog leads you to an animal well past its prime. But think hard before turning away. Even a few fabulous years with just the right dog is an opportunity worth seizing, as illustrated by the story of this golden oldie.

MAGNIFICENT MAXWELL

Found by a fisherman, the forlorn, old Doberman Pinscher was waiting beside a back country bridge for owners who never returned. The fisherman took him to the pound where the employees' hearts went out to the gentle red dog with the graying muzzle. They called volunteer Myni Ferguson and told her to come down and see their "old baby" because they knew Dobes were her favorite breed.

Myni wasn't in any hurry to see the dog because she was afraid she would end up taking him home and she really didn't want to adopt an elderly pet. So she procrastinated. Hours later, when she felt she couldn't put it off any longer, she made the visit. On her way, she stopped by the office of the veterinarian who worked for the shelter and asked him if he had seen the old Dobe yet. He told her the dog had undescended testicles (orchidism) and the testicles were tumorized and should be removed immediately. Other than that, all the dog needed were regular meals and affection and he'd be in fine shape for his advanced age.

When Myni arrived at the pound, she was greeted by a sad employee. "That sweet old Dobe has tumors," the young woman said with tears in her eyes. "He has to be euthanized."

"Not if the person who adopts him pays for an operation," Myni said. "I just talked to the vet and he said it's a simple surgery."

The employee's face paled and her breath caught in her throat. "Oh no," she wailed and ran from the room.

A few minutes later she returned, helping her co-workers lug the nearly unconscious dog down the hallway. The shelter workers were laughing through their tears. In another moment, the big dog that had captured their hearts would have died by lethal injection. Now he was almost unconscious because they had sedated him heavily to prep him for euthanasia. They didn't want the trusting old soul to realize something bad was happening.

Myni took him straight to the veterinarian who quipped, "Looks like he's already prepped for surgery."

When Myni returned to the veterinarian's office the following day to pick up the dog that had never met her, a grinning nurse said, "Wait till you see the old boy now."

Maxwell Plum, a Doberman Pinscher, shares a snooze with his feline friend, Marvie.

A few seconds later, the door to the kenneling area opened and a jovial red flash bounded through. He trotted around the waiting room visiting each dog owner and staff member briefly, then circled Myni, sat by her side, and leaned against her leg.

Myni named her new dog Maxwell Plum and took him along when she gave animal education presentations at the mall. "His idea of heaven was being covered with babies," she said. Maxwell also became a therapy dog, cheering other oldsters at the local nursing home. He lived three more years and brought smiles to hundreds of faces.

Since Maxwell, Myni has continued rescuing abandoned or abused Doberman Pinschers, carefully matching them up with new families and educating their owners in dog care and training. It's an ongoing avocation. "Only one in five dogs remains in its first home forever," she said. "There are always wonderful pets in need of new homes through no fault of their own."

If you are captivated by a graying muzzle and don't know if you should take a chance, this bit of philosophy may help. At best, dogs have short life spans when compared to people. Almost everyone who loves a dog eventually endures loss and grief, but we cherish our marvelous memories and learn to love another dog.

CANINE SPECIALISTS

With so many opportunities to acquire an adult dog, finding one that already has good house manners may be easier than you think. But many people have done even better than that. Mature dogs with specialized training are often available. For the livestock owner, this could mean a herding dog that's already accomplished at working stock. For the animal-assisted therapy volunteer, it could be a retired show dog who loves hamming it up for an adoring audience. For the hunter, it could mean a professionally trained hunting companion, like George R. Quittner's second start English Springer Spaniels, Chip and Dream.

Until a few years ago, George competed in field trials and went hunting with dogs he had raised and trained from puppies. But when cancer took the last one just as the 1990 hunting season was about to begin, George needed a dog who already knew how to hunt. He wanted a trained adult.

George called some of the kennels that advertise in *Gun Dog* magazine and inquired about purchasing a mature hunting dog. He was soon networked to a kennel where there was a five-year-old English Springer Spaniel named Chocolate Chip. Originally purchased as a puppy by a family with young children, Chip had been professionally trained for the home before being sent out for field trial training. But she failed as both a field trial competitor and a house dog, and was returned to her breeder. Believing she could still become a winner in the field, the breeder sent her to several professional handlers, but nothing helped. Bred and trained for excellence, Chip's field work was considered only "very good," and that's not enough to win in tough competition. Her breeder told George, "Chip did everything right, but she never did win a field trial."

Many dogs that aren't quick enough to win field trials are exactly the right speed to be ideal hunting companions, and George knew it. Two weeks after he purchased Chip they went hunting and have been successful partners in the field ever since. During the mid-90s, George wanted a second dog and acquired Dream, another field trial dog who failed to win trophies. "I waited only three weeks after getting Dream till I hunted over her and she is the happiest and most biddable dog I've ever worked," George said.

Now George is an advocate of acquiring older dogs and says the advantages far outweigh the cuteness of those puppy years. "I can't

Chip, an English Springer Spaniel and hunting specialist, makes a stylish retrieve.

imagine anyone really enjoying the teething, puberty, or the terrible twos stages of a growing dog," he says. His wife agrees. She calls Chip "robo dog" because the first day Chip entered the house she was shown her place in the family room and stayed there until told it was okay to go elsewhere. Chip never has had an accident in the house and doesn't touch anything unless someone gives it to her. Dream also has impeccable manners, and both dogs are good travelers.

George also found that older dogs bond easily. "Early in its first week of transition, I fuss over a new dog," he says. "This includes generous doses of petting and gentle talk, making sure it eats, and brushing its coat. Spending time together helps us get used to each other. Also, I do nothing negative during the transition period so the dog builds trust in me and my family. Chip adjusted instantly while Dream took about a week until she eagerly came to any family member who called her. Both are extremely affectionate and obey all of us. Some dogs I've raised from puppies only responded to me as their trainer, in spite of being raised as family dogs.

"The bottom line is I am committed to buying older dogs and letting others raise pups," George says. "The cost of a fully trained gun dog is about the same or less than that of a good pup, and a pup has to go to the veterinarian regularly and may need professional training to hunt as well as my old girls. It's such a pleasure to go afield right after acquiring my new partner without having to go through the frustrating years of yard work and field training. There are so many opportunities to ruin a pup, and sometimes it doesn't even have the strong hunting instinct it was bred for. With a grown dog, you see what you get and you can get what you want. The older dog just wants someone to care for it and fuss over it. It's a fair trade and the owner wins. Who knows how many older dogs would relish a home, close friendship, and an opportunity to do the work they were bred for?"

MOVING ALONG RIGHT

Does acquiring an adult make dog ownership sound more like a possibility? Can you almost feel a dog's silken head leaning against your knee? If so, it's time to ask yourself the most important question of all: Do I really want a dog? Not just today, but ten years from today? So read on. The next chapter will help you decide.

Kate, a Labrador Retriever, relaxes with the Werner children, Nikolas, 18 months, and Taylor, 3.

Kirk Werner and his wife of Monroe, Washington, were about to buy a Labrador Retriever puppy when they decided that a seven-week-old pup was not a good idea. The Werners' two children were both under four, so the puppy wouldn't get the time and attention it needed and deserved. An adult dog that already had some training sounded like a better idea.

Kirk had heard that adult dogs don't forge nearly as close a bond with their new owners as puppies raised from infancy, but still believed an adult made sense in his situation. So the Werners started looking for an adult Labrador Retriever with a nice, calm temperament.

They located one-year-old Kate through an ad in the newspaper and the whole family went to "interview" her. She had been raised with children, dogs, and horses, and greeted the Werners with sweetness and charm. When they left, they were a family of five and Kate bonded in no time.

"Kate has always been a sweet-natured and tolerant friend to our kids, who climb on her and treat her with all the respect that toddlers have historically shown dogs," Kirk said. "She has taken to our home as if it were the only one she ever had, and we're happier now than before she arrived."

With age often comes good sense. Ten-year-old Odie, a mixed-bred, baby-sits a two-week-old chick.

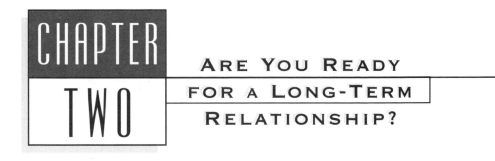

CHAPTER TWO

ARE YOU READY FOR A LONG-TERM RELATIONSHIP?

Can money ever buy you love? Sure. Just use the money to buy a dog. Dogs don't waffle when it comes to making permanent commitments. Without hesitation, they promise to love and protect you for the rest of their lives (but if you want "obey" added to the oath, you'll have to earn it through training). Having a dog makes you healthier. Medical science has proven that enjoying an animal's companionship helps you relax and may even lower your blood pressure. Besides, dogs give you an incentive to enjoy long walks on lovely spring days. A dog will also enhance your circle of friends. Dog owners naturally gravitate to each other when out walking their pets, and it's easy to meet people with common interests while attending training classes or other dog-related events.

But while dog ownership usually adds exciting new dimensions to a person's life, it doesn't always work out that way. An occasional owner views the dog as nothing more than a burdensome responsibility; an incredibly sad situation for dog and owner. Yet these unhappy owners must have thought they wanted a dog or they wouldn't have gotten one. What went wrong with their owner-dog relationships, and how can you keep it from happening to you?

SOMETIMES TIMING IS EVERYTHING

People often become impatient and acquire their dog too soon—before they have the time and stability to enjoy it. Bad timing is one reason why many nice dogs are neglected or even lose their unhappy homes. So before debating what kind of dog you want, it's smart to decide whether owning any dog fits into your life right now. Asking yourself the following questions should help.

Can I Afford a Dog?

The initial price of a dog is only one of the costs to consider. All dogs need food and shelter, annual vaccinations, regular worming, preventative medication for heartworm, a collar and leash, grooming equipment, their own dishes, a variety of toys, and occasional treats. They also need veterinary care when they are sick or hurt, and should be spayed or neutered. Some dogs also need professional grooming at a salon every six weeks or so. If none of those items poses a financial burden, ask yourself if you could afford emergency treatment if your dog broke its leg. Priorities may come into play. If your dog's accident would put you on a budget of beans for a month, be sure you and your family would be willing to make the sacrifice.

Will I Enjoy a Dog's Dependence?

Unlike children, dogs don't grow up and become independent enough to take care of their own hair, make their own breakfast, or bathe themselves. In fact, your dog will depend on you for daily care all its life. For most dog owners, the brief daily routine is relaxing and warm; a favorite, fun part of their day. But if years of caring for a dependent dog sounds like a drag, that's exactly how it will feel.

If you're thinking about getting a dog because your children want one, I bet they promised to do all the grooming, feeding, potty training, walking, and cleaning chores. Don't believe it. Yes, children can acquire a sense of responsibility from helping with dog care, but they shouldn't be left totally in charge of the process (the exception is an older child who spent several years working with the family dog in a 4-H project and is probably ready for a dog of his or her own). Dog care should be a family affair with other family members ready to substitute if Junior has basketball tryouts on his night to feed and walk Prince.

Division of labor should be discussed before a family acquires a dog, but don't expect it to be set in stone. In the end, someone has to take overall responsibility to make sure Prince has fresh water, is fed on schedule, is walked when he indicates a need to go potty (or allowed out if the yard is fenced), is exercised, trained, groomed, and has his feces removed from the yard. Since you are the one reading this book, that person will probably be you. So you should be the one who decides if you will relish or resent the responsibility.

Is My Life Missing a Dog?

Dogs purchased for the sole purpose of improving a boring life are often ignored once their novelty wears off. This is heartbreaking and incredibly unfair to a loyal pet. Before acquiring a dog, ask yourself if you are prepared to love one for its entire life, not just use it for a brief interlude of entertainment. But that doesn't mean it's wrong to think a dog will add zest to your life. Loving a dog is life-affirming in itself, and involvement in dog activities, such as agility trials and animal-assisted therapy, can add excitement and accomplishment to a once mundane existence. Still not sure? Ask yourself this: Is ten years of love and commitment from a dog what I really want, or would two weeks in Tahiti be equally gratifying?

Do I Have Time to Give a Dog Affection, Training, and Exercise?

A new dog will need more of your time during the period of adjustment (your first few months together) than at any other time, but it will always need and deserve some of your time. One of the reasons we love dogs so much is because they are social animals. Dogs give and desire affection. They also need daily exercise, grooming, and an occasional brush-up on their training. You may have time on your hands today, and wish those hands were petting a Pug or throwing a Frisbee for a frolicsome retriever, but think to the future before getting a dog. Do you have a demanding career? Climbing the corporate ladder might mean moving every few years, or working such long hours that a gleeful dog greeting you at the door might feel more like pressure than privilege. Are you planning to raise a family? Once the babies come, will you have enough time and energy to tend them without ignoring your dog? Are you in college? Inexpensive rentals in university towns often accept dogs, but when you move on and start your career it might be hard to find an affordable rental that permits pets.

Will a Dog Fit Into My Home, Family, and Lifestyle?

Your spouse's feelings, your children's ages, the size and location of your home, your activity level, and your travel plans are all important considerations when deciding whether to make a dog part of your family. Bringing a dog home when your spouse doesn't want one is unfair to everyone. Sure, there are cases where the reluctant spouse learns to love the dog, but there are even more cases where one partner never came around. Having to defend your dog on a daily basis

Kids and dogs go together like milk and cookies. This is happy Odie, the mixed-bred we met in Chapter 1, and his friend is Amelia Thornton.

becomes tiresome and reduces the pleasure of dog ownership. In fact, many perfectly nice dogs are residing in the pound because their owners decided keeping them wasn't worth the hassles at home.

If your children are still babies or toddlers, do yourself a favor and wait a few years before acquiring a dog. Children and dogs go together like milk and cookies, but only after the kids are old enough to understand the difference between a living animal and a stuffed toy.

Dogs need daily exercise, and while a few breeds can get their workout in a studio apartment, most of them need either a brisk walk or access to a fenced yard. They also need to go outdoors to relieve themselves. If you have a fenced yard, that's no problem, but it's a big consideration if you live in a fifth floor walk-up. And yet millions of people in city apartments delight in their dogs and walk them before and after work—rain, snow, sleet, or shine. Also, many city parks include a safely-fenced area where dogs can run and play with each other while their owners watch and chat.

How you feel about your home is another consideration. Is the atmosphere casual and relaxed, the kind of place where the kids eat popcorn in their bean bag chairs while watching cartoons? Or is it immaculate and perfectly appointed, the kind of place where the family removes their shoes before walking on the cream-colored carpet? While some dogs are exceedingly clean and some breeds shed very little, even the cleanest and most reliably trained dog may become ill one day and make a mess in spite of itself. When that day comes, will the accident be treated as a brief annoyance or a major tragedy?

When dog-owning families go on vacation, they either board their dog or take it along (unless they are blessed with reliable friends or relatives who volunteer to dog sit). With a little advance planning, it's easy to find motels and campgrounds that accept dogs. But if you live alone and are a frequent business traveler, consider the expense of boarding your dog or hiring a house sitter every time you have to leave town.

MOVING ALONG RIGHT

If you've answered these questions and are still ready to leap into loving a dog, slow down. That old saying, "Look before you leap," was never truer than it is here. For a happy owner-dog relationship, both partners must be right for each other. So read on. Chapter 3 will help you determine what type of dog matches your personality and lifestyle.

Dog Wanted: *Mannerly, intelligent, and affectionate small- to medium-sized dog that gets along well with people and other dogs and enjoys going for walks, sitting on laps, and being babied. Curly hair and learning tricks easily are plusses. I will care for you all your life. You will be nice to my grandchildren and put up with them playing dress up with you. Please respond to 555-8765.*

Owner Wanted: *Someone to cuddle me. I'm small and smart with curly hair. Also housebroken and easy to get along with. I like friendly people, well-behaved dogs, and nice kids of all ages. Sitting beside you, or on your lap, is my favorite hobby. Going for walks is good too. My owners and I loved each other but their adopted baby is allergic to me. Please call the boarding kennel at 555-5678.*

Dog Wanted: *Strong, athletic, and active large dog that's into jogging, playing ball, cross-country hiking, and camping out. Cool if you look tough, but must be enough of a gentleman so my girlfriend likes you too. Prefer short hair. If you can hunt, that's a plus. No couch potatoes. Beep me at 877-555-1234.*

Owner Wanted: *Macho and muscular big dog with sleek coat wants an active owner who likes outdoor sports. Mean mug, but big heart. Willing to learn manners if you'll teach me. Don't answer if you're the type who will give me away because I need lots of exercise. Been there and done that. Want lasting relationship. Ask for tag #1357 at the animal shelter.*

CHAPTER THREE

MAKING A MATCH

Opposites often attract, but they seldom make for a rewarding relationship between people and their dogs.

WHY PEOPLE "DIVORCE" THEIR DOGS

Mismatches occur between owners and dogs just as they do between human couples. Sometimes it's a no-fault situation. For example, a young computer programmer who lives alone in a studio apartment in uptown Manhattan fell in love with a retriever puppy. A dedicated cybernaut, Laura purchased Zack and assumed he would be her patient companion while she spent her evenings on-line. Bred to be both enthusiastic and intelligent, Zack soon grew into a large athletic animal, starved for attention, exercise, and an outlet for his inherited retrieving talents. In his frustration, he became a destructive and noisy nuisance. In her frustration, Laura placed an ad in the paper offering the retriever to a good home. Adopted by a family with three active children who include him in games of fetch and catch, Zack thrives. Meanwhile, Laura felt lonely in her empty apartment and tried again. This time she went on-line and asked her cybernaut friends for advice. They sent information on several suitable breeds and a few leads on available adult dogs. Laura soon found her perfect match in Muff, a tiny Maltese whose owner was moving to a nursing home. Muff is easily exercised in an apartment and loves cuddling on Laura's lap while she surfs the Internet.

It would be great if all mismatches were resolved so easily, but Zack was lucky. Many human halves of a mismatch resolve their frustration by discarding their dog at an animal shelter and telling themselves that it will probably get a good home. In truth, it probably will not. Many shelters are crowded, understaffed, and poorly funded. They have no choice but to euthanize animals that aren't adopted within a given brief time period. And depending on the shelter and the situation, that period may be as short as a week.

While housing a large, active dog like Zack in a small space without regard for his physical or emotional needs was an obvious mistake, there are many other potential mismatches. For example, large, active dogs and speedy, small dogs are both a poor match for a senior citizen (or anyone else) who has trouble getting around. Tiny dogs and temperamental breeds seldom fit into families with toddlers. Profusely coated dogs soon become matted if their owners neglect grooming requirements, and tiny, fragile dogs are often overwhelmed by a houseful of lively children.

While mismatches are often tragic for dogs, they are also disheartening for their owners. After all, they wanted a dog's companionship or they wouldn't have brought one home in the first place. So when it doesn't work out, they endure feelings of loss, guilt, and failure. The good news is mismatches are preventable. And here's how.

FRIENDS HAVE THINGS IN COMMON

Think about your close friends. I bet you enjoy their company because you have similar interests. But what about all the perfectly nice people you meet at social functions, talk to politely, and get away from as fast as you can? Are they truly boring people, or just uninteresting to you because you have nothing in common with them?

You may live with your dog for ten years or more, so choosing a dog that matches your personality, activity level, and lifestyle is vital. After all, you can't be roommates with just anybody. Accessing your likes and dislikes before choosing a dog will provide you with a road map through the maze of adult purebreds, or keep you on the right path at the animal shelter. Once you have charted your course, stick with it. Don't let pleading eyes or a wildly wagging tail entice you into taking a shortcut or detour. Instead, do yourself and the wrong dog a favor by resisting its appeal if it's way off your road to a happy partnership.

DOTSIE'S PERFECT MATCH

"Everyone hopes for the 'perfect match' of adopter and dog," says Judy Marden, of the East Coast German Shorthaired Pointer Rescue Network. Of all the placements she's made, Judy says Dotsie's was the most satisfying of all.

As Judy tells it:

"Dotsie, a gorgeous, dark-eyed, solid liver Shorthair, was found running loose in Pennsylvania with no form of identification, and extensive advertising failed to turn up her legal owner. When we picked her up for inclusion in rescue she was extremely thin and in poor coat. Myriad spots of lost hair on her head made her appear as if she'd been attacked by a flock of woodpeckers. In addition, she obviously had whelped a litter within the last two to three months. Yet none of this dampened her outstanding roll-with-the-punches attitude toward life and new situations.

"When we had her spayed, we asked the veterinarian to examine a small lump on her spine. The lump turned out to be a glistening, new .22 caliber bullet which was removed! Someone had apparently taken a pot shot at her while she was running loose.

True friends have many things in common. Dotsie, A German Shorthaired Pointer, and her new owner clowning together for the camera.

"Dotsie was lovely to look at but it was her intensity on game birds, with high tail, high head pointing style, and excellent retrieving agility, that put the icing on the cake. The first time we tried her on a released quail, she hit her point hard and stood like a statue while we took picture after picture. We vowed that unless we could find a combination house pet and hunting home for her, we would keep her forever.

"Dotsie got along with our dogs and adapted to her new situation with ease. With one exception. She had probably lived outdoors all her life and was never housebroken. This was not a problem with other kennel dogs we had fostered. Two to three days of crating night and day, with time out for play and training only, is our method of housebreaking kennel dogs. Normally that's all it takes. But in Dotsie's case it didn't work. She urinated in her crate by 6:00 a.m. if we didn't take her outside very early each morning. We had her tested for urinary problems but there weren't any. So we adapted to her schedule.

"Eventually, Dotsie was matched with a retired couple from New England. She accompanies them on frequent camping expeditions and the husband is an avid hunter with membership in a local hunting preserve. Best of all, he doesn't mind getting up in the middle of the night to let Dotsie go potty. Truth is, he gets up every night to go to the bathroom anyway, so he lets Dotsie out at the same time. He goes, she goes, then she's back on their bed for the rest of the night. How's that for the perfect lifestyle match-up?"

YOUR IDEAL DOG

Your ideal dog likes as much or as little activity as you do, has as much hair as you want to groom, is as friendly or as aloof as you prefer, enjoys some of your hobbies with you, loves your children, and is of a size you can train and handle. How will you recognize your ideal dog when you find him (or her)? Start by considering the following questions.

What Does My Dream Dog Do?

Close your eyes for several seconds and visualize your dream dog. What is your imaginary dog doing? Is he jogging beside you during your daily run? Or is he basking in the warm glow of the fireplace, the picture of canine contentment? Are the two of you play-wrestling on the rug? Is he jumping for a Frisbee? Retrieving a ball? Pointing a covey of quail on a crisp autumn morn?

Is he snuggling on your lap as you watch TV? Guarding your home? Romping in the yard with the kids? Flushing a pheasant? Performing tricks during a party? Greeting you at the door with happy kisses? Watching you with loving eyes as you knit mittens for your grandson? Swimming after a stick? Retrieving a duck? Winning a ribbon in Obedience competition? Racing across a field? Hiking through the woods? Sharing the sofa as you read a book? Maybe your dream dog enjoys several different activities—some active and some quiet.

Does your dream dog . . . win an Obedience competition like this Shetland Sheepdog? . . . swim after a stick like this mixed-bred? . . . have long, profuse hair like this Bearded Collie? . . . or does he fit perfectly in your lap like this Yorkshire Terrier?

Photo credit: Pets by Paulette.

What Does My Dream Dog Look Like?

Now visualize what your imaginary dog looks like. Is he big, medium-sized, or little? Is his hair long or short, straight or curly? Is he black, white, brown, or spotted? Are his ears alertly erect, or long and bouncy? Do his looks matter, or is happy and healthy beautiful enough?

Besides giving you unconditional love, Mr. or Ms. Right Dog will enrich your life by sharing many of your favorite activities. So let's continue searching for your kind of dog.

MY KIND OF DOG QUIZ

When answering the following questions, circle the letter of the answer that best describes a trait you would like in a dog. There are no right or wrong answers, only different answers. That's why dogs come in different breeds.

1. **When it comes to attention, my kind of dog**

   (a) can't seem to get enough

   (b) enjoys it for awhile, but likes doing his own thing too

   (c) likes being near me, but doesn't require much petting

   (d) is cool, detached, and indifferent to attention

2. **When my friends visit, my kind of dog**

   (a) constantly runs from one to the other, seeking each person's attention

   (b) sits near them so they can pet him if they want to, but isn't insistent

   (c) greets them at the door, then is content to be in the same room with us

   (d) turns his back on them, but will accept petting if they insist

3. **In the house, my kind of dog**

   (a) tries to attract my attention constantly and is often underfoot

   (b) is content to be in the same room with me

   (c) spends a lot of time sleeping

4. **In the yard, my kind of dog**

   (a) is only happy if a family member is with him

   (b) will play alone for a while, then wants to come back inside and be with people

   (c) will occupy himself for hours

5. **My kind of dog**

   (a) often tries to initiate active games such as catch and fetch

   (b) is content to play with his toys without begging me to join in

   (c) is so laid back he seldom gets excited enough to play

6. **When I come home, my kind of dog**

   (a) greets me with gleeful kisses and much excitement

   (b) wags his tail happily and waits to be petted

   (c) looks up from his nap and thumps his tail

7. **My kind of dog**

   (a) loves to gallop at top speed

   (b) moves along at a lively trot

   (c) makes his way at a walk

8. **My kind of dog is always ready for**

   (a) a lively game or a long run

   (b) a brisk walk

   (c) a nap in my lap (or beside my chair)

9. **My kind of dog could best be described as**

   (a) always on the go

   (b) playful and moderately active

   (c) sweet and sleepy

10. **After his walk, my kind of dog**

    (a) is soon ready for more exercise

    (b) is content for a few hours

    (c) sleeps until he hears me preparing his dinner

11. **When visiting a new place, such as a friend's home, my kind of dog**

    (a) is confident, secure, and eager to look around

    (b) doesn't hesitate to enter but stays close to my side

    (c) hesitates at the door, and moves forward slowly and carefully

12. **When startled by a sudden noise, such as a pan falling, my kind of dog**

> (a) recovers quickly and investigates the source of the sound
>
> (b) runs to me and trusts my judgment that everything is fine
>
> (c) avoids the invading army by hiding behind the couch

13. **When my kind of dog sees a noisy new object, such as a vacuum cleaner, he approaches it**

> (a) quickly and fearlessly
>
> (b) carefully and sensibly
>
> (c) hesitantly, if at all

14. **When the doorbell rings, my kind of dog**

> (a) barks his hello and races happily to the door, hoping the visitor will play with him
>
> (b) goes to the door with me and stays beside me
>
> (c) usually ignores it
>
> (d) charges the door in a barking, growling rage

15. **When company arrives, my kind of dog**

> (a) is so happy he's almost too friendly
>
> (b) likes a little attention, but minds his manners
>
> (c) is quiet and subdued
>
> (d) goes into another room

16. **My kind of dog enjoys getting attention from**

> (a) any friendly person
>
> (b) my friends, but is aloof with strangers
>
> (c) only my immediate family

17. **In a crowd of people, my kind of dog**

> (a) shows off or wants to play
>
> (b) is pleasant, but not excited

(c) stays close to me

(d) keeps his guard up

18. **My kind of dog prefers the company of**

(a) children and adults equally

(b) children

(c) adults

19. **My kind of dog loves**

(a) every friendly person he meets

(b) our family best, but likes meeting other people too

(c) only me

20. **When he meets strange dogs, my kind of dog**

(a) wants to play

(b) checks them out briefly and goes on his way

(c) ignores them

(d) challenges them with barks and growls

21. **When my friend brings her familiar dog over for a visit, my kind of dog will**

(a) share his toys with his friend

(b) play with the visiting dog but won't share his belongings

(c) make it clear that he wants to be left alone

(d) be aggressive enough to show he's the boss on his own turf

22. **My kind of dog knows**

(a) lots of tricks

(b) a couple of tricks

(c) no tricks

23. **My kind of dog obeys**

(a) lots of commands

(b) basic commands like sit, down, and come

(c) no commands, he's a free spirit

24. At obedience school, my kind of dog

(a) passes advanced courses and earns obedience titles at dog shows

(b) graduates near the top of the beginner class

(c) isn't an honor student, but learns to obey well enough to be a polite companion

(d) doesn't go to obedience school

25. My kind of dog's most important occupation is

(a) warning me of intruders and scaring strangers away

(b) just being his friendly self

(c) being my children's best buddy

(d) winning ribbons in competition such as obedience or agility

(e) hunting

26. My kind of dog loves

(a) his role as watch dog

(b) keeping me company

(c) playing with the children

(d) learning new tricks or commands

27. My kind of dog barks

(a) every time a stranger comes near the house

(b) seldom

(c) at the slightest provocation

28. My kind of dog is

(a) a purebred with registration papers

(b) a purebred, but he doesn't have to have papers to prove it

(c) a mixed breed

(d) any of the above is okay as long as he's a nice, healthy dog

29. When it snows, my kind of dog

    (a) can't wait to go outside and play in the drifts

    (b) thinks it's fun for a few minutes, but comes back inside quickly

    (c) wears a coat on walks and still shivers

30. When it rains, my kind of dog

    (a) splashes happily in every puddle

    (b) doesn't seem to mind

    (c) would rather stay inside

31. At feeding time, my kind of dog

    (a) cleans his dish immediately

    (b) takes his time and enjoys every morsel

    (c) eats slowly and doesn't always finish his dinner

32. When it comes to size, my kind of dog is

    (a) absolutely enormous

    (b) big

    (c) medium-sized, not too big but not little either

    (d) small enough to fit on my lap, but not real delicate

    (e) so tiny he tucks right under my arm

33. My kind of dog

    (a) has long, thick hair

    (b) feels fluffy, but his hair isn't real long

    (c) wears a curly coat

    (d) has short, sleek hair

34. My kind of dog is

    (a) agile and athletic

    (b) solid and steady, but not particularly fast

    (c) clumsy and comical

35. When strangers see my kind of dog they

    (a) comment on how pretty he is and sometimes ask to pet him

    (b) usually ignore him

    (c) look a little scared and give us lots of room

Interpreting Your Answers

Draw a line down the length of a sheet of paper to make two columns. Label the left side "Dream Dog Check List," and the right side "Not For Me List." Then use the following instructions to create a list of the attributes you want, and do not want, in a dog. When you finish, your lists may need a little more personalization. An explanation of how to personalize your lists will conclude this section.

Need for Attention and Activity Level (Questions 1–10)

SECTION 1 (QUESTIONS 1–6)

Questions 1 through 6 evaluate the amount of attention your dream dog desires or demands. Checking mostly (a) answers means your ideal dog wants to be with you all the time and also seeks attention from your friends and friendly strangers. Are you home most of the day? Then an attention-loving (a) dog would be good company, provided you really do enjoy having your dog close to you all the time. There are several reasons why a dog may have a strong need for attention. Some dogs are born super friendly. Others may have been starved for attention during part of their lives and simply can't get enough of your love. In some cases, their security depends on your constant presence. Most attention-loving dogs are a pleasure to train. They like learning tricks and delight in performing them for you and your friends. They are also attentive at obedience school, because they want your praise even more than they want to check out the other dogs and investigate the new smells. On the downside, an especially needy dog could be problematical when you have to leave it alone. If you choose an attention junkie, confine your dog when you are away until you are certain it can handle separation anxiety without eating the sofa to console itself. Are you away for hours at a time every day? Perhaps your dream needs adjusting. A (b) dog would also bask in your attention, but would soon learn to occupy itself with its own toys until you come home. If you checked mostly (a) answers, write "needs constant attention" in the left column.

Mostly (b) answers on questions 1 through 6 indicate that your dream dog is affectionate and likes attention, but doesn't need to be right beside you all the time and is capable of entertaining itself. While not as compulsive in its quest to please as an (a) dog, a (b) dog is still easy to train. At obedience class, it may be distracted at first by the strange dogs and new sights and sounds, but it will soon concentrate on its lessons and delight in your praise. A splendid compromise between a clinging vine and a cool customer, there is no downside to a (b) dog's attention-seeking level. If most of your answers were (b)'s, write "likes moderate attention" in the left column.

There is something comforting and relaxing about a (c) dog's presence. If you selected mostly (c), and no (d) answers on questions 1 through 6, your dream dog reminds you of a soothing stuffed animal, but much better, because it gives, and gladly receives, affection. Cozy (c) dogs are content to lie by your feet, where they thump their tails in subdued glee when you speak to them or pet them. Extremely adaptable, they seldom suffer from separation anxiety. On the downside, (c) dogs seldom get elated about anything, so training won't tickle them either. That doesn't mean they aren't good students. They learn quickly, and once they know a command, they can be counted on to give the correct response. They just don't perform with a lot of flair. Don't expect a (c) dog to be the quickest dog in obedience class to hit the deck on the "down" command. But do expect a (c) dog to learn house manners easily, and when it comes to obedience school, value your dog's consistency over some of the other dogs' speed. If your answers were mostly (c)'s, write "content to be close by" in the left column.

If one or two of your answers to questions 1 through 6 were (d)'s, your dream dog is cool and distant, and may be rather regal in bearing. Unaffectionate, but not necessarily unfriendly, (d) dogs have an independent nature and sometimes seem to put up with attention rather than seek it. They are not the best dogs for children. Most kids want lots of interaction with their dogs, and (d)'s are likely to walk away from games and hugs. But if you admire an animal with an "attitude," and a dog in the same room is close enough, then a cool, composed, and indifferent (d) may be just the dog for you. A (d) will learn house manners as well as any other dog, and can do well in obedience class too. He just won't enjoy it. Praise isn't important to him, but ending the training session is, and he'll learn the right response just to get you to stop teaching. If you checked the (d) answer to question number one, it overrides your other answers. If you already wrote an attribute on your "Dream Dog" list, cross it out and replace it by writing "cool and distant" in the left column.

At this point, you should have one entry on the "Dream Dog" side and nothing under "Not For Me." The four possibilities were "needs constant attention," "likes moderate attention," "content to be close by," and "cool and distant." Would you just hate to have a dog with one or two (or more) of those attributes? Then write the attribute or attributes you wouldn't want your dog to have in the right-hand column to start your "Not For Me" list.

SECTION 2 (QUESTIONS 4–10)

Questions 4 through 10 evaluate how active you want your dog to be. If you checked mostly (a) answers, you want an energetic dog that is into prancing and galloping instead of walking, and would rather play games with you than be petted. This is the dream dog of joggers, back-country hikers, and mothers of spirited children who play alone in a fenced yard and could use a frisky playmate. This is also the dream dog of Agility competitors and hunters. But this dream dog turns into a nightmare when it doesn't get enough exercise. Bored and bursting with energy, an (a) dog's need to let off some steam can result in rearranged furniture and shredded drapes. If you don't have a fenced yard, an (a) dog will need more than one long, brisk walk every day to stay on its best behavior. Of course, retrieving and other ball games (see Chapter 9) will also help put the lid back on your (a) dog's tea kettle. An (a) dog is a marvelous addition to the right family. It can help you lose weight without dieting, and wear down your children so they will actually be sleepy at bedtime. But consider your lifestyle before becoming enamored of an (a) dog. Do you jog before work every day, and come home every night raring for a rowdy romp and a long, brisk walk? Then by all means, get an active (a). But if "every day" sounds like too often, a somewhat less active, but still lively dog might fulfill your dream. Perhaps a bouncy (b) is just right for you.

If you selected mostly (b) answers to questions 4 through 10, your dream dog is moderately active, and lively enough for most families. A (b) dog will enjoy long walks, the brisker the better, but will be content to relax when you get home. It will also join in games with your children, but will quietly curl up for petting when play time is over.

A sweet and sleepy (c) dog makes few demands and is happy just to sit beside you and be petted. If you selected mostly (c) answers to questions 4 through 10, your dream dog is friendly in a laid-back way and seldom initiates activities. Even so, remember that a contented (c) dog needs exercise too, so keep your (c) dog healthy and fit by taking it for long, unhurried walks. The comforting charm of a (c) dog may help a stressed executive lower his or her blood pressure, and (c) dogs are also ideal for senior citizens.

SCORING QUESTIONS 4–10

If you checked mostly (a) answers, write "extremely active" on the "Dream Dog" side. If you had an abundance of (b) answers, write "moderately active," and if you selected (c)'s, write "couch potato." Next, look at the three possibilities and write the one or two you wouldn't want your dog to have on your "Not For Me" list.

Temperament (Disposition) and Sociability (Questions 11–21)

SECTION 1 (QUESTIONS 11–14)

Questions 11 through 14 evaluate your dream dog's temperament or disposition. If your answers were mostly (a)'s, your dream dog is the happy-go-lucky, throw-caution-to-the-wind type. This dog likes everyone and fears no one. And, believe it or not, this dog usually makes a good watchdog. Dogs that distrust people often back away when approached by a real-life bad guy. But trusting (a) dogs aren't afraid of people at all, so they are more apt to discern when something really is wrong and take a stance between you and trouble. In thousands of cases, the cheery dog that always gave friendly strangers a big slurp, hurled itself at a dangerous intruder without hesitation.

Mostly (b) answers to numbers 11 through 14 indicate that your dream dog relies on your presence for its confidence, and trusts your decisions. Chances are this dog would be protective if need be, and would probably scare an intruder away by barking. Never stop socializing your (b) dog (see Chapter 7), as it could backslide into shyness.

If you answered mostly (c)'s to questions 11 through 14, your dream dog is rather timid. Even though you might think it would be fun to "mother" a fearful friend, your (c) dog would have a fuller life if it was socialized, or if its past wasn't haunting its present. If you like long-term projects, an overly cautious (c) dog might by your perfect partner. With time, you might even give it the courage to face new adventures with its head high and its tail untucked. How? Read "Socialization" in Chapter 7 and work on your (c) dog's fears slowly and patiently. Expect improvement but not miracles. Depending on your dog's past, it might stay shy forever.

If your selected the only (d) answer in questions 11 through 14, your dream dog defends you fiercely and scares intruders away with its gruff growl and sharp bark. Unfortunately, that dream could quickly turn into a nightmare. What happens when you open the door and the object of your dog's ire is a nine-year-old Girl Scout taking orders for cookies? You could hold your ferocious (d) dog so it can't hurt anyone, but what if it gets past you?

On the other hand, maybe your wildly barking (d) dog is all bluff behind closed doors and changes into a pussycat when you greet your visitor. In that case, its fierce act could be useful, especially if you live alone. Good watchdogs come in all sizes. They are natural guardians and need no special training to warn their family when a stranger approaches. These alert, but inherently friendly, noisemakers save lives and property simply by barking a warning when they scent or spy an intruder. But attack dogs are a whole different story. In their case, (d) stands for dangerous. Leave attack dogs to the professionals who train them for specific duties. Bringing such a dog into your family is like letting Junior play with a loaded gun.

SCORING QUESTIONS 11–14

Mostly (a) answers—fearless and curious; mostly (b) answers—needs me nearby for confidence; mostly (c) answers—cautious and timid.

Write the attribute you selected most often in your "Dream Dog" column. Were you evenly split between two attributes? Then think over both of them and choose the one that suits you best.

Did you have one (d) answer? In addition to your selection above, add "fierce defender" to your "Dream Dog" list.

Now look at the attributes you didn't select. If you really dislike one or two of them, add them to your "Not For Me" list.

SECTION 2 (QUESTIONS 15–21)

Questions 15 through 21 include sociability along with temperament. Mostly (a) answers suggest that your ideal dog is everybody's best friend and gets along with other dogs too. Cheerful and affectionate, this dog's amiable attitude is contagious. Most people smile when meeting an (a) dog. When you walk your (a) dog, be cautious for him when he approaches a strange dog. Your charming pet may want to play, but the other dog may not be as friendly.

If your answers are mostly (b)'s, your dream dog is sociable enough, but doesn't go out of its way to meet friendly strangers or other dogs. A (b) answer to question 18 indicates a dog that will remain in the playroom with the kids while the adults watch the football game. Is your ideal dog a (b) on question 21? It isn't unusual for a dog to be possessive of its belongings when other dogs enter its territory. Prevention pays off here. When your dog-owning friends visit, remove all your dog's toys and chews. Chances are the dogs will play with each other just fine when none of their priceless possessions are involved.

Mostly (c) answers to questions 15 through 21 indicate that your ideal dog is the "one-person" or "one-family" type. Some dogs are (c) dogs from birth, as a few breeds love and respect only their owners. Other dogs are subdued around strangers due to lack of socialization or unpleasant experiences. A (c) dog may work out fine for a single adult or a mature couple, but it's not a good idea to seek out a (c) dog if you have children of any age living at home. Kids tend to bring other kids home with them, and the combination of strangers and noise will make a (c) dog uncomfortable at best. At worst, that kind of environment could turn it into a nervous wreck and potential fear biter (snapping at people out of anxiety).

If you chose (d) answers on questions 15 and 17, you want a dog that is distrustful of everyone but you and your family. Perhaps you are mistaken in what constitutes a good watchdog. The best family guardians are friendly and confident, not nasty and nervous. A dog that leaves the room because it is uncomfortable around your guests, and is apprehensive when walked through a crowd, is seldom a suitable pet for anyone but a hermit.

Did you check (d) answers to questions 20 and 21? If so, you want a feisty dog, the type that tries to display dominance over every dog it meets. Many of the dogs that match this personality type are terriers, and their owners have to take responsibility for their actions in one of two ways. Most terriers are small, but some of them will bravely challenge dogs five times their size if permitted to do so. Surprisingly, most large dogs will gallantly back away from a gutsy little terrier's assault, but an occasional big dog will answer the challenge. So, if your dream dog is small but scrappy, you'll have to stay alert on your daily walks to keep it out of trouble.

The second way owners have to take responsibility for their (d) dog's actions is if their quarrelsome pet is large. When a large terrier or any other big, strong dog picks a fight, the results could be deadly to someone else's dog. So have a peppery pet if you want to, but be alert to potential problems so your dog, and every dog it encounters, stays safe.

SCORING QUESTIONS 15–21

From the attributes listed below, put the one you selected most often on your "Dream Dog" list, and the attribute(s) you absolutely don't want on your "Not For Me" list.

Mostly (a) answers—friendly and outgoing; mostly (b) answers—moderately sociable; mostly (c) answers—subdued around strangers.

If you answered (d) to questions 15 and 17, it overrides your other answers. Write "distrusts everyone but family" in your "Dream Dog" column instead of any of the other attributes.

If you answered (a) or (b) to questions 20 and 21, add "gets along with other dogs" to your "Dream Dog" list. If you answered (d) to questions 20 and 21, write "displays dominance with other dogs" under the "Dream Dog" column.

Trainability and Occupation (Questions 22–28)

SECTION 1 (QUESTIONS 22–24)

(Note: If you checked (c) on question 24, it counts as a (b) when scoring.)

Questions 22 through 24 evaluate your dream dog's trainability. If you answered (a) to these questions, your dream dog enjoys learning and responds to many cues and commands. Since dogs only learn tricks or obedience if someone teaches them, your ideal dog is either already well trained, or you plan to put some time into its training. An (a) answer to question 24 means training and exhibiting your dog may even become a hobby.

Mostly (b) answers to questions 22 through 24 indicate that your dream dog responds to basic commands and may perform a trick or two for your friends. A (b) dog is easily trainable but doesn't perform with the zest of an (a) dog. If you chose (b) answers, you will probably train your dog until it is a pleasure to live with and let it go at that.

If you answered (c) to questions 22 and 23, and (d) to question 24, you believe dogs should be free spirits and people shouldn't burden them with training. That kind of thinking underestimates dogs. The truth is that dogs are intelligent and curious and will learn whether their owners train them or not. The only difference between a trained and an untrained dog is what it learns. When allowed to live as free spirits, dogs learn to topple the garbage, soil the carpet, annoy your guests, and steal the steaks you were defrosting for dinner. Soon all that learning earns them a demotion to "outdoor dog," and from there it's a small step to "ignored dog." A dog is a social animal and banishing your dog because you failed to train it is sad and unnecessary. If you like independent animals and don't believe in training, consider getting a cat. Cats make charming companions and are the ultimate free spirits.

SCORING QUESTIONS 22–24

Mostly (a) answers—outstanding trainability; mostly (b) answers—average trainability; mostly (c) and (d) answers—untrained free spirit.

Put the attribute you chose on your "Dream Dog" list and any you especially dislike on your "Not For Me" list.

SECTION 2 (QUESTIONS 25–28): EXPLANATION AND SCORING

Questions 25 through 28 concern your dream dogs chief occupation. Answering (a) on questions 25 through 27 means you want an alert watchdog and natural guardian. Write "alert watchdog" in the left column. It's doubtful that you absolutely hate any of the other attributes listed below, but if you do, write them on your "Not For Me" List.

If you answered (b) to 25 and 26, your dream dog will have a full career as your loving companion. Write "friendly companion" in the left column.

Your ideal dog is your children's best friend if you answered (c) to questions 25 and 26. Write "children's pet" in the "Dream Dog" column.

Competition calls if you answered (d) to 25 and 26. You want an animal that performs happily and reliably in public. Write "performs well in public" in the left column.

An (e) answer on 25 means you want your dog to go hunting with you. That limits your choices to sporting breeds or some hounds (depending on what you want to hunt) as you will see later in this chapter. If hunting is the chief reason why you are acquiring a dog, try to find out all you can about the dog's background so you can avoid getting a gun-shy dog. It is nearly impossible to correct gun-shyness, and this problem prevents a dog from being useful in the field no matter how good its nose is. If you checked (e), write "hunts well" in the left column.

A (b) answer on 27 means you want a dog that seldom barks. Perhaps you live in a residential area where continuous barking would not be tolerated, or maybe you just want a quiet, peaceful pet. Write "seldom barks" in the left column, and if you are dead set against a noisy dog, write "barks often" on the right.

Answering (c) to 27 means you like dogs that bark long and often. Perhaps you believe a noisy pet will provide better protection. In truth, people tend to tune out dogs that bark false alarms, so, like the boy who cried "wolf!", a non-stop barker is often ignored. Here's hoping you live in a rural area, as few neighbors will sleep through your dream dog's constant mouthing off. If a (c) dog is for you, write "barks often" on your "Dream Dog" list.

Question 28 is self-explanatory. If you have a preference, write it on your "Dream Dog" List. If one or two of the choices are definitely not for you, you know where to jot them down. After reading Chapter 9, you may want to rethink your answer. It deals with activities for you and your dog. While the American Mixed Breed Obedience Registry (see Appendix) offers competitive performance events for mixed-bred dogs, there may or may not be an AMBOR chapter in your area. If taking part in these events is important to you, do a little research before choosing a dog. In some parts of the country, the majority of events are American Kennel Club (AKC) sanctioned and open only to AKC registered dogs. If United Kennel Club (UKC) events are held in your area, mixed-bred dogs belonging to AMBOR may participate in obedience and agility. Also, purebred dogs without registration papers, if they qualify, may be granted an Indefinite Listing Privilege by the AKC. This listing allows them to participate in specified events. Write to the AKC (see Appendix) for details.

Hardiness and Appearance (Questions 29–35)

SECTION 1 (QUESTIONS 29–33)

(Note: When scoring, (b) or (c) answers to questions 32 and 33 count as (a)'s; (d) answers to questions 32 and 33 count as (b)'s; and an (e) answer on 32 counts as a (c).)

Questions 29 through 33 evaluate whether your dream dog is the hale and hearty type or on the delicate side. Mostly (a) answers point to a dog that is probably medium to large in size and has a protective coat (long, fluffy, wiry, or curly). This dog isn't particularly bothered by changes in weather and never misses a meal. A stalwart companion for outdoor adventurers, an (a) dog is ready and willing to accompany you anywhere.

If most of your answers were (b)'s to questions 29 through 33, you want a sound dog, but your pet doesn't have to be as rugged an animal as an (a). Perhaps you want your dog to be on the small side, or to have a short, sleek coat. While small dogs are often extremely hardy, as are smooth-coated dogs (dogs with short hair), neither one can take as much harsh weather as a medium or large dog with a protective coat.

Mostly (c) answers? Your ideal dog is a homebody and doesn't enjoy the rigors of nature. Perhaps it is so tiny that snow drifts swallow it up and puddles loom as large as lakes. Although sometimes a bit on the finicky side, most (c) dogs are top-notch companions and ideal for a city apartment. The great outdoors isn't their "thing," so they are usually content with a few visits to the curb every day to relieve themselves, and one nice walk—weather permitting, of course! Dog sweaters help easily chilled dogs stay cozy on winter walks, and are available in a variety of styles and colors. The best ones are functional and protect the chest and belly, not just the back.

SCORING QUESTIONS 29–33

Mostly (a) answers—write "robust and sturdy" on the Dream Dog side; mostly (b) answers—"fit, but prefers creature comforts"; mostly (c) answers—"dainty."

Is anything above exactly the opposite of what you want in a dog? Put it on your "Not For Me" list.

SECTION 2 (QUESTIONS 32–35)

Questions 32 through 35 give you a rough idea of what your dream dog looks like. There's no need to add up answers. Instead, add the four attributes you selected to your "Dream Dog" list. For example, if you selected (e) on 32, write "tiny." When you get to 35, shorten your answers. If you answered (a), write "pretty." For (b), write "plain," and for (c), write "looks intimidating." Now read the other possible answers to those four questions, and add the attributes you want to avoid to your "Not For Me" list.

Modifying Your Lists

Your "Dream Dog Check List" may not cover every attribute you need in a dog, so think about your lifestyle and add a few if necessary. For example, do you have a cat? Then add "safe around cats" to your "Dream Dog" list and "hates cats" to your "Not For Me" list. Do you spend months on the road in a recreational vehicle? Then "enjoys traveling" is an important attribute, and "gets carsick easily" wouldn't do at all.

SELF-EVALUATION QUIZ

Now you have lists to help you discover the dog of your dreams and keep you from waking up with a nightmare. But before you start searching for superdog, try the following test as a reality check. Are you ready to have a dog? Do you know what you're getting into? Do you have time? Will you make time? Now's the time to find out.

Answer the following questions according to your current lifestyle, not what you think it should be or wish it was. In other words, if watching sports on television is your favorite hobby, but one of these days you're going to take up cross-country skiing, answer like a TV sports fan, not a cross-country skier. If a question doesn't pertain to you, leave it blank. For example, don't answer a question that asks about the other pets in your household if you have no pets. Again, there are no right or wrong answers, only different answers. That's why different people like different dogs.

1. **I've wanted a dog**

    (a) for a long time

    (b) recently

    (c) never, but my spouse or children do

2. **When I visit a friend who has a dog, I**

    (a) can't stop fussing over it

    (b) greet it briefly, then let it alone

    (c) push it away if it demands too much attention

3. **Concerning my friends' dogs, I know**

    (a) their names, breeds, ages, and habits

    (b) their names

    (c) very little about them

4. **I'm getting a dog because**

    (a) I really want one

    (b) it will make me feel safer

    (c) my spouse or children want one

5. **There is a pet other than a dog in my household and I**

    (a) enjoy its company and give it lots of attention

    (b) attend to its needs but don't enjoy it

    (c) wish I could get rid of it

6. **I've enjoyed the same sport or hobby for**

    (a) three years or more

    (b) one to three years

    (c) under a year, or participate in no hobbies or sports

7. **The best part about dogs is their**

   (a) zest for life and loyal affection

   (b) attractive appearance

   (c) ability to guard the house

8. **I usually finish projects**

   (a) earlier than I planned

   (b) right on schedule

   (c) a little later than planned

   (d) very late, if ever

9. **My job is**

   (a) stressful, but challenging and rewarding

   (b) okay, but nothing special

   (c) boring

   (d) miserable

10. **I always seem to be**

    (a) in a hurry

    (b) rather calm

    (c) bored

11. **I plan to spend _____ training my dog**

    (a) fifteen minutes or more almost every day

    (b) fifteen minutes or more at least three times a week

    (c) very little if any time

12. **Training a dog sounds like**

    (a) fun

    (b) a challenge

    (c) just another job I don't have time for

13. **Combing or brushing a dog several times a week**

    (a) is probably pleasant and relaxing

    (b) should soon become a habit

    (c) sounds more like work than fun

14. I plan to groom my dog

    (a) every day

    (b) three or four times a week on a regular schedule

    (c) never, grooming will be a good chore for the children

    (d) never, I'll get a breed that doesn't need coat care

    (e) never, I'll take my dog to a professional groomer on a regular schedule

15. During my dog's first week or so in my home, I can arrange to

    (a) stay home most of the time

    (b) come home at lunch time, or have someone else walk my dog at noon

    (c) I can't schedule that far ahead and I'm making no promises

16. I am usually home

    (a) most of the day

    (b) some of the day

    (c) during the evening

    (d) seldom

17. I live

    (a) in a house with a securely fenced yard

    (b) on a farm

    (c) in a house, but the yard isn't fenced

    (d) in an apartment or condo that has a dog walk, but no private yard

    (e) in a big city high rise

    (f) in a rental that doesn't allow dogs, but I'm going to hide a small one

18. My household consists of _____ adult(s)

    (a) one

    (b) two

    (c) three or more

19. My household consists of _____ children under the age of 8

    (a) none or one

    (b) two

    (c) three or more

20. In my household

    (a) one adult is at home most of the time

    (b) one adult is usually home for at least half a day

    (c) all the adults are away from home during the day

21. Between working and commuting, I am away from home

    (a) very little, I work at home

    (b) under 25 hours a week

    (c) 25 to 40 hours a week

    (d) 40 to 60 hours a week

    (e) over 60 hours a week

22. I would rather

    (a) go hiking, fishing, hunting, or camping

    (b) go dancing

    (c) go to the movies

    (d) surf the Net with my computer, read a good book, or watch TV

23. On vacation, I prefer sleeping

    (a) in a tent in the back country

    (b) in a recreational vehicle at a campsite with a breathtaking view

    (c) in a hotel or motel

24. I most enjoy

    (a) participating in an outdoor game or sport

    (b) conversation or a card game with friends

    (c) reading or watching television

25. **I participate in**

    (a) team or league sports, such as softball, soccer, or bowling

    (b) individual sports, such as golf, handball, or tennis

    (c) no competitive sports, but I jog, walk, bike, or work out regularly

    (d) no sports or exercise on a regular basis

26. **I prefer associating with**

    (a) a group of people

    (b) one or two good friends

    (c) only my family

    (d) myself

27. **If I'm doing something outdoors and it starts raining, I**

    (a) ignore it and continue my outdoor activity

    (b) put on rain gear and continue my outdoor activity

    (c) go indoors immediately

28. **Making some adjustments in my daily schedule, such as getting up 15 minutes earlier to walk a dog, would be**

    (a) no problem

    (b) a pain, but I'd do it

    (c) absolutely unacceptable

29. **Learning to train a dog by taking it to obedience school sounds like**

    (a) a good idea and a good time

    (b) a necessity

    (c) something the kids might like to do

    (d) a waste of time and money

30. **I'm a patient person**

    (a) most of the time

    (b) sometimes

    (c) never

31. I had a dog

   (a) most of my life, and know how to care for one

   (b) when I was a child, and I did some of the dog-related chores

   (c) when I was a child, but my parents did the chores

   (d) never

32. I trained a dog

   (a) within the last ten years

   (b) more than ten years ago

   (c) never

33. If my dog made the mistake of relieving itself on the rug, it would be

   (a) a minor inconvenience

   (b) a serious annoyance

   (c) grounds for getting rid of the dog

34. If I get a dog that needs professional coat care, it will visit the groomer

   (a) once every six weeks

   (b) only when absolutely necessary

   (c) never

35. My kids want a dog, and they will probably

   (a) leave the care to me

   (b) help out with dog chores

   (c) take over its care completely

36. I had a dog before but it

   (a) died of old age, or was euthanized because it was suffering from an incurable disease

   (b) didn't work out so I sold it or gave it away

   (c) didn't work out so I left it at the animal shelter

   (d) got hit by a car, or died of a dog disease because its vaccinations weren't up to date

37. **Dogs that occasionally race through the house for no reason except high spirits are**

   (a) comical and fun to watch

   (b) a little too wild for me

   (c) liable to break something expensive

38. **When unexpected company arrives, my living room looks like**

   (a) a comfortable place to relax

   (b) a show place

   (c) a tornado just tore through

39. **An emergency veterinary bill would**

   (a) be easy to pay

   (b) go on my credit card so I could pay in installments

   (c) create a financial crisis

40. **My neighbors**

   (a) live a quarter mile or more away

   (b) live in the house next door

   (c) live in the condo or apartment on the other side of the wall

41. **The children in my household are between the ages of**

   (a) eight and seventeen

   (b) five and eight

   (c) newborn to five

42. **I have**

   (a) one or two other pets

   (b) several other pets

   (c) never had a pet

43. **My home is usually**

   (a) neat, but lived in

   (b) immaculate

   (c) cluttered and chaotic

44. I get around

    (a) very well, thank you

    (b) a little slower these days

    (c) with difficulty

WHAT DO YOUR ANSWERS TELL YOU?

Desire for a Dog and Lasting Interests (Questions 1–7)

Your answers to questions 1 through 7 should help you decide if your desire for a dog is strong enough to make the relationship work. Bringing home a dog means inviting an intelligent creature with a personality of its own to live with you. Adjustments have to be made for any relationship to succeed, and if you really want a dog in your life making some minor modifications will be easy. In fact, you will soon savor a new schedule that includes time for daily walks, occasional training, and spontaneous fun.

On the other hand, if you're being coerced into getting a dog by another family member, or just want an early warning system, you may resent the demands of dog ownership. Soon you may set up the relationship for failure by stretching the time between walks beyond your dog's best efforts to remain housebroken, or by failing to groom your dog until it is too matted and smelly to be housed indoors. If you're reluctant to get a dog, don't do it. No one deserves to have a dog forced upon them, and no dog deserves to be put in such a potentially unhappy situation.

SCORING YOURSELF ON QUESTIONS 1–7

If you chose mostly (a) answers and no (c) answers, your eyes light up whenever you see someone walking your type of dog, and you can hardly wait to have a dog of your own. Choose carefully, not quickly, and you will be on your way to years of enjoyment.

If you chose mostly (b) answers, with an (a) answer or two mixed in with your (b)'s, ease into dog ownership slowly. You like looking at dogs, find some of them quite appealing, and might even feel safer if you had one around. But you really don't know dogs very well. Getting a dog without getting to know a few dogs is as sensible as getting married without ever dating. Spend some time with a few dogs (one at a time, of course) before making a decision. One way to get to know dogs and find out if you enjoy their company is by volunteering to dog-sit when your dog-owning friends go away for the weekend.

If some (c) answers are mixed in with your (b)'s, think about why you're interested enough in dog ownership to read this book. Does your spouse or child want a dog? Is your spouse going to take responsibility for its care and training and only wants you to put up with its presence? Could that work, or will your spouse be gone most of the day, leaving you home and in charge of the dog?

Getting a dog for your child is not a step that should be taken lightly. When kids want a dog they make all kinds of promises, but don't count on them taking over all the dog duties, because it simply won't happen. At least, not for long. Even the most responsible children occasionally have after-school activities, or appointments in the evening, and have to ask another family member to take over that day's dog care. A dog is not a disposable object like a worn-out shoe or a broken bat, so give in and get a dog only if you want one in the family and are willing to share in its care. Threatening to get rid of the dog every time your child forgets to walk it sends a sorry message about relationships, and is grossly unfair to the dog.

If most of your answers to questions 1 through 7 were (c)'s, you seem to have no desire at all for a dog's companionship and should steer clear of dog ownership. Along with those (c)'s, did you answer (b) on question 4? If your only interest in dogs is having a watchdog, consider installing an electronic alarm system instead. It's probably less expensive in the long run, and it won't put any demands on your time.

Available Time and Lifestyle (Questions 8–16)

There is a saying that goes, "If you want something done, ask a busy person to do it." That's because most busy people have learned how to schedule and prioritize their time so everything that has to get done, does get done. Being busy, or even having a stressful job, does not make you a poor candidate for dog ownership. In fact, training and petting a dog, and doing simple chores such as walking and feeding, may be a great tension reliever after the pressures of the day. Questions 8 through 16 deal with how much time you plan to set aside for your dog.

SCORING QUESTIONS 8–16

Either (a) or (b) answers, or a mixture of the two, indicate a responsible person who has given some thought to the daily details of dog ownership and is willing to set aside time to train a dog and keep it clean and healthy. Dogs respond quickly to regular attention, and it won't be long until dog care and training time is one of the prime times of your day. Without a doubt, it will be the high point of your dog's day.

If you answered (c) or (d) to questions 8, 9, or 10, and the rest of your answers were (a)'s and (b)'s, the above paragraph also applies to you. But if you answered (c), (d), or (e) to any questions from 11 through 15, you don't want to make time to help a dog fit into your family. Even if you acquire a reliably housebroken dog, it still has to learn your schedule or accidents will happen.

It's also unrealistic to expect a dog to have good manners unless you teach it the house rules. Even more important, if training or grooming a dog sounds more like work than fun, steer clear of dog ownership altogether. Many other pets need no training and are easier to care for than dogs.

Question 14 deals with grooming. All dogs need some grooming to stay clean and healthy, even dogs with extremely short coats (see Chapter 8). Some breeds, such as Poodles and Schnauzers, look their best when clipped and shaped at the grooming salon about every six weeks. But even they need a bit of care between appointments to keep their skin healthy and their coat inviting to the touch. Grooming is a good chore for an older child provided he or she has been taught the correct method for the dog's coat type, and is sensible enough to be gentle. But don't make your dog's life depend upon it. Kids have a way of neglecting chores, and dogs can look and smell so disagreeable when their coats are neglected that insensitive owners may banish them to the outdoors—sometimes forever—instead of cleaning them up or taking them to a professional groomer.

Many people answer (c) to 16. If you are one of them, give the relationship a good start by acquiring your dog when you have a long weekend or some vacation days to spend at home. Confine your dog sensibly when you are away, and your dog will soon adjust to your schedule. If you leave at dawn and work until late every night, and there is no one else at home and no dog walkers for hire in your neighborhood, don't get a dog until your situation changes. Most healthy, housebroken dogs can hold off relieving themselves much longer than people can, but there are limits.

Evaluating Your Lifestyle (Questions 17–21)

Your lifestyle may help you ease into dog ownership. For example, if you work at home, have a spouse who loves dogs, a ten-year-old who wants to help care for a dog, and a fenced yard, the adjustment should be a joy. On the other hand, if you are the single parent of three young children, work long hours outside the home, and live in a fifth floor walk-up apartment in a large city, you will adjust to a dog's needs with difficulty. While few of you fit either extreme, questions 17 through 21 will help you evaluate how your lifestyle affects dog ownership.

SCORING QUESTIONS 17–21

If most of your answers were (a)'s, your lifestyle lends itself to dog ownership. While (b) answers are a little less ideal, they also point to a suitable situation, provided you choose a dog that adores kids and teach your kids to respect the dog. A dog should never be used as a baby-sitter for small children. In fact, an adult should always supervise when toddlers and dogs are together.

If you checked (c), (d), and (e) answers, your lifestyle makes having a dog more difficult. If your yard isn't fenced, or if you live in an apartment, condo, or high rise, you'll have to walk your dog (and clean up after it) in the morning, early evening, and before you go to bed. Depending on the dog, you might have to make arrangements for a noon walk too. This schedule may sound demanding, but thousands of people in skyscraper apartments take their dogs up and down on elevators and gladly exercise them in all kinds of weather. Obviously they find a dog's company well worth the effort.

Three or more adults in a household may indicate young career people rooming together, a couple caring for an elderly relative, or an extended family. None of these situations has an adverse effect on dog ownership provided everyone is consistent with the house rules so the dog doesn't get confused. Being away for long hours is far from ideal dog ownership, but has been practiced successfully by thousands of career-oriented singles and couples. Your dog may adjust to your hours by sleeping when you are away. His real day will begin when he hears the welcome sound of your return.

Three or more small children in the house are a handful, so if you have young children and toddlers, it's a good idea to wait a few years before acquiring a dog. Toddlers are rough with dogs and too young to know better, so their play time with a dog should always be supervised for their own safety. While most dogs are tolerant of tiny tots, pulling a sleeping dog's tail or poking its nose could cause an unfortunate incident. And while the dog may be contrite the instant it wakes up and realizes what happened, the damage will already have been done.

If you chose (f) as your answer to 17, please don't try it. When your landlord discovers your dog (and they always do), you'll probably be asked to get rid of the dog or move.

Your Likes and Dislikes (Questions 22–27)

There are no appropriate or inappropriate answers to these six questions, so there is no need to score them. They were included to help you identify your preferences, so you can consider them when choosing a dog. For example, if you love outdoor sports and enjoy associating with other people, you may want to join a dog club and participate in some of the competitive or non-competitive dog sports outlined in Chapter 9. If any of them appeal to you, select a dog that meets the qualifications for participation.

Are you the ultimate outdoor person? Then get a dog sturdy enough to hike the mountains and woods with you, while carrying its food and supplies in its own backpack. (Yes, they do make backpacks for dogs!)

Do you go camping in your recreational vehicle? So do many other people with pets. Look for a dog that's pleasant and friendly, tolerant of strange dogs, and quiet at night.

Would you rather relax at home? A small dog that can get enough exercise indoors may be ideal, but keep in mind that your dog will have to be walked no matter what the weather, unless you have a fenced yard.

Reality Check (Questions 28–44)

A dog that eagerly shares your favorite activities is a warm and wonderful companion, but few partnerships are perfect. And wouldn't they be boring if they were? It takes a pinch of pepper to make a tantalizing stew or a lively relationship, so let's find out how much spice you think is nice.

SCORING QUESTIONS 28–44

All (a) answers to questions 28 through 44 is almost impossibly ideal. These answers mean you have had a dog before, know how to train one, and won't turn a minor mishap, like muddy paws or vomit on the rug, into a major crisis. Your last dog (no matter how long ago that was) lived a good long life. You are at ease with expenses such as veterinary care and professional grooming, and realize that your kids may leave the daily dog chores for you. There is a pet in your home now, and your children understand the difference between living creatures and stuffed toys. And if that isn't enough, your neighbors live far enough away not to notice if your dog impersonates a werewolf when the moon is full!

A mixture of (a) and (b) answers is more realistic. This indicates that you understand the realities of dog care even though you may not relish every facet of it. Don't worry. If you scored high on desire for a dog, you'll do fine. Most of us aren't perfect dog owners, and don't demand perfection from our dogs. Being a good owner, and teaching your pet how to be a good dog, is all it takes to have an excellent relationship.

A few (b) answers warrants further thought. If you take pride in keeping your home spotless, choose your dog with that in mind. Be certain to get one that is already house trained, then stay home with him for the first few days and confine him when you leave, until you're sure he is reliable in your home. Due to nervousness or confusion, many housebroken dogs make a mistake or two soon after moving into a new home. But after being told "No!" firmly, hustled out the door (on lead of course), and shown the area where they are supposed to relieve themselves, they soon recall their fastidious manners. If your new dog makes a mistake, don't clean the soiled area with an ammonia-based formula. The scent is similar to urine and may make your dog think that spot is his designated toilet.

Shedding is another scourge of impeccable homemakers. Short-coated breeds shed just as much as long-coated breeds (it just looks like less), and dark hairs of any length won't enhance your cream carpet, but there is a solution. Select a type of dog that is professionally clipped and seldom sheds, such as the Poodle, the Miniature Schnauzer, or several others (information on the various breeds appears in the next part of this chapter). There's no need to fear muddy tracks on your clean floors either. Just leave a towel by the door when you walk your dog in the dew or rain, and use it to wipe his feet as soon as you get home.

UNDERSTANDING THE POWER OF INSTINCT

Instinct is more than just a desire to perform a certain function. Instinct is an internal force, programming a dog to behave in a certain way. Many breeds were selectively bred to have certain instincts, such as the instinct to herd or the instinct to hunt. When a stock owner makes a match with a herding dog or a hunter makes a match with a hunting dog, it's pure pleasure all around. The following story illustrates the power of instinct. In this case, it was strong enough to act as an anesthetic during what would have been a painful procedure. But first, a little background.

When Paul Scheffer, of Colorado Springs, CO, acquired Elke, the German Shorthaired Pointer was eighteen months old and living in a small kennel with another dog. Her original owners had purchased her for hunting, but they divorced before they ever took Elke afield, and she ended up kenneled and for sale. Undaunted, she was still inquisitive and friendly, with all the energy typical of her breed.

The bonding process with her new owner began as Elke quickly adjusted to camper traveling, learned to swim, and accompanied Paul on fishing trips. Paul also taught her basic manners and had her spayed. They spent a lot of time on obedience training, as well as a long, slow program to ensure that she wouldn't be gun-shy. Elke was not a quick study when learning obedience and needed much repetition, but training her for hunting was a breeze. Her instincts were strong and all Paul had to do was focus them. He describes the power of those instincts:

"I think one of my most chilling experiences with Elke was when I acquired first-hand an appreciation of the transformation a pointing dog undergoes when it catches scent. We were out on a beautiful, clear, dry, and breezy day—not the best of hunting conditions but certainly a joy to be afield. As with most scaled quail habitat, cactus was plentiful. Elke had adapted quickly to dog boots and seemed to avoid the worse spots with just some front shoes. But she had picked up a few spines in her hind pads and we stopped on the shoulder of a shallow draw so I could remove them. I perched on a rock and maneuvered her rear around to where I could handle the hind feet much like a blacksmith would. This left Elke with her nose to the wind. With my right arm around her back and the left grasping her foot, she stood patiently on three legs. Suddenly I felt her whole body tense up rigid. Then her nose inched forward and her eyes almost glazed over. Following her line of sight across the little draw, I saw a very fresh quail roost. Clearly it had engulfed her nose, making her oblivious to my cactus removal operation. I can't say that I noticed a difference in her pulse, but I swear she stopped breathing and would have continued the rigid point even if she had fallen off her three point stance."

Elke is seven now and Paul says she's in her prime as a hunter and he's never seen a better quail dog that operates the way he likes to hunt.

The perfect match? Probably as close as it gets.

"Elke is also a wonderful companion on trout fishing trips," Paul says. "On hot days she stands right behind me in the stream and follows the flow as I move. We are content to relax together, indoors or out."

A cherished dog living in an immaculate home is nothing unusual, but there is one undeniable reality. Sometimes dogs get sick. Your dog may vomit, or suffer a bout of diarrhea. It won't happen often to a healthy dog, and it may never happen to your dog, but ignoring the possibility would be dishonest. How would you react if your reliably housebroken dog suddenly got sick and soiled your carpet? Only you know the answer. Consider it before acquiring a dog.

Another (b) answer that warrants thought is to question 36; the previous dog that didn't work out and was sold or given away. You've read this far, so you must be trying for a successful relationship the second time around. Using the failure as a learning experience should help. Why wasn't the dog suitable? Did he have nasty habits you couldn't break, or did you choose the wrong dog for your lifestyle? Was he destructive? Could it have been your fault for not teaching him house manners and confining him until he was reliable? As you read this book, think about what you could have done differently that might have helped your first dog work out. Habit is a powerful force, so try to resist the temptation to fall into the same pattern with a new dog that you had with the last one. If it didn't work last time, it probably won't work again.

If you already have several other pets in your house (question 42), be certain you will still have time to give them all sufficient attention after you acquire a dog. Also, depending on what type of pets you have, your new dog could shock you by treating them as prey. Make sure all small pets, such as gerbils, birds, and reptiles, are safely caged well out of your dog's reach. They can be killed in one horrid instant— and your dog's curiosity can kill them as quickly as viciousness can. So it's better to be extremely safe than very sorry. Dogs and cats can get along wonderfully well together, provided they have mutual respect. If you get a dog through a rescue organization (see Chapter 4), it probably has been tested out with cats, and its foster family will be able to tell you how it reacted.

If you get around a little slower these days (question 44), choose a mature dog that is well past its puppy foolishness and is a size you can easily handle. Extremely tiny dogs or quick-moving terriers may not be the best choice for you either.

Mostly (c), (d), and (e) answers to questions 28 through 44 indicate that you have unrealistic expectations no dog could ever live up to, and are unwilling to put any time, effort, or money into essentials like training and grooming. But a few of the (c) and (d) answers aren't bad at all. If you answered (c) or (d) to 31, 32, and 42, it just means you have no experience with tending and training dogs or other pets. That's no problem, as long as you want to learn. This book will help you with selection, care, and training. Plus, there are hundreds of other books and videos to help you delve deeper into the areas you find most interesting. Dog training classes welcome new students, and veterinarians are happy to give tips on preventative health care. So don't let lack of experience stop you. If you scored strong on desire, your dog will be lucky to have you.

Neighbors on the other side of the wall (question 40) just means you should select a dog that's on the quiet side. It's probably already on your "Dream Dog" list, but if not, be sure to include.

If you have tiny tots (question 41), your dog absolutely has to be good with children. Even so, stay nearby when they are playing together.

Thousands of happy people and happy dogs live together in cluttered houses (questions 38 and 43). The only reason this was included in the quiz is because a dog is more apt to chew something valuable in a cluttered house than in a neat one. If your dog was raised in a home where its toy was on the floor, but everything else was put away, and now lives in a home where shoes and purses are strewn about, it may not understand the difference between your leather goods and its rawhide chew.

If you get around with difficulty (question 44), select a calm dog of a size and strength you can easily handle—not too big and not real tiny either. You will have to walk your dog if you don't have a fenced yard, but the mild exercise may be a blessing. If you're in a wheelchair, don't let that keep you from the joys of dog ownership. Many wheelchair-bound people not only have dogs, but successfully compete with them in Obedience competition.

MEET THE BREEDS

Over 150 different dog breeds are recognized by the American Kennel Club and even more by the United Kennel Club. Each of these breeds is unique, but when classifying dogs we have to start somewhere, and the American Kennel Club's system is as good a place to do this as any. It divides all AKC-recognized breeds into seven variety groups, according to the work each breed originally performed. An introduction to these groups will help you expand your choices while seeking the right dog for you. If you already have a dog, it will also help you understand your dog's intriguing instincts.

The following is a brief description of each Group, including its historic work and its present-day function. The breeds that make up each Group are listed, along with their size and coat type. That should help you decide which individual breeds you want to research further at your local library. A good place to start your research is with "The Complete Dog Book," the official publication of the American Kennel Club. It has information on every AKC-recognized breed, in the Group order listed here. Many books on individual breeds may also be available.

When doing your research, take along your "Dream Dog" list and your "Not For Me" list. No matter how beautiful, elegant, or intriguing a dog appears in pictures and print, these lists will remind you to look for the qualities you selected as most suitable in temperament, activity level, size, and coat type. That will help you narrow down your selections in a hurry. There are individual books available on almost every breed, either in your library or in major bookstores, so take your time and thoroughly study the breeds that seem suitable. Remember, you are who you are, and it's doubtful you will make a major change in your personality or lifestyle to suit a dog's needs. Along the same line, your dog's original purpose will always have some impact on its behavior. While training does wonders for dogs, it doesn't wipe out generations of breeding for specialized instincts.

Following are descriptions of AKC's seven variety groups.

KEY TO ALL BREEDS

S = size

C = coat type

feathering = longer fringe of hair on ears, legs, tail, or body

THE SPORTING GROUP

The Sporting group is AKC's official name for the breeds that are commonly called bird dogs or gun dogs. It is made up of three basic types of hunting dogs: retrievers, pointing breeds, and spaniels. Each type has its own style of hunting.

Retrievers patiently wait with their owners in small boats or duck blinds. Their job begins after ducks or geese are shot down. Through

English Springer Spaniels are beautiful and active and some make marvelous hunters. This is T.J.'s Broadway Connection (Scooter), owned by Dennis, Marilyn, and Kim Bain. The dog is handled by Marilyn.

Many Golden Retrievers make wonderful obedience dogs because they love to please. This is Beckwith's Panjandrum, CD with Dave Wedum.

dense reeds and often frigid waters, these dogs retrieve fallen birds and carry them back to their owners. And they do it with a mouth so soft that the meat will not be bruised.

The pointing breeds use their incredible sense of smell to hunt upland birds such as grouse, pheasant, and quail. When they locate a game bird, their stylish pose is the stuff many hunter's dreams are made of. At the first scent of a bird, they stop several feet away and stand rigidly with their nose facing the bird and one fore leg often lifted. They remain in this statuesque position until the hunter flushes the bird (spooks it so it flies) and shoots it. Many pointing dogs are also trained to retrieve the shot bird for the hunter.

Spaniels do a three-part job. They merrily hunt through dense vegetation until they find a bird, then they rush in and flush it. After the hunter shoots it down, they retrieve it gently and look for another.

Sporting dogs don't have to hunt to be happy. Games of fetch and catch, backpacking in the mountains, or jogging in a city park are just a few activities that keep Sporting dogs in high spirits. But they are hardy dogs, bred to work for long hours serving their masters. Consequently, they require enough training to know how to please their owners and are most content and well-mannered when they get plenty of exercise.

Mature Sporting dogs that were never used for hunting often make excellent hunting companions once they have sufficient training. Instinct is crucial, of course, but it isn't the only element that makes a fine gun dog. Some training, especially in basic hunting manners, is always required. But making a match with a member of the Sporting group does not automatically mean you have acquired a hunting companion. Many Sporting dogs need a second start because they failed as hunters due to gun-shyness, lack of sufficient instinct, or improper training.

Failed hunting dogs often become fantastic family dogs. Since Sporting dogs were bred to work with man, it's natural for them to be devoted partners. In fact, the Labrador Retriever, the Golden Retriever, and the Cocker Spaniel are in the top ten of America's most popular companion breeds.

There are many differences between members of the gun dog breeds even though they are in the same group. But that's a plus, because it means there are Sporting dogs to suit many human personalities. For example, the jaunty, active English Springer Spaniel is in its element when it has plenty of exercise and a job to do. Meanwhile, the sedate, heavier Clumber Spaniel is content to curl up and nap if its owner dozes off during the news.

If you think a Sporting dog might be the right partner for you, study the personalities, histories, and hunting styles of the breeds that match the size and coat preferences you have.

THE SPORTING GROUP
RETRIEVERS
Chesapeake Bay Retriever:
S—medium/large, C—thick and rather short
Curly-Coated Retriever:
S—medium/large, C—rather short, tight curls all over the body
Flat-Coated Retriever:
S—medium/large, C—medium length with some feathering
Golden Retriever:
S—medium/large, C—medium length with feathering
Labrador Retriever:
S—medium/large, C—rather short and dense
Irish Water Spaniel (classified as a retriever for hunting purposes):
S—medium/large, C—tightly curled

POINTING BREEDS
Brittany:
S—medium, C—rather short with some feathering on legs
Pointer:
S—medium/large, C—short
German Shorthaired Pointer:
S—medium/large, C—short

German Wirehaired Pointer:
S—medium/large, C—rather short, dense, and wiry
English Setter:
S—large, C—medium length with feathering
Gordon Setter:
S—large, C—medium length with feathering
Irish Setter:
S—large, C—medium length with feathering
Vizsla:
S—medium/large, C—short
Weimaraner:
S—large, C—short
Wirehaired Pointing Griffon:
S—medium/large, C—medium length and wiry

SPANIELS

American Water Spaniel (some hunt retriever style):
S—medium, C—medium length with waves or curls
Clumber Spaniel:
S—medium, C—medium length with feathering
Cocker Spaniel:
S—small, C—medium length with thick feathering
English Cocker Spaniel:
S—medium/small, C—medium length with feathering
English Springer Spaniel:
S—medium, C—medium length with feathering
Field Spaniel:
S—medium, C—medium length with feathering
Sussex Spaniel:
S—small, C—medium length with feathering
Welsh Springer Spaniel:
S—medium, C—medium length with feathering

THE HOUND GROUP

Ancient drawings found on the walls of caves prove the antiquity of hounds. They were man's hunting partners, bringing down animals ranging from rabbit to bear, long before there was a written language.

Modern hounds are available in a variety of shapes, coats, and sizes and are capable of hunting game from the frozen North to the equator. They are also capable of pleasing those who want the most elegant or the most comical of pets. From the stately Irish Wolfhound, one of the tallest of all breeds, to the brash but diminutive Miniature Dachshund, the Hound Group mixes similarities with diversity.

From the elegant to the comical, hounds come in a variety of shapes and sizes. These two charmers are a Greyhound (above) and a Basset Hound (below).

Photo credit: Pets by Paulette.

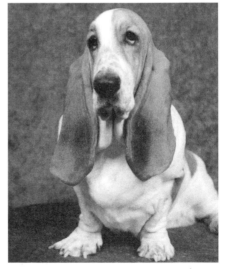

There are two basic types of hunting hounds: those that track by scent and those that give chase by sight. Scent hounds use their astounding sense of smell to track game until they locate it for the hunter. Once on a scent trail, they give voice at intervals during the hunt, enabling the hunter to follow. As they close in on the game and the cold trail gets hotter and hotter, their pitch changes in intensity, thereby serving as a signal.

Some scent hounds are a challenge to train because it's hard to get their noses off the ground long enough for them to concentrate on the lesson being taught. But with a little persistence, they make loyal, jovial, and cooperative companions. In fact, Dachshunds and Beagles, two of the smallest scent hounds, are included in America's top ten breeds in popularity.

Sight hounds use their superior vision to locate game and their extraordinary speed to catch it. Though few people hunt with sight hounds in America, the sport of coursing a mechanical lure simulates a real hunt and is fun for the dogs and their owners. Sighthounds are among the swiftest and most graceful of all breeds, yet most of them are laid-back companions. While they need daily exercise (as all dogs do), it doesn't take a lot of space to keep them comfortable and content.

Although hunting with hounds is still a popular sport in some parts of the country, most hounds are kept as companions today. If you think a hound might be the right match for you, read as much as you can about the breeds that interest you. They are divided below into scent hounds and sight hounds.

THE HOUND GROUP
SCENT HOUNDS
Basset Hound:
S—medium, C—short
Beagle:
S—small, C—short
Black and Tan Coonhound:
S—large, C—short
Bloodhound:
S—large, C—short

Dachshund:
S—small, C—short, fairly long, or wiry depending on variety

American Foxhound:
S—medium/large, C—short

English Foxhound:
S—medium/large, C—short

Harrier:
S—medium, C—short

Norwegian Elkhound:
S—medium, C—medium length and dense

Otterhound (hunts by scent, sight and in water):
S—large, C—medium length, dense, and course

Petit Basset Griffon Vendeen:
S—medium/small, C—long and rough

Sight Hounds
Afghan Hound:
S—large, C—long

Basenji:
S—medium/small, C—short

Borzoi:
S—large, C—medium long with long feathering

Greyhound:
S—medium/large, C—short

Ibizan Hound:
S—large, C—short

Irish Wolfhound:
S—very large, C—medium length and wiry

Pharaoh Hound:
S—medium/large, C—short

Rhodesian Ridgeback:
S—large, C—short

Saluki:
S—medium/large to large, C—short usually with feathering

Scottish Deerhound:
S—very large, C—medium length and rough
Whippet:
S—medium/small, C—short

THE WORKING GROUP

From the regal Great Dane to the powerful Saint Bernard to the playful Boxer, the Working breeds traditionally helped man by performing a multitude of jobs. The northern breeds pulled sleds, enabling man to traverse the polar ice caps and live successfully in a hostile environment. Other Working breeds served as war dogs, draft animals, fishermens' helpers, and guardians of estates and livestock. Many still serve in the capacity they were orignally bred for, and all are happiest when they are trained to perform some type of useful activity. Bred for generations to work with man, they are simply too intelligent, too big, and too strong to be left to their own devices.

While Working dogs come in a variety of shapes and coats, all of them are medium to large in size and some are downright huge. Particularly popular breeds from this group are the Rottweiler, the Boxer, the Siberian Husky, and the Doberman Pinscher. Because they were originally bred to perform so many different jobs, there is great variation in temperament, trainability, and activity level within the Working breeds. If you think a Working dog may be the right companion for you, study the following breeds and compare their attributes to your "Dream Dog Check List."

THE WORKING GROUP

Akita:
S—large, C—medium/short and dense
Alaskan Malamute:
S—large, C—medium/short and dense
Bernese Mountain Dog:
S—large, C—medium/long and thick
Boxer:
S—medium/large, C—short
Bullmastiff:
S—very large, C—short

Bred for generations to be mans' helpers and friends, Working dogs, like this Rottweiler (left) and these Boxers (right) are most content when they are well trained.

Photo credit: Pets by Paulette.

Doberman Pinscher:

S—large, C—short

Giant Schnauzer:

S—large, C—dense and wiry

Great Dane:

S—very large, C—short

Great Pyrenees:

S—very large, C—long with profuse feathering

Komondor:

S—very large, C—long and corded

Kuvasz:

S—very large, C—medium/long

Mastiff:

S—very large, C—short

Newfoundland:

S—very large, C—medium/long

Portuguese Water Dog:

S—medium, C—wavy or curly

Rottweiler:

S—large, C—short

Saint Bernard:

S—very large, C—short or medium

Samoyed:

S—medium/large, C—long

Siberian Husky:

S—medium, C—medium length

Standard Schnauzer:

S—medium, C—wiry and thick

THE TERRIER GROUP

The word "terrier" comes from the Latin word "terra," meaning "earth," and describes dogs with the courage and determination to go to ground (dig underground) in pursuit of prey. Although a few Terrier breeds are too large to go to ground, they are still deadly on vermin above the ground. Rats and mice are typical Terrier prey, but good working Terriers take on all types of vermin, including badgers, foxes, and weasels. Their ability to keep stored grain free of mice, and poultry safe from foxes, makes them especially valuable to rural families.

Although few Terriers are still used for hunting or herding, today's terriers are mostly loved as loyal family companions and alert watchdogs. Healthy, hardy, and so happy their moods are contagious, Terriers use their jaunty attitudes and big hearts to charm their owners. On the downside, these breeds sometimes have a stubborn streak and are also brave to a fault. Many have no respect for other dogs, and will challenge animals several times their size without hesitation.

From the elongated Skye to the muscular American Staffordshire, Terriers are found in a variety of coat types, sizes, and some unique shapes. Each breed has its own history, ranging from bull and dog fighting to hunting with handlers on horseback. Most are small enough to easily adapt to apartment living, provided they have daily walks or some other form of regular exercise.

Small dogs with big hearts, the West Highland White Terrier (left) and the Miniature Schnauzer (right) are two of the bright and brave members of the Terrier group.

Photo credit: Pets by Paulette.

The most popular Terrier breeds today are the Miniature Schnauzer, the West Highland White Terrier, and the Scottish Terrier. If Terriers intrigue you, learn all you can about the following breeds before making a selection.

THE TERRIER GROUP

Airedale Terrier:
S—medium/large, C—wiry

American Staffordshire Terrier:
S—medium, C—short

Australian Terrier:
S—small, C—medium

Bedlington Terrier:
S—medium/small, C—soft and curly

Border Terrier:
S—small, C—wiry

Bull Terrier (Colored or White):
S—medium, C—short

Cairn Terrier:
S—small, C—medium length and coarse
Dandie Dinmont Terrier:
S—small, C—medium length and crisp-textured
Fox Terrier (Smooth):
S—small, C—flat, close but not too short
Fox Terrier (Wire):
S—small, C—wiry
Irish Terrier:
S—medium, C—wiry
Kerry Blue Terrier:
S—medium, C—soft wavy or curly
Lakeland Terrier:
S—small, C—wiry
Manchester Terrier (Standard):
S—medium/small, C—short
Miniature Bull Terrier:
S—medium/small, C—short
Miniature Schnauzer:
S—small, C—wiry
Norfolk Terrier:
S—small, C—medium length and wiry
Norwich Terrier:
S—small, C—medium length and wiry
Scottish Terrier:
S—small, C—medium length and wiry
Sealyham Terrier:
S—small, C—medium length and wiry
Skye Terrier:
S—medium, C—long
Soft Coated Wheaten Terrier:
S—medium, C—medium/long with slight wave, soft

Staffordshire Bull Terrier:

S—medium/small, C—short

Welsh Terrier:

S—small, C—wiry

West Highland White Terrier:

S—small, C—medium length and coarse

THE TOY GROUP

Toy dogs are living proof that terrific things really do come in tiny packages. They fit anywhere, some will even snug in your pocket, and are usually highly intelligent with bold, fun-loving temperaments. Some Toy dogs, such as the Toy Poodle, are down-sized versions of their larger cousins. Others, like the Miniature Pinscher, have actually been around longer than the larger dogs that resemble them.

Toy dogs were created to be companions to man and are very good at their job. Able to get enough exercise in even the smallest apartment, and equally happy in the city, the suburbs, or the farm, these dogs thrive on attention and affection. From the exotic Chinese Crested, to the Papillon that performs with all the zest of a full-sized spaniel, the Toy breeds love to play games and entertain people. All members of this group make extremely popular therapy dogs, provided their temperaments are suitable. Most also make fine obedience and agility dogs, but there are exceptions. The beguiling Pekingese, for example, is not a good choice if you want a high-scoring performance dog, because its unique gait is too slow to make it competitive.

Today's most popular Toys are the Pomeranian, the Yorkshire Terrier, the Shih Tzu, and the Chihuahua. All the Toy breeds are small and loving lap-warmers, but those are the only two things they all have in common. Toys come in a variety of shapes, coat types, and colors, and their temperaments and activity levels are also quite varied. If you believe a Toy dog will warm your heart, research the following breeds. One of them may be your perfect match.

The Toy Group

Affenpinscher:

S—small, C—rather short and coarse

Toy dogs may be tiny, but they are just as smart and just as healthy as larger dogs.
This Pomeranian sports a pretty smile.

Photo credit: Pets by Paulette.

The smallest of all breeds, Chihuahuas can be long coats, as this alert pair, or the
more familiar smooth coats.

Photo credit: Pets by Paulette.

Brussels Griffon:
S—small, C—rather short, wiry, and dense

Chihuahua (Smooth or Long Coat):
S—tiny, C—short or rather long

Chinese Crested (Hairless or Powderpuff):
S—small, C—almost hairless or rather long

English Toy Spaniel (Blenheim, Prince Charles, King Charles, and Ruby):
S—small, C—long

Italian Greyhound:
S—small, C—short

Japanese Chin:
S—small, C—long

Maltese:
S—tiny, C—very long

Manchester Terrier (Toy):
S—small, C—short

Miniature Pinscher:
S—small, C—short

Papillon:
S—small, C—rather long

Pekingese:
S—small, C—long and thick

Pomeranian:
S—tiny, C—long and thick

Poodle (Toy):
S—small, C—long and curly

Pug:
S—small, C—short

Shih Tzu:
S—small, C—long and thick

Silky Terrier:
S—small, C—medium length
Yorkshire Terrier:
S—tiny, C—long

THE NON-SPORTING GROUP

Non-Sporting. What a terrible name for an excellent and diverse group of dogs. Where did it come from?

The earliest dog shows in the United States were open only to dogs used in sporting activities, such as hunting. Later, as dog shows became more popular, other breeds were allowed to compete in a category called "Non-Sporting." "Sporting" and "Non-Sporting" were the only groups at dog shows until the increasing multitude of Non-Sporting dogs were eventually divided into several Groups (such as Hound, Toy, and Terrier), according to the work they did. But a few dogs had been permanently laid off their jobs; not because they didn't do them well, but because the jobs had become obsolete. For example, humane laws stopped bull baiting (dogfights and bullfights), so the Bulldog was out of work. Automobiles replaced the horse and buggy, putting the world's best coach dogfights the Dalmatian, out of business. The Schipperke (Flemish for "little captain") couldn't find employment in America at its traditional job, guarding canal boats. So these, and all the other fine breeds that were unemployed through no fault of their own, remained in the Non-Sporting Group.

From the winsome white powder puff called the Bichon Frise to the comical French Bulldog, the Non-Sporting Group is made up of a variety of dissimilar breeds. The most popular of these are the Poodle and the Dalmatian. That so many Non-Sporting breeds remain popular even though their traditional jobs no longer exist is a tribute to how well they perform the most important job of all—family companion. In addition, many excel at new jobs and some of those jobs are decidedly sporting. For example, the Poodle and the Schipperke are exceptional Obedience and Agility competitors; while the Bichon Frise, Boston Terrier, French Bulldog, and Keeshond make outstanding therapy dogs.

Some of the breeds in this group have high activity levels, while others move slowly and are dignified in their demeanor. A few are aloof

This elegant Standard Poodle is groomed for a dog show.
Photo credit: Pets by Paulette.

The flashy Dalmatian, the original fire-house dog and coaching dog, still has an affinity for horses.
Photo credit: Pets by Paulette.

with strangers, while others adore all their owners' friends. If you enjoy grooming you can find your dream dog here, and if you prefer a wash 'n wear breed, plenty of them are in this group too. If some of the dogs in the Non-Sporting group attract you, study them carefully and compare them with your "Dream Dog Check List."

The Non-Sporting Group

Bichon Frise:
S—small, C—thick and rather curly

Boston Terrier:
S—small, C—short

Bulldog:
S—medium, C—short

Chinese Shar-Pei:
S—medium, C—short

Chow Chow:
S—medium/large, C—long and thick

Dalmatian:

S—medium/large, C—short

Finnish Spitz:

S—medium, C—medium length and dense

French Bulldog:

S—small, C—short

Keeshond:

S—medium, C—long and thick

Lhasa Apso:

S—small, C—long

Poodle (Miniature):

S—medium/small, C—curly

Poodle (Standard):

S—medium/large, C—curly

Schipperke:

S—small, C—medium length

Shiba Inu:

S—medium/small, C—rather short and very thick

Tibetan Spaniel:

S—small, C—medium

Tibetan Terrier:

S—medium, C—long and thick

THE HERDING GROUP

Dogs with strong herding instincts have worked side by side with man for centuries, moving large flocks of sheep or herds of cattle great distances. While some Herding breeds would qualify as large (though none are enormous), others weigh under thirty pounds. When you imagine a thirty-pound dog handling a stubborn steer, you'll understand why Herding dogs must be agile, with quick intelligence, superior stamina, and the trainability to respond precisely to their handlers' commands in any situation. Although only a small

Active and hardy, Herding dogs like this Border Collie (above) and these Cardigan Welsh Corgis (below) are happiest when they have a job to do. Many of them excel in Obedience competition.

Photo credit: Pets by Paulette.

percentage of Herding dogs have the opportunity to perform their original jobs today, many, especially Border Collies, German Shepherd Dogs, Shetland Sheepdogs, and Corgis, showcase their tremendous trainability during Obedience and Agility competition.

All Herding breeds are loyal and affectionate with their owners, but not all of them befriend strangers easily. While some Herding dogs quickly accept their owner's friends, others are suspicious of strangers and remain aloof, showing affection only to those they learn to know well. A reserved attitude is perfectly acceptable in these breeds, but shyness is not. Herding dogs have traditionally been effective natural guardians and fine watchdogs, and should not cower at the sight of a stranger.

Herding dogs were developed to work stock in many countries, and the variety of coat types, sizes, and shapes in this group reflect what was most suitable for the climate and terrain of each breed's native land. From the comely Collie to the corded Puli, Herding dogs make dependable and versatile companions. In fact, one of the top ten most popular breeds in the United States is the German Shepherd Dog, and the Shetland Sheepdog is also a favorite. If you think a Herding dog may be the faithful friend you seek, study the following dogs and rate them against your "Dream Dog Check List."

The Herding Group
Australian Cattle Dog:
S—medium, C—rather short
Australian Shepherd:
S—medium, C—medium length
Bearded Collie:
S—medium, C—long
Belgian Malinois:
S—large, C—rather short
Belgian Sheepdog:
S—large, C—long

Belgian Tervuren:

S—large, C—long

Border Collie:

S—medium, C—medium long

Bouvier des Flandres:

S—large, C—medium length and coarse

Briard:

S—large, C—long

Collie (Rough):

S—large, C—long

Collie (Smooth):

S—large, C—rather short

German Shepherd Dog:

S—large, C—medium length

Old English Sheepdog:

S—large, C—long and thick

Puli:

S—medium, C—long and curly or corded

Shetland Sheepdog:

S—small, C—long

Welsh Corgi (Cardigan):

S—small, C—medium length

Welsh Corgi (Pembroke):

S—small, C—medium length

SEARCHING FOR SUPERDOG

You've listed your likes and dislikes, faced the realities of dog care, and researched the breeds that seem most suitable. You're ready to move on. Where to? Out of the library and into the world of dogs. It's now time to go looking for love in all the right places.

A dog that is nothing but trouble for one person could be exactly what another person wants. After reading this story, imagine a dog like Gator living in a small apartment with no one at home most of the day. Then imagine how hard it must be for people who want a dog just like Gator to find one with the right combination of speed, intensity, intelligence, determination, and coordination.

GATOR FINDS HIS NICHE

Lonnie Olsen came home from a trip to find an extra dog in her kennel. Her husband Ed confessed that the Australian Cattle Dog had been rescued from the shelter by the local herding breed rescue group and he brought it home because he believed it would make a great flyball dog (flyball is a fast, competitive relay team sport for dogs). "Let's see," Lonnie said, and took a ball along when she went out to meet the dog.

Lonnie held the ball high and the muscular dog ran toward her full speed and gave her a full body tackle. She held the ball out at arm's length, about five feet off the ground, and the dog leaped up and snapped most of her hand and wrist in his jaws along with the ball. Lonnie looked at her husband. "We're keeping this one," she grinned.

Lonnie named the dog "Gator" and he responded to the name quickly. In fact, even before he had training he would spin in his tracks and come galloping back when he heard his name, even though he had been heading off at the dead run to chase the neighbor's horses. With training, Gator became a well-mannered and playful housedog; gentle with puppies and tolerant of the family cat.

Lonnie, who served as president of the National Association of Dog Obedience Instructors, understands that a dog as intense and active as Gator is certainly not for everyone. But he was perfect for her. "Gator has exactly the traits I was looking for in a good flyball dog," Lonnie said. "He has a strong prey drive, limitless energy, is possessive of his ball or toy, and is dauntless in his effort to capture and control any plaything. These are exactly the kinds of traits which could cause a dog to lose his happy home. I could just see this guy zooming up on a baby with a blanket, Snoopy and

Super flyball competitor Gator, an Australian Cattle Dog, takes a break with his favorite toy.

Linus style, and zinging off with the blanket, baby still attached or not. Or I could visualize him chasing joggers, knocking down little kids, or killing livestock."

Of course Gator did none of these things as Lonnie and Ed's dog. Instead, he behaved at home, excelled at his game, and won his Flyball Championship. "Gator is loving, playful, and very expressive," Lonnie says, "and when I think about how he was almost put to sleep because nobody wanted him, it makes me want to cry. We love his adorable personality so much that we bought another Australian Cattle Dog. Our Gator's story has a good ending, or rather a good middle. I hope Gator will be with us for many years. I know he'll be with us for the rest of his life."

CHAPTER FOUR

FINDING A DYNAMITE DOG

Would you like a beautiful purebred dog? Perhaps one that's already had some training. Finding a dynamite dog may be easier and less expensive than you think.

SHOW KENNELS

Dogs bred for the show ring often become available, and at reasonable prices too. Many of them don't live up to their perfect puppy promise and grow into maturity with some minor imperfection that keeps them from becoming top-notch competitors. These unsuccessful show dogs are usually extremely attractive animals, and only a discerning judge or breeder would be able to find the subtle conformation fault that halted their show career. In most cases, failed show dogs are well socialized, walk in a mannered fashion on lead, and are completely crate trained.

Even champion show dogs sometimes become available for adoption, or may be sold for about the same price as a quality puppy. When a champion is past its prime for breeding, its caring owner may try to place it in a home where it will enjoy the balance of its life as someone's special dog, not just languish to no purpose in a breeding kennel. Besides benefiting the dog, this also helps the kennel owner by making room for younger breeding and show stock.

Retired champions and unsuccessful show dogs both make wonderful companions and may excel at entirely new careers, such as agility, obedience, or therapy. But don't expect to use them for breeding. They have either earned their retirement or shouldn't be bred in the first place, so they will either be spayed or neutered before being offered for sale, or the adoption contract will make the new owner responsible for having this minor surgery performed. Since spayed and neutered dogs make the best companions and avoid some potentially major health problems, everyone benefits from the procedure.

Finding kennels that raise show dogs is easy. Many of them advertise in magazines such as *Dog Fancy, Dog World,* and the *AKC Gazette.* Also, you can contact the American Kennel Club (see Appendix) and request a geographical list of show and obedience clubs or field trial and hunting test clubs (both are free). Write to the clubs in your state that represent the breeds you are interested in and request a list of breeders in your area.

When you contact breeders, tell them you prefer an adult and explain why you selected their breed. The more they know about what you want in a dog, the better match they can help you make. Will the dog serve as a companion to senior citizens or a playmate for children? Will it be indoors all the time or will it live in a fenced yard during the day and inside at night? What other plans do you have for the dog? For example, will you compete in obedience or agility competitions, go hunting, or volunteer for animal-assisted therapy in a nursing home?

It's a good idea to write to the breeder first, then follow with a phone call in about ten days. That gives the breeder time to think about your letter and imagine their dog in your home. Many a breeder who didn't plan to place their favorite brood matron for at least another year can't resist an outstanding home when it presents itself. A typical introductory letter might read like this:

> *Dear Mr. and Mrs. Weiss,*
> *My name is Carolyn Wilson and I am interested in getting a West Highland White Terrier. My husband and I are retired and spend several months a year traveling in our motor home, so we would like a small, sturdy dog to keep us company at home and on the road. The dog will live indoors but will have to adjust to both the house and the motor home and should be a good traveler. Since we often stay in campgrounds with other travelers for neighbors, it's important that the dog be friendly with people and not too noisy. It should also accept other dogs as there is usually a common area in campgrounds for walking dogs. My husband and I enjoy hiking and fishing all year long, so our dog will get plenty of exercise. We would prefer a female between two and five years old, but would consider the right male.*

*I'll call you during the week of September 1st to find out if you have
a suitable dog.*
Sincerely,

Carolyn Wilson

When you call the breeder, expect to answer questions about your history of dog ownership and why you're interested in this breed. The
breeder may ask how much time you spend at home, the ages of your
children, and whether you have a fenced yard. Answer honestly and
don't be insulted. Good breeders love their dogs and want to make
sure their retired darling will have a safe and loving home.

If a show champion has a genetic fault or a breeding problem, it may
become available when it's still relatively young. Top-quality kennels
have their animals tested for hereditary problems before breeding
them, and carefully find homes for those dogs deemed unsuitable for
breeding. That's how Tom Coyne, of New Vernon, New Jersey, got the
dog of his dreams, Ch. Eden Ruffwood Genuine Risk, JH, WC.

NOT SO RISKY

Risky, a champion Flat-Coated Retriever with a Junior Hunter title
and a working certificate, was four years old when Tom Coyne heard
about her. Flat-Coats aren't easy to find, and Coyne had been looking
for one for a long time before he finally located Risky through the
Flat-Coated Retriever Society of America, Inc. She was owned by
Debbie Porter of Chicago.

On the plus side, Risky was as beautiful as one would expect of a
champion show dog and was trained for hunting too. She was also a
gentle and protective nursemaid to the Porters' baby, alerting the family at the first hint of a cry. But Risky had hip dysplasia, and Porter
was too responsible a breeder to consider using her in a breeding program. So she selectively put out the word that if the right person came
along, one who met her criteria, she'd consider placing Risky.

Porter's criteria were stringent. First of all, any prospective owners
had to be willing to come in person, so Porter could see if they had
a rapport with Risky, and vice versa. Secondly, since Risky loved

hunting, they had to be willing to utilize her talents in the field. And of course, they had to offer Risky a secure and loving home.

Porter had already turned down several people when Tom Coyne called from New Jersey. He wanted a Flat-Coat as a house dog and hunting companion and was willing to fly to the Midwest to meet her. The meeting went well, and after several hours of talk and a brief training session, Porter kissed Risky good-bye and the dog flew east with Coyne.

The Coynes and the Porters have remained friends over the years. At last report, Risky had accepted another full-time job in addition to being best buddy and hunting partner. She's back in the nursery, but instead of helping Porter with one baby at a time, she's watching over three at once. The Coynes are the proud parents of triplets. "The last time I spoke with Tom and Ann, Risky was licking formula off three little faces," Porter said. "Tom also told me he was using Risky's side as sort of an infant seat. He'd rest one baby against her while he fed another. Now that's what I call a multipurpose dog in just the right house!"

Ch. Eden Ruffwood Genuine Risk, JH, WC (Risky), a Flat-Coated Retriever, was a successful show dog before she became the Coynes' fabulous family pet.

"When someone is in the nursery, Risky is in the nursery," says her owner, Tom Coyne. "With at least one eye and one ear always open, she is our living, breathing nursery monitor. We couldn't have asked or expected anything more from this wonderful retriever."

FIELD TRIAL AND HUNTING DOG KENNELS

Kennels where dogs are bred for either competitive field trialing or hunting often have adults available. A dog that is bred for field trials, and returned to the breeder because it wasn't fast enough to win in competition, could make a splendid companion and an ideal hunting dog. A female kept for breeding may not produce puppies, but could become someone's lovable pet. A puppy sold to a hunter may have been returned due to gun-shyness, but that's no problem for someone is search of a house dog. A dog may have sustained an injury that would keep it from winning field trials, but would have no impact whatsoever on its leading a healthy, happy life. Sometimes an adult dog becomes available simply because its first owner couldn't keep it and returned it to the breeder. That's how an English Springer Spaniel named Buddy became one of the most famous canine cops in Canada.

Buddy—The Nose that Knows

Pheasant Run Kennels in New Castle, Pennsylvania, is known for its top-quality field-bred English Springer Spaniels, so it wasn't surprising when an elderly gentleman stopped by to look for "a good bird dog." During the pre-purchase interview, owners David and Kimberly Richards learned that the man was newly separated from his wife and returning to his boyhood home in Denver, Colorado. He wanted to buy a puppy and take it with him.

The puppy that appealed to the buyer was one David had other plans for, as he believed it had "superstar" potential. The man had never trained a field-bred English Springer Spaniel and David felt obligated to warn him that this pup was bold, energetic, and aggressive. In other words, it was "wired for sound." But the man assured David that he could handle the pup.

"It was love at first sight," David said. "He was crazy about the pup and the pup thought he was pretty neat too. So I decided to let the pup bring some happiness into this old bird hunter's life."

The old man named his puppy Buddy, and took off for Denver with the dog beside him. Over the next several months, he often sent letters and pictures to David and Kimberly. In the photos, Buddy was happily hunting and retrieving pheasants in the snowy Colorado hills. He was well trained and everything was going fine.

Then one day the old man and Buddy reappeared at Pheasant Run. David remembers, "Although he was pleasant, he was obviously very disturbed about something. He regaled me with stories of Buddy and his outstanding ability to hunt and retrieve. Most important of all, Buddy was his best friend. However, he had reconciled with his wife and moved back into their condo in Pennsylvania, whereupon his wife told him the dog must go. So he was returning Buddy in the desperate hope that I would place him with someone who would care for him as well as we both had. He also told me I was right. Buddy would be a "superstar" someday. Tearfully, the old man gave Buddy a hug and a big kiss. Then he got into his truck and never looked back."

David kept Buddy for a few weeks just in case the old man managed to change his wife's mind. Then he called his friend, Constable Mike Bowman of the Peel Region Police in Ontario, Canada. Mike had recently relinquished an English Springer Spaniel that he had trained for narcotics detection, and he and his family missed the dog terribly. When David offered to give him Buddy, Mike arrived at the kennel in no time. He and Buddy were delighted with each other, and as David watched them depart, he knew his early assessment of the puppy would come true. Buddy would be a "superstar."

The rest is history. Born to be a superior hunting dog, Buddy fulfilled his breeder's dreams. But instead of hunting the woods and fields looking for pheasant, he hunts for drugs. Buddy started his second career by finding hashish that was wrapped in a package and stuffed in the air filter of a car. Since then he has found cocaine, heroin, crack, and marijuana, no matter how elaborately they were wrapped and hidden. With Mike's training, and the help of the Peel Police, Buddy is famous today as the all time highest scoring Narcotics Detection Dog in Canada. At competition in Toronto, the judges called him "Buddy the Wonder Dog." He also won the United States Police Canine Association York Regional Trials two years in a row, achieving the highest points in history—198.44 out of a possible 200.

To find field trial and hunting dog kennels, check the advertisements and/or classifieds in *Gun Dog Magazine*, *Pointing Dog Journal*, *Spaniels in the Field*, *Retriever Field Trial News*, and the *AKC Hunting*

Narcotics Detections Dog, Buddy, an English Springer Spaniel, finds drugs that were wrapped up and placed in the air filter of a car.

Test Herald (see Appendix). Tell the breeder if you want a hunting dog, or are just looking for a terrific companion.

PUREBRED RESCUE ORGANIZATIONS

Purebred dog rescue organizations are made up of volunteers who offer foster home care to dogs (usually of a particular breed) that have lost their home for any reason. Some of the dogs have registration papers, while others are purebreds whose papers were lost or never issued. People who can no longer keep their dog often contact their breeds' rescue organization directly, and dogs whose owners have died are often fostered by a rescuer until a new owner is found. In addition, rescue volunteers take dogs of their breed out of animal shelters, help dogs that were victims of abuse, and provide medical treatment when necessary. Later, when these dogs are medically and temperamentally sound and have been thoroughly screened, they are offered for adoption. The potential adopter is also screened, as rescue organizations emphasize making a good match. For example, they won't place a dog that hates cats with a cat owner or one that is afraid of children with a family of five.

Judy Marden, of the East Coast German Shorthaired Pointer Rescue Network, explains why putting dogs in foster homes until they are adopted works better than housing them in shelters:

"It's impossible to completely evaluate a dog in a shelter situation. In some instances, a shelter dog may exhibit lethargy, disinterest in humans, and an attitude indicating he has simply given up. On the other hand, he may appear to be a pacing, jumping, raging maniac. When a dog is taken from a shelter and fostered, the foster caregiver might be in for a surprise as the dog settles into its new environment. For example, the lethargic dog may actually have excess energy, while the raging maniac may have exemplary house manners and be an easy acquisition for a new owner. Fostering is truly the key to proper placements, as this is how we ascertain exactly what the dog is like, what obedience training he may still need, how he gets along with children, toddlers, adults, other dogs and cats, and how well he may be able to do the job for which the breed was developed."

Somebody's Buddy Now

Another Buddy, this one a year-and-a-half-old German Short-haired Pointer fostered by Judy and Ken Marden, is an example of how rescue volunteers give dogs a makeover and a match up. As Judy tells it:

"The dog we called Buddy had lived his entire life chained to a doghouse. He was rescued from an owner who was going to shoot him because that was a cheaper way to get rid of him than putting him in a shelter (some shelters require a donation). He got along fine with our dogs, crated well, housebroke in two days, but didn't respond to people. Changing situations didn't faze him—he spent his time in la-la land and knew absolutely nothing, not even his name if he ever had one. Upon entering rescue, he was dangerously undernourished, had ulcerations of the sclera of both eyes, a severe sprain in one leg, ear mites, and deep-seated ear infections. Luckily, the veterinarian was able to correct all the physical problems.

"After two weeks of building Buddy up nutritionally and giving him some solo training, he still didn't respond to people. It was obvious that he would need serious training to progress to the point where he would be adoptable, so we enrolled him in a basic obedience course. After a slow start, he suddenly caught on and began to show awareness of his handler and learn what was expected of him. From then on, there was no stopping him. In eight weeks he graduated first in his class and breezed through AKC's Canine Good Citizen test.

"Today Buddy resides happily in Norfolk, Virginia, with a Navy helicopter pilot and his wife. The pilot is at sea six months a year and his

After his rescue, Buddy was enrolled in an obedience school by his foster family. He graduated first in his class and passed the AKC Canine Good Citizen Test.

wife wanted a substantial-looking dog who would bark when strangers came to the door. Buddy is perfect for the job. He's large, not shy, and has a thundering bark. Of course, he's really a wimp who just wants to say, 'Hi!' to everyone, but strangers don't know that. Now a well-loved and well-behaved member of the family, Buddy has come a long way from the no-personality, non-responsive lump that entered the rescue program."

To locate purebred rescue, call the *AKC Gazette* (see Appendix). A publication of the American Kennel Club, it maintains and annually publishes a list of breed rescue organizations nationwide, and provides names and phone numbers by breed, on request. On a local level, most shelters can supply the name of the nearest breed-specific rescue contact. In some areas, individuals involved in rescues are members of an All Breed Rescue Alliance. This group maintains a list of rescuers who specialize in specific breeds, and places classified ads in the pet section of major newspapers. Also, in most states there are federations of dog clubs which publish, in major metropolitan newspapers, the phone number of a person who can refer you to either breed rescue or to responsible breeders. In addition, most dog clubs have a designated person who can refer you to a rescuer.

When you contact a rescue organization, expect the third degree. Rescue workers devote considerable time and expense to every one of their charges and want each new home to be successful. To ensure this, those adopting a rescue dog must answer a battery of questions. Don't let the personal questions put you in a huff. The volunteer wants to make sure you and the dog are a suitable match and that the dog will be well provided for in a permanent home.

Classified Ads in the Newspaper

"Free to good home: five-year-old Labrador mix. Good with children. Phone: 555-555-2123."

Classified ads similar to the one above appear daily in many newspapers and offer a variety of adult dogs for sale or for free. While some of these dogs are darlings, and others are destructive devil dogs from hell, all of them have owners who are responsible enough to find them a new family instead of dumping them at the shelter. This gives you the advantage of being able to talk to the dog's owner in addition to testing the dog's temperament. Phrases like "He needs room to run," could simply mean the dog needs more exercise than the owner has time to give, but it could also mean the dog never adjusted to being a house pet and paces or whines continuously or is destructive or noisy. Rather than trying to read between the lines, ask honest questions. If you live in an apartment house and it's important that your dog be reasonably quiet while you are at work, say so. Here are some examples of questions that could be worked into your conversation, and you can tailor others to your needs:

- How long have you had your dog?

- Why are you getting rid of your dog?

- Did you get the dog as a puppy? If not, when did you get it and who had it before you?

- What training has your dog had?

- Can it be trusted around children, men, women, and strangers?

- Is it housebroken?

- What are your dog's favorite games? (If you get a blank stare in response, you'll know the dog doesn't get a lot of attention.)

- Does your dog have any habits that a new owner should be aware of? For example, is the dog an escape artist, or a furniture muncher, or does it make so much noise that the neighbors complain?

- What time does your dog eat and what brand of dog food do you feed? (A dog with no regular schedule, that is fed whatever brand happens to be on sale, might be impossible to housebreak. Dogs need to be fed on a regular schedule and are healthiest and easiest to housebreak when they receive the same high-quality dog food day after day without variation.)

- Are you going to get another dog when you find a home for this one?

ANIMAL SHELTERS

Sometimes dynamite dogs are turned in at animals shelters and humane organizations. Not everyone is aware of the rescue networks, so if someone dies without making provisions for their pet, the animal could end up at a shelter. Likewise, an owner's sickness or a sudden move could put a pampered pet with the destitute dogs at the local humane facility. So don't rule out the "dog pound" in your search for a dynamite dog. That's where Suzette M. Wood found her dream dog, Chumley.

Chumley, a Wirehaired Pointing Griffon, was adopted from the pound. Since then he has earned titles in Obedience competition.

From Shelter Dog to Obedience Star

When Suzette M. Wood of Kissimmee, Florida saw a newspaper photo of a Wirehaired Pointing Griffon at the animal shelter awaiting adoption, she could hardly believe it. Not only are Griffons rather rare, but Suzette had failed to find one twenty years earlier when she wanted to buy one.

Suzette adopted Chumley right off death row, and the dog was so handsome and sweet that she couldn't believe her good luck. A shelter worker said the Griffon had been picked up as a stray, and Suzette was certain he had been lost or stolen and someone probably missed him very much. So, instead of giving in and loving him, she tried to find his owners. She contacted his national breed club, called several breeders, and waited for return calls. While waiting, she started loving Chumley in spite of herself. The dog responded and soon regained the happy confidence typical of his breed.

Most important of all, there should be some chemistry between you.

When four months went by with no call from Chumley's owner, Suzette finally considered the dog hers. It was all uphill from there. Chumley earned his Companion Dog (CD) and his Companion Dog Excellent (CDX) titles in AKC Obedience competition and was featured on the cover of his breed's national publication, *The Griffonnier*. Today he is working toward his Utility Dog title and training for hunting tests.

"I'm enjoying Chumley so much," Suzette says. "Over the past several years he brightened my life with companionship, entertainment, and his many accomplishments."

ASKING THE DOG

Making a match with your dream dog doesn't entail a long engagement, but it's good to find out as much as you can about your intended companion. So learn about your potential partner by asking questions of the breeder, rescue volunteer, current owner, or shelter staff—but above all, ask the dog. Whether you want a registered purebred or a pet from the pound, putting it through the tests described below will help you discover its disposition.

Testing for Temperament

- Pet and talk to an adult dog to check for mental stability and a willingness to please, but don't force it to stay close to you. Does it enjoy affection? Is it loving and attentive? Or is it excitable or independent? Does it overwhelm you with affection or does it show its delight delicately? Does it tense up at your touch or cringe in terror? Is the dog so passive that it doesn't seem to notice if you pet it or not? If so, it may be traumatized by its stay at the pound or mourning the loss of its owner. Time and loving attention may give it back its spirit and personality. Do you have the time? If so, you could have the satisfaction of seeing this dog learn to live and love again. If not, select an adult dog that doesn't need so much extra attention.

- Ask if you and the dog can have a few minutes alone together in a room with the door closed so the dog can be off lead. Now watch the dog. It may be confused at first, but does it orient itself quickly and start exploring its new surroundings? Or is it afraid to move when it finds itself in a new situation? How fast does it move during its exploration? Does it trot around or take its time? That gives you a clue about its activity level. When the dog is on its own, does it ever check to see where you are or what you are doing? After watching awhile, walk to the other end of the room. Does the dog follow? Call it and walk away again. Does it come?

ADOPTING A RETIRED RACING GREYHOUND

Until rather recently, young Greyhounds that weren't speedy enough on the track, and successful racers past their prime, were euthanized to make room for faster stock. Thankfully, that's changed at most dog tracks in the United States. In the last ten years, agencies have sprung up all over the country dedicated to matching retired Greyhounds of all ages with loving owners.

Retired racers make wonderful companions, but because they were raised in kennels and trained for the track, they have to make a few unique adjustments. No one can explain the process of adoption and adjustment better than someone who is enjoying a retired racer's company right now. So here's . . .

Cinder's Story
by her owner, Barbara Furman

"It all started at a sidewalk sale in West Hartford Center, Connecticut. We had seen advertisements on television about adopting Greyhounds and even discussed the possibility, but there they were in the flesh,

The Furman family with Muffin the cat, Smoky the Poodle, and Cinder their adopted Greyhound.

nuzzling our sides, yearning for affection. WAG (We Adopt Greyhounds) had brought them to the sale to entrap passersby, and it worked. We were trapped. Then and there we filled out the adoption application and prepared to wait while the organization checked to see if we would make a good adoptive family.

"This included talking to our veterinarian to see if we were taking good care of the two pets we already had. Two days later the phone rang—we were Greyhound parents! We were given two numbers. One was for an ex-Greyhound trainer who houses Greyhounds he rescued from the racetrack until they are adopted. The other was for a woman who had adopted numerous Greyhounds and was willing to help out by answering questions.

"Since Smoky, our Toy Poodle, is a male, we had requested a female Greyhound. As we waited outside Paul's noisy basement kennel, two female brindles were brought out to us. "Choose," Paul said. One

Greyhound pranced around playfully, coming to each of us for attention. The other stood there shaking and hiding her head between her
legs when anyone came near. I think my husband and son were leaning
toward the playful one, but my heart went out to Cinder. Actually,
"Forever Elegant" was her name, if you can call it a name, for she'd
never actually been called by it. On the track and in training a very
impersonal "Here Girl," was all she'd ever heard. Property was all
she'd been. She would be our own personal Cinderella story, so Cinder
she became.

"As excited as we were, we knew there was one possible problem.
When Greyhounds race, they chase a small, furry simulated animal, so
of course they are trained to chase a small, furry simulated animal,
something that comes quite naturally to them in any case. Now we
were about to bring a Greyhound home to live with two small, furry
real animals, Smoky, our Toy Poodle, and Muffin, our cat. With this in
mind, Paul gave us a muzzle for Cinder with instructions to put it on
her when she was introduced to Smoky and Muffin and to continue
using it when they were left alone together, until we were sure she was
used to them.

"As it turned out, Cinder's introduction to Smoky went very smoothly.
They sniffed each other in Paul's front yard, then we took a family picture on his porch and drove home with Smoky in the front seat on my
lap and Cinder stretched comfortably across the back seat with our
son, Seth.

"With our arrival home, it became quite apparent that Cinder had
never been in a house before. Led by Smoky, her little host, she went
from room to room, sniffing everything, and became fascinated with
her reflection in the front of our dishwasher.

"Her initial reaction to Muffin, our cat, was somewhat bizarre. At first
she cried as if she was totally confused by this plump ball of fur in
front of her. Then her cry suddenly turned into a growl and she lunged
at Muffin. I don't know if she would actually have harmed the cat, but
we were grateful for that muzzle. For a while after that, Muffin simply
kept her distance from Cinder. Then one day she brazenly came up to
Cinder and sniffed her nose, leaving before the surprised Greyhound
had a chance to react. From that point on, it was as if Muffin simply
decided it was her house and she shouldn't have to 'pussy foot' around
some dog. She stopped taking the long way around to keep out of
Cinder's reach, and Cinder became accustomed to Muffin and accepted
her as a member of her new family.

"As for Cinder and Smoky, things seemed to be going almost too
smoothly. Cinder took a somewhat subservient role to Smoky's 'boss-
man' act. In fact, she even hid in my closet the day Smoky snapped at
her for trying to steal some of my attention from him. Then, one day

when we were outside, Smoky started darting playfully around the yard and Cinder's mind shifted suddenly into racing gear. She lunged at him, almost pulling her leash out of my hand. I pulled her back, reprimanded her strongly, and got Smoky to stop running and come over to Cinder. This happened on several other occasions until Cinder finally understood that the bounding little black ball of fur in the yard was the same less active little friend from the house.

"Cinder's adjustment to living in a house faced two major obstacles. The first was actually somewhat comical—she had never walked up stairs. At night, fourteen stairs stood between Cinder and sleeping comfortably with her family. So my husband, son, and I took turns, one at each end, walking her front and back legs step by step up those stairs. Finally, after many nervous solo practice sessions, desire to be with her family overtook fear of stairs and she made it to the top by herself—yea Cinder!

"The second obstacle was housebreaking. Having been walked from kennel to run to racetrack, Cinder had no idea what the rules were in a house. To assist in her training, we had been advised to put her in a crate at night and when we weren't at home. She was taken out to the same area of our yard morning, noon, and night, and within half an hour of each feeding was told to "find a spot" and highly praised when she was successful. There were accidents, always in the same spot in the house (our living room, of course), but after several weeks of being consistent, both in the timing of outings and the words used for command and praise, she seemed to be getting the idea. There was still an occasional accident, but we knew she was an older dog and that we had changed the rules on her, so we were patient and continued to be consistent. Eventually our patience paid off in a well-housebroken dog.

"In the two years since we adopted Cinder, she and Muffin seem to have learned to coexist with just an occasional bark or hiss to show who is boss—but also, an occasional nuzzle. Smoky and Cinder have become good friends. They play together in the house (with Smoky always on higher ground, the bed or a couch, so he won't get trampled), sniff the same telephone poles together on walks, and even occasionally share a bed together for a nap. Smoky is still the dominant one, with Cinder apparently happy to follow his lead. Their only clashes occur as a result of Smoky's possessiveness. When Smoky's snuggling with one of us he still doesn't want Cinder to share the attention and lets her know it in no uncertain terms, and Cinder, many times his size, backs off. Some care still has to be taken outside, but only because when their play gets too rough, there is no high ground for Smoky to get on to keep him from getting hurt accidentally.

"It's hard to imagine our house without Cinder. Her Greyhound antics have made her the family clown. She always has a friendly "goose" for you when your back is turned, and if you're missing a sock or shoe, you'd be wise to check her (and our) den where she loves to hoard them. The contortions she can twist her body into while at rest are nothing short of amazing. Most notable was the morning she was found curled up, or perhaps coiled is a better word, in a small laundry basket that was less than half her size—and sleeping comfortably! Cinder has also proven to be something of a thief, but even that has had some comical results. One night she stole the remaining half of an apple strudel off our dining room table, carried it into the den and started to eat it right in front of me!"

"Comedy aside, Cinder is a sweet, gentle, loving dog who craves affection like no animal I have ever had. She wants nothing more than to be stroked and spoken to lovingly and she returns the favor with tender nuzzles and wet, sloppy kisses.

"So that's Cinder's story. A true Cinderella story of a Greyhound who made the trip from a frightened ex-race dog who couldn't even look a person in the eye, to a friendly, affectionate pet and a much-loved member of our family."

Greyhound Adoption

Gentle but playful, and elegant but comical, retired racers make marvelous pets. If you're interested in obtaining one, the agencies listed under "Greyhound Adoption" in the Appendix are a good place to start.

- Take a ball or dog toy out of your pocket or purse and show it to the dog. Is the dog interested? Is it eager to frolic with you, or is it fearful? Is it so bold that it tries to snatch the toy? Roll the toy on the ground away from (not toward) the dog. Does the dog respond? Roll the toy three times to give the dog time to understand the game. Does it chase or examine the toy, perhaps even pick it up in its mouth and carry it toward you?

- Wait until the dog is looking away from you, then blow a whistle or drop a metal pan about ten feet behind it. Watch the dog's reaction. After being startled, does it recover quickly?

- Put a long leash on the dog and take it outside. Does it still show interest in you? Will it play? Or is the dog so distracted by the outside world that it no longer notices you?

- If the dog knows how to walk on lead, take it for a walk. Does it trot along by your side or a little in front of you? Or does it hang back in fear, tail tightly tucked between its legs? Does it notice which direction you turn and go your way, or does it choose the direction and stretch your arm hauling you down the street? If the dog is pulling, don't give up on it right away. Perhaps no one ever trained it to walk nicely.

To find out if the dog will easily accept you as leader and learn to walk with you, put it on a six-foot-lead. Hold the loop of the lead tightly against your waist with both hands and start walking without talking to the dog. After a few steps, change directions quickly and silently by making a sudden right turn. If the dog is momentarily yanked off balance, so much the better. Keep moving, and eight or ten steps later, make another right turn. If the dog catches on and starts to watch where you go and keep up with you, praise it and keep going. Repeat the test continuously for two minutes by walking about eight or ten steps and then suddenly making a right turn. When you finally stop, ask yourself: Has the dog learned anything? Have I learned anything about the dog?

- While parents can select a puppy and bring it home as a present for their children, an adult dog should never be a surprise. Something in the dog's past may cause it to be aggressive with men, dislike children, or fear women, so every member of the family should meet the dog before a decision is made. While these meetings take place, the dog should be on leash and under control. The children must also be under control and not approach the dog. Walk the dog near but not within touching range of the children and watch its reaction. If it seems nervous, angry, or frightened, don't let the children pet it. When a dog reacts badly to any member of your family, look for a more suitable dog—one that reacts well to all of you.

- Most important of all, there should be some chemistry between you and the dog. Do you automatically smile when you see the dog? Is the dog happy to see you and content in your company? Is this the dog you want beside you as a constant companion? No dog is perfect. Some day even the nicest dog may leave dirty paw prints on your newly washed floor or get sick on your carpet. That's why the chemistry is so important. It makes life's little accidents more than worth the trouble.

PEDIGREE OR PUREBRED?

Every dog can have a pedigree, but not every dog is a purebred. A pedigree is simply a list of ancestors, just like a family tree. For example, one of your grandparents may be Irish, another Cuban, another French, and the fourth, Australian, but you still have a family tree. Along the same line, a dog's four grandparents may be a Collie, a Boxer, a Springer Spaniel, and a Golden Retriever, and that is the dog's family tree. The dog has a pedigree even though he isn't a purebred. Generally, when you see an ad for a "pedigreed dog," the seller really means a purebred dog and is guilty only of improper usage of the word "pedigreed." But just in case, ask to see an AKC or UKC registration certificate if owning a purebred dog with "papers" is important to you.

Purebred dogs are descended from dogs that were all of the same breed. That means a purebred Doberman Pinscher's parents, grandparents, and great-grandparents were all Doberman Pinschers, as were all the other ancestors as far back as records were kept.

A purebred dog's pedigree can tell you more than just the names of the dog's ancestors. If any of those ancestors won a title, its abbreviation will appear as part of the ancestor's name on the pedigree. For

Good breeding shows. Purebred dogs, like these Boston Terriers, were descended from all dogs all of the same breed for many generations.

Photo credit: Pets by Paulette.

example, if a dog earned a championship, the letters Ch. will appear before its name. If it won an Obedience title, such as Companion Dog, the abbreviation (CD) will follow the dog's name on the pedigree. Performance titles such as Agility, Herding, Lure Coursing, or Hunting will also appear on the pedigree. But no matter how outstanding it appears, a pedigree is only as impressive as the dog it represents. A quality dog with a quality pedigree is a treasure, but an inferior dog with a magnificent pedigree is still an inferior dog.

LOVING SACRIFICE

Dove Hill Labradors, owned by Ann Parris and Dave Altman of Culpeper, Virginia, is an example of a small, quality kennel that places retired breeding stock and older dogs that have reached the end of their competitive careers.

College student Christine Roberts and seven-year-old Cassie are roommates and best friends. Christine worked part-time for Dove Hill Labradors and she and Cassie were fond of each other from day one. So when Cassie was retired from breeding, the kennel owners gave her to Christine.

"Emotionally, this is a very difficult thing to do," Ann says. "We try to remind ourselves that each one of our dogs receives the chance to be a 'one and only' rather than just 'one of many.' The dogs respond quickly to a loving environment. Sometimes they come back to visit. After I get over having my feelings hurt, it's heartwarming to see them have eyes only for their new families."

AMIABLE APRIL

For those who like big, friendly dogs, 167-pound April, a housebroken Mastiff with a pleasing personality and gentle manners, is ideal. But she had three owners before finding her fourth and final home. April's third owner dropped her off at an animal shelter when she was five years old, and shelter workers contacted Mastiff Rescue.

Easy-going April with her friend, Chelsie.

John and Linda Greene, of Virginia Beach, Virginia, wanted to adopt a Mastiff and had their name on a waiting list with Mastiff Rescue. They were glad to adopt the overweight but engaging April, and were amazed at how easily she fit in with their cats and Rottweilers. Linda can't understand why a dog with April's kind disposition and perfect manners had four homes in five years. "Too many animals are obtained with little or no thought," she says. "People give more planning to buying a pair of shoes than obtaining an animal. I can't imagine anyone getting rid of April."

CHAPTER FIVE

ADOPTING A DESTITUTE DOG

Kilo, a three-year-old Rottweiler, was confiscated by the Norfolk, Virginia SPCA when her owner was arrested for dealing drugs. She was found chained to a fence, nursing a litter of puppies. Bred twice a year and practically starved, Kilo weighed only forty-one pounds. She was severely sway-backed and her inch-long, deformed nipples, the result of having so many litters, hung loosely. Her sparse coat was dry and straw-like, and the skin showing through was irritated by hot spots, dermatitis, and a severe infestation of fleas and ticks. Cigarette burns on her ears attested to the abuse she had endured, and a deep scar around her neck, caused by her puppy collar becoming imbedded in her skin as she outgrew it, attested to the neglect she had survived.

Meanwhile, John and Linda Greene of Virginia Beach, Virginia, wanted a friend for Max, their neutered male Rottweiler. They contacted a rescue organization, requested a female, and were told Kilo's story. But they were also told not to get their hopes up as there was a strong possibility Kilo wouldn't be adoptable. Not only did she have to be held until her owner went to court, but she was in deplorable physical condition, and no one knew how severely the long-term abuse had affected her personality.

Two months later, Kilo's owner went to court and the charges were dropped. He wanted Kilo back, but couldn't come up with the impound fees. Since the dog gave no evidence of aggression during her confinement, the Greenes were notified that she was finally available for adoption.

"When I saw her the first time I felt anger and horror," said Linda Greene, "but I also looked into a beautiful face. She wasn't aggressive and didn't cower from me. In fact, she looked at me as if to say, 'What took you so long? I've been waiting for you.' One look and I knew I wouldn't leave the shelter without her."

Soon the Greenes learned that saving a destitute dog can play havoc with a budget. Kilo had no medical records and needed all her inoculations. They also had her spayed, tested for fecal- and heartworms, and treated for skin problems. "During all the poking, prodding, and needle sticking, she behaved with dignity and seem thrilled at just being touched," Linda said. "Our veterinarian even commented that taking a blood sample is probably a kindness to her."

Kira (far right), and her friends Max and April (a Rottweiler and a Mastiff), show off their Down-Stay.

To mark Kilo's second start, the Greenes changed her name to Kira. Since she didn't respond to her old name anyway, there was no need to keep the moniker bestowed upon her by a drug dealer. On the road to recovery Kira explored the house, learning for the first time what it's like to live indoors. She and Max became good buddies and she thrived with enough to eat, toys of her own, and affectionate attention. Even while adjusting, Kira never bothered the family cats and was always calm and trusting with people. "It's as if we had her from a puppy," Linda says.

Today Kira weighs eighty-four pounds and she and Max have a new friend, a rescue Mastiff named April. Except for continuing skin problems, which her veterinarian believes are permanent, she is healthy and secure. "Kira's a most welcome addition to our family," Linda says, "and in spite of the money we invested in her health we've never regretted giving her a second chance."

LIFESTYLES OF DESTITUTE DOGS

Destitute dogs may be registered purebreds or unrecognizable mixes, but they all have a few unfortunate things in common. They are all unloved, unwanted, unkept, and unhealthy. Some have been starved, abused, or thrown out to fend for themselves. Others were born behind the dumpster in a filthy alley and never had a home to be thrown out of.

Some destitute dogs have never walked on a leash, or navigated stairs, or been petted, or fed a biscuit, or heard pots and pans rattle, or the sounds of a dishwasher, a toilet, or a hair dryer. In fact, many have never even seen the inside of a house.

Other destitute dogs lived in houses where they were regularly kicked or beaten. They may panic when someone buckles or unbuckles their belt, cringe at the sight of a rolled-up newspaper, back away if someone lights a cigarette, tremble at the scent of alcohol, or hide when they hear loud, male, or children's voices.

Destitute dogs often have bad manners at feeding time because memories of starvation seldom fade quickly. They may inhale their food almost without chewing and strike a protective stance over their dish.

Destitute dogs are often completely untrained and uncivilized. To understand how completely, imagine what would happen if a young man who grew up deep in the jungle was suddenly snatched up, put on an airplane, and deposited on your doorstep as your permanent house guest. A virtual wild man, he would be used to hunting, even fighting for food. He wouldn't understand your language, manners, clothing, appliances, or even your music. He would miss his freedom, even though freedom meant a meager diet, raids by hostile tribes, disease, and a constant struggle just to survive. He would also miss his tribesmen, even though they competed with him for the scant supply of available food.

Now imagine some of the incidents that might occur during the early weeks of your wild man's visit as he learns about table manners, television sets, radios, doorbells, phones, indoor plumbing, cars, and clothing—all without the benefit of a common language. Eventually he will learn to communicate with you, and you'll learn to "read" his body language. Finally he'll start trusting you and enjoying the conveniences of a modern home. And so will your destitute dog. But the first weeks won't be easy. Not for you and not for your dog.

WHY BOTHER TO ADOPT A DESTITUTE DOG?

Turning a destitute dog into a desirable pet is an act of faith, mixed with an aura of magic, backed up by a lot of hard work, and sometimes, more than a little money. Is it for you?

Do you want a dog that adjusts quickly or are you willing to take on a project? Will veterinary bills be a major or minor sacrifice? Do you look forward to walking your dog with pride right away, or would you enjoy seeing your pathetic pet slowly blossom into a beauty? Do you have patience, extra time, and a history of saving strays? Was Cinderella your favorite bedtime story?

Destitute dogs need more understanding, more love, more socialization, and more training than dynamite dogs. Many people relish the challenge. If you always root for the underdog, this could be your opportunity to turn one underdog into a lucky dog. It isn't hard to find a homeless dog. Unfortunately, there are thousands of unwanted dogs in shelters. And while you can't do anything about all of them, you can make all the difference in the world to one of them.

FINDING A DESTITUTE DOG

Divorce in a family, allergic reactions to a dog in the household, irritating behavior on the dog's part, and all the other reasons dogs are discarded explain why they end up viewing the world through the barred cages of an animal shelter or pound. Most of the dogs in shelters were given up by their owners, but others were reported running loose or lost. Picked up by a local government agency such as Animal Control, they were brought to the shelter to await owners who often don't bother to claim them. A few of the dogs lived horrendous lives and were deposited at the shelter by local authorities as neglect or abuse cases.

You won't have to look far to find plenty of destitute dogs. Animal shelters and humane organizations have them in all sizes, shapes, and

CULTIVATING PEPPER

No one knows how long Pepper lived as a wild animal in the forests of Oregon. When she was captured, the Wirehaired Pointing Griffon had dysentery and every internal and external parasite imaginable. She had been running with another young Griffon and both of them were sent to their breed's rescue program where they were treated, nursed back to health, and put up for adoption.

From nearly wild to happy house dog, Pepper (right) learned how to relax and enjoy life with her friend, Dinah (left).

Carol Svoboda's elderly Griffons had died during the previous year and she wanted to give a home to a needy dog and provide company for her young Griffon, Dinah. So she and her husband adopted Pepper. The skinny, shivering dog arrived by plane and rode from the airport to its new home in Fox River Grove, Illinois, on Carol's lap.

It was a challenge from day one. Although Dinah was delighted with her new friend, Carol discovered that teaching Pepper simple rules was a complicated problem. The half-wild dog was an escape artist. As Carol tells it, "The first night she squeezed under the fence and took off into the woods. She was wearing a collar, but no identification yet. We have no immediate neighbors to call for help, so while my husband called the police to alert them about our loose dog, I stayed outside and continued to call her. As I started for the woods she came streaking back to the yard. We secured the bottom of the fence but she dug under again; we extended the top but she still climbed over. One night when we were away, she went through the temporary cover we put over the kennel fence, jumped over the yard fence, and tore through the porch screen. When we came home we found her curled up by the fireplace wood. We finally managed to keep her home by putting a three-foot lip on the inside of the fence, a secure wood cover on the kennel, and staking the bottom of the fence every few feet."

"The next challenge was training. Pepper didn't respond to any commands and she didn't react to sweet talk or praise. I took her to obedience school for socialization and we walked and walked. Eventually, with the help of a whistle, a pocket full of cookies, and low stimulus from a tritronic collar, she learned to stay with me on a walk, and often beats Dinah when running back to me for a reward. She will sit, stay, and down on command, and has even learned to stay off the couch; plus she does it all with a happy wag and a smile. It has been rewarding for us to see her progress from a semi-wild animal to a dog that's fairly well socialized and fun to have around. It's also been a learning experience. There were times when we would have been tempted to give her to the first taker, but now we wouldn't part with Pepper for any price. She's a sweet dog, but has been a trial, and we would do it again in a minute."

ages. Some will be purebreds, but most will have mixed ancestry. Does it matter? Usually not. So why do so many puppy buyers prefer purebreds?

Purebred or Mixed-Breed?

One of the main advantages of acquiring a purebred puppy is that you have a clear picture of how the dog will look as a grown-up, including its size and coat type. But that reasoning doesn't apply here. You are adopting an adult dog, so what you see is what you get. In time, your loving care will round off the rough edges, brighten the eyes, and give gloss to the coat. But for now, the basic animal is already visible.

Another advantage of acquiring a purebred is that certain breeds hunt, others herd, and still others are born ratters. You may get a mix that can hunt, herd, or keep mice out of your basement, but don't count on appearances. For example, a mix that looks like a retriever or a spaniel may have no hunting dog ancestors at all.

People who want to show their dog will seek registered purebreds because they can compete in American Kennel Club (AKC) and United Kennel Club (UKC) dog events. But if you fall for a mix, you can still compete in a variety of activities through AMBOR, the American Mixed Breed Obedience Registry (see Appendix). In addition, mixed-breds registered with AMBOR are welcome in UKC Obedience, Agility, and Hunting Retriever events.

So, should you search for a purebred or will a mix make you just as happy? It depends on why you want a dog. If companionship and fun are the major reasons, by all means consider a mix. A dog doesn't need "papers" to be your best buddy.

SHELTERS AND SUCH

Try to be tough-minded when visiting animal shelters and humane facilities. Yes, it's true that unadopted animals will be euthanized in many shelters. But thousands of animals await their fate in these institutions. You can't save them all, so take your time and take along your "Dream Dog Check List." Then save the dog that's right for you and your family; one whose chemistry attracts all of you. Making the right match brings joy to everyone. You, your family, the dog, and even the shelter workers.

Shelter Employees and Volunteers

Most shelter workers adore animals. That's why they work at institutions for unwanted pets. It's obvious they don't apply for the job because it pays well, or because the work is easy. It doesn't and it isn't. Idealistic at first, the workers want to make a difference, make the animals more comfortable, help people find the right pet, and feel good because they made the world a little bit better for pets and people.

So what happened? You're asking questions about a charming dog and getting short, impersonal answers—not the outpouring of details you hoped for. Why, the young shelter worker doesn't even seem to notice how cute that spotted dog with the perky ears is. Doesn't she care if it gets a home?

What happened is that the young woman probably cared too much when she started working at the shelter. No doubt she already adopted all the dogs she can support. Still, she fussed over special favorites, calling them pet names and bringing them treats. But the animals kept arriving much faster than they were adopted, and many of her special friends were euthanized. Some were adopted, of course, and that gave

THE MAKING OF MAX, THE WONDER DOG

When Tim Elkins of Dearborn Heights, Michigan, lost his year-old Miniature Schnauzer, he felt a tremendous void in his life and decided to fill it with an adopted dog. Although he didn't have a particular type of dog in mind when he visited the humane society shelter, he certainly didn't plan to pick one with serious personality problems. Nevertheless, that's exactly what he did.

"I remember when I approached his cage in the shelter, he retreated to a far corner and trembled," Elkins says about the little mixed terrier that later became famous as Maxwell's Second Chance. "When I tried to coax him out of the crate, he wouldn't come. He was the most shy, fearful dog I had ever seen. He had obviously been given a very bad time by someone. I can't explain what motivated me to pick this frightened little guy to be my new companion. There was just something very appealing about him that I can't explain."

Obedience training turned a terrified Max into terrific Max. He became the first mixed-bred to ever make the top ten in obedience's tough Superdog competition.

After a month of living together, Maxwell was still terrified. "I'll never forget one day when I picked up the *TV Guide*," Tim says. "Max ran to a corner and shook violently. I didn't want us to go on like that."

Tim had never obedience-trained a dog, but when his veterinarian suggested that attending classes might help socialize Max and give him the confidence to overcome his painful shyness, he decided to give it a try. Instruction at the first school was too firm for fearful Max, but eventually Tim found the type of instruction they needed. He learned how to show Max what he wanted and reward him with praise and treats when he complied. Eventually Max became proud of his accomplishments, gained confidence, and learned to trust.

Tim continued taking Max to training classes even after confidence reshaped the dog's personality. "We discovered we both enjoyed obedience work, so we just kept at it," Tim says. And the rest, as the cliché goes, is history.

Once Max overcame his fears, he mastered new obedience exercises with incredible speed. Tim registered him with the American Mixed Breed Obedience Registration (AMBOR) and they earned their Companion Dog (CD) title, followed by their Companion Dog Excellent (CDX), and the coveted Utility Dog (UD) title. But that was only the beginning. Tim and Max earned such high scores that they became eligible to compete at the Gaines/Cycle Classic, an annual tournament featuring the top obedience dogs in the nation. It was the first year mixed-bred dogs were allowed in the prestigious Classic, and Max was AMBOR's only representative, so all eyes were upon him. Those eyes saw him make history. Maxwell's Second Chance, once a pitiful shelter dog, is now known in obedience circles as "Max the Wonder Dog." He's the first mixed-breed to place in the top ten of the Superdog competition, the highest level offered at the Obedience Classic.

her joy, only to double her heartbreak when a few of them were picked up running loose, or confiscated as abuse cases, and brought back to the institution. And so many people who appeared to mean well returned pets instead of training them that gradually she lost some of her high hopes, as well as a lot of her faith in people's promises.

She's numb now. She has to be, or working at the shelter would destroy her. So she feeds the animals, keeps their kennels clean, gives them the benefit of her kind voice and gentle hands, but doesn't dare get too involved with pets or people. She'll tell you what she knows about the spotted dog you keep coming back to, but she may not know much since she learned to distance herself from doomed relationships. If there is space, and it's not against shelter policy, she'll let you "Ask the Dog" (see Chapter 4). Take along treats, a toy, an adjustable collar, and a lead, so you'll be ready. It may be up to you to find out if the soulful face peering out from the chain-link cage is an undiscovered dream dog, or every dog owner's worst nightmare.

Prices and Policies

Prices and policies vary among animal shelters and humane societies. Some take care of vaccinations, spaying, and neutering, and any other necessary treatment before offering an animal for adoption, and add those costs to the adoption fee. Others encourage spaying and neutering by charging a higher fee for an intact pet and rebating a portion of it when shown proof that the animal was spayed or neutered within a given time period. Shelters incur many expenses, so don't expect to get a dog for free. When you visit a shelter, ask about prices and policies before you enter the kennel area. Then you will know if you can afford to fall in love.

PUREBRED RESCUE, CLASSIFIEDS ADS, AND BREEDERS

Destitute dogs and dynamite dogs often come from the same places. A dog may be in purebred rescue because it was starved, neglected, or abused. The pet in the classified ad may have been chained behind the garage for years with no human companionship. The breeder may be bottom rung instead of top-notch, and keep dogs in filthy cages, breeding them every season until they are too weak or too ill to raise a litter. (Real breeders call these disgraces "puppy mills.") While the rescue volunteer will gladly tell you each dog's history, the puppy-mill owner will tell you only what he or she thinks you want to hear, and the classified ad writer may or may not give you the whole truth. But you know how to find out for yourself—just ask the dog.

IS THERE A DESTITUTE DOG IN YOUR BACKYARD?

Does a glance out your kitchen window reveal your very own destitute dog? Perhaps he's chained to a stake or pacing back and forth in a kennel run. Sure, Prince gets food and water and you've provided shade, but it has been months since he's been brushed, walked, petted, or allowed inside the house. What do you feel when you look at him? Guilt? Regret? The emptiness of unfilled promises—yours and his?

Forget guilt, it doesn't solve anything. Then get rid of regrets and fulfill those promises. Would you . . . could you . . . still love Prince if you could break him of his bad house habits? Yes. You can do it. Just give it one more try. The next few chapters will tell you how.

After reading Chapters 6 and 7, treat that lonely dog in your backyard as if you just acquired him today. Wipe the slate clean. It's a second start for both of you. Begin by having Prince checked by a veterinarian to make sure he's healthy and parasite-free. Bathe and groom him (or have it done professionally) so he looks, feels, and smells lovable. Then bring him inside for crate training and teach him basic commands like "Sit" and "Down." You can even add a trick or two just for fun. Everything you need to know for your own successful second start is in the next few chapters.

A SHELTER VOLUNTEER'S STORY

Gee Weaver, of Kalispell, Montana, volunteers through the local humane society's foster care program. She has a lot of stories and this is just one of them:

"I was sitting in the Humane Society booth at the fairgrounds. It was next to the Animal Control booth and we were sharing stories. They had a call that morning from a woman in a trailer court where no dogs were allowed. She said a stray dog just had puppies under her steps. The Animal Control workers were in no hurry to pick up the brood as they knew the puppies would have to be euthanized within 48 hours.

"I was just the one to tell. When I left the fairgrounds I went straight to the trailer court and picked up the large mixed-bred momma dog and her 17 puppies. She was loaded with lice, very protective of her newborns, and appeared to be a mixture of Collie and Airedale.

"Soon momma dog started getting sick from feeding and cleaning up after so many puppies and I had to help her by tube and bottle feeding and washing tiny butts. Then her nipples became so sore she couldn't nurse them at all and she got mastitis. Hot towels, a breast pump, and medication helped, but the puppies got sick from all of that and were off the bottle at three weeks. Twelve puppies survived and momma dog was spayed as soon as she regained her strength.

Humane volunteer Gee Weaver and her son Chris after walking their Standard Poodles in the Humane Society Walk-a-Thon. Gee walked 12.5 miles and Chris walked 9 miles.

"Healthy, spayed, and free of lice, momma dog became gentle and obedient. Eventually a family with a little girl adopted her. Momma dog is now Sara. She's housebroken, loved, and sends me gifts of brushes, collars, dishes, and monetary donations for the humane society. Her family even paid back the cost of her food, spay, and medical expenses.

"The twelve puppies weren't as lucky. After they had their first vaccination and were free of lice, a close friend and a local pet store helped me find homes for them. Unfortunately, the litter came down with

Parvovirus. Momma dog probably gave them little, if any, protection through her milk, and puppies need a series of vaccinations before they can be considered safe from this disease. Two of the puppies were taken to the veterinarian by their adoptive families. They were put on I.V.s and soon recovered. Other families returned their puppies when they got sick and I treated them with medication and I.V.s. We saved them all and found an adoptive home for the last one when it was four-and-a-half months old.

"When the pups were five months old, the first one showed up at the Animal Control Shelter. By the time they were eight months old, I had adopted three of them from the shelter and gave them foster care. After grooming, training, breaking bad habits, and spaying, they were adopted into new homes that seem to be permanent. I often wonder about the other pups. I stressed to their new owners that the females should be spayed or they could also have 17 puppies."

FROM ABUSE CASE TO DOG SHOW CHAMPION

Sir had a permanent scar on his elegant face. The English Setter had asked for a little attention while his owner was playing pool, and had a cue stick broken over his muzzle. Rescued from his abusive home when he was three years old, Sir was adopted by Marcy Desmond and her family of Hayden Lake, Idaho. Along with him came AKC papers. His registered name was Lord of Blue Hills.

"Sir was afraid of fast movements and loud noises, yet he was desperate to be needed and appreciated," Marcy said. "For almost a year my husband and I patiently taught him that he was important to us; that we would never harm him; that he could put his paw on our arm to ask for a pat and receive affection, not rejection." During that year, Sir suffered chronic ear infections and two bouts of pneumonia resulting from his weakened condition. But even while he was adjusting mentally and strengthening physically, he made himself useful by guarding the door at night and watching over his family while they slept. He also occupied himself by pointing the family parrots.

When Sir was four, he was taken on his first pheasant hunt and his excellent breeding became apparent. Instinctively, he hunted with fine style and retrieved tenderly to hand. Over the years, Sir not only kept food on the family table, but won and placed at several field trials. He also earned a Companion Dog (CD) title in obedience and overcame tremendous odds to win his AKC Conformation Championship.

In later years, Ch. Lord of Blue Hills (CD) retained his gentle temperament and even played nursemaid to a litter of rambunctious German

Shorthaired Pointer puppies, giving their dam an occasional well-deserved rest. "I can still see him lying there with puppies crawling all over him, pulling his ears and tail and hanging from his flews (lips)," said Marcy. "Sir was very dear to us. He enriched our lives for ten precious years."

Ch. Lord of Blue Hills, CD (Sir) on point at quail. The English Setter was abused for the first three years of his life and became a show champion, earned an obedience title, and learned to hunt after he was rescued and adopted.

Have you already tried everything and nothing worked? Has the chemistry between you fizzled from too much frustration? Do you wish you had known more about matchmaking before you selected Prince? If you and Prince aren't having any fun together, it's useless to waste the next several years and the rest of your dog's life. You and your dog both deserve a second start with more suitable partners. Chapter 10 will help you place Prince in a good home and get on with it.

DID A DESTITUTE DOG FIND YOU?

Sometimes a destitute dog finds you. You don't see him at first but you know something was out there because your garbage bag was ripped opened and your trash was scattered on your lawn. When it happens again you get angry and glance out the window occasionally, hoping to catch the culprit in the act. Is it a raccoon? Or is one of your neighbors letting their dog run loose? When you finally spy the trash bag burglar, your anger melts into pity.

The creature is gaunt with a sparse coat and dark, scared eyes. He sees you looking at him and slinks off, defeated. Haunted by his eyes, you decide to buy a little dog food and put it in a bowl at the end of the driveway. That will keep him out of the garbage, you tell yourself.

The next night you watch through the window as he gulps the dog food, then yell "No!" when he heads for the garbage anyway. He leaves in a hurry but you know he'll return. And he does. Night after night. Soon you stand quietly while he eats his dog food—first watching from the window, then the porch, then the edge of the lawn, and finally within a few feet of him. By now you've named him in your mind and he is yours, even if you don't know it yet. Soon he stays over, spending the night curled up on the old rug you just happened to toss into a corner on the porch. You move his bowl to just outside the door. Soon he looks a bit better. Not quite as skinny; not quite as scared.

Eventually this dog will trust you enough to take food from your hand. But don't rush him. And above all, don't corner him. Remember, he's wild and frightened, and probably hasn't been vaccinated against rabies.

Does he growl at you sometimes and bristle the hairs on his neck? He has problems you don't need. Call Animal Control and let the professionals decide if he's capable of becoming a companion animal. They'll pick him up, take him to their shelter, and check him out.

Does he creep a little closer to you each day, sometimes even tentatively wagging his tucked tail? He wants your friendship, but his past makes him fear relationships with humans. Be patient. He'll come around.

Taking food from your hand is the first big step. It won't be long until he lets you touch him, then caress him. Eventually you'll bribe him into the house. For his sake, and yours, have him examined and vaccinated by a veterinarian who makes house calls (he's still too timid to handle a ride in the car and a busy waiting room). When the veterinarian fills out the paperwork with your name as owner, you've accepted responsibility for this dog's —your dog's—health and heart. Now the period of adjustment begins. And that's a whole new chapter for both of you.

FROM MISERY TO MAGNIFICENCE

Maude the Mastiff has survived starvation, neglect, physical abuse from adults and children, a blow to the face that permanently blinded her left eye, an infected tail that developed gangrene and required surgery to remove it, heartworm, bloat, serving as guard dog for a towing company, and the devastation of Hurricane Andrew. "In spite of her past, she is still sweet, gentle, magnificent, and a perfect example of a Mastiff," says owner Sara Robertson of Palm Beach, Florida.

Maude the Mastiff wears her lace necklace and the medal she earned in the rescue class at the Mastiff National Specialty Show.

Originally Sara was supposed to give Maude a foster home until the dog could be placed with permanent owners. But the starved and wounded Mastiff had so many problems it was several weeks before she was ready for adoption. By then, her gentleness and nobility had impressed Sara so much that she bonded with the big dog. So Maude became a city dog; living in an apartment on the 22nd floor with Sara and her thirteen-year-old male Mastiff.

Today Maude accompanies Sara everywhere and adores meeting most people, but is still terrified of large men with equipment at their waist, as well as children. Sara calls Maude her "gentle giant" and marvels at how she was able to throw off most of her bad past and take to her new life with zest. She's also come a long way from the scrawny ninety-eight pounds she weighed when she was rescued in the aftermath of the hurricane. "She's a solid 170," Sara says proudly. "All muscle and no fat." She's also a celebrity of sorts, having earned a rosette and a medal in the rescue dog class at the Mastiff National Specialty Show.

PART TWO

HAPPILY EVER AFTER

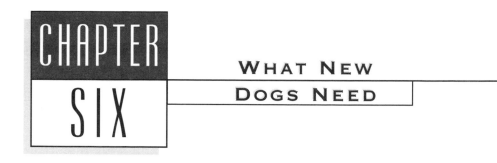

CHAPTER SIX

WHAT NEW DOGS NEED

Congratulations! You've made the decision to get a dog and you even found the dog of your dreams. You don't need a diamond to cement your new relationship, but a little advance planning will help you enjoy your new friend and keep him happy and healthy. The following are must-haves for the new dog owner.

THAT GREAT CRATE

Dogs descended from denning animals that spent a great deal of their time in the relative security of their lair. That's why it will take only a brief period of adjustment before Prince feels comfortable and protected in a dog crate. Contrary to being cruel, as some new dog owners imagine, dog crates have saved dogs' lives and owners' tempers, not occasionally, but routinely.

Buy Prince a crate that's large enough for him to stand up and turn around in comfortably. If he isn't full grown, take that into consideration and buy a crate big enough to be useful all his life. The crate will be a tremendous help with housebreaking, because Prince will soon learn not to soil his bed (details in Chapter 7). It will also keep him from swallowing something dangerous or destroying something expensive while no one is home to supervise.

The inside of Prince's crate should be snug, soft, and comfortable. Bedding should be easy to clean or change in the event of a mishap, and not dangerous if chewed or swallowed. For example, several layers of newspaper (black and white, not color like the Sunday comics) make good bedding for an indoor crate. For extra coziness, rip one newspaper section into long, thin streamers and place them in the crate on top of the whole sections. For something more permanent, washable pillows, cushions, or carpet samples all make a comfortable bed for a crated dog.

Every time you put Prince in his crate, toss a favorite toy or a special treat into the crate ahead of him. Say "crate" and very firmly, but as gently as possible, put Prince in and shut the door. Then walk away. Don't wait to see what Prince will do because that will entice him to react. Pretty soon he'll learn the word "crate" and enter it himself, without your help.

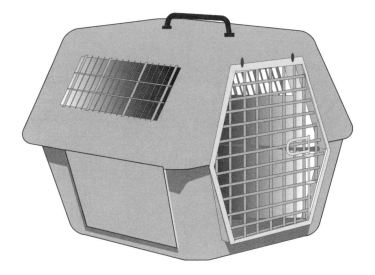

Dog crates keep their occupants safe and secure both indoors and out.

The crate should never be used as punishment, and it should not be used too much. A few hours at a time is fine, but Prince shouldn't be forced to spend the majority of his life in a crate. If the crate is being used properly, eventually Prince's attitude toward it will become neutral. If he either hates his crate or loves it too much, something is wrong.

Prince may struggle or cry the first few times he is introduced to his crate, but if you walk away, and don't take him out of the crate until he settles down, he'll soon become accustomed to it. If he still complains after a week, see "Noise Stoppers" in Chapter 7.

Once you trust Prince's house manners, you may prefer that he spend the night outside his crate. Some owners welcome their dogs into their beds, and if allowed to choose, Prince will probably want to sleep with you or with one of your children. Others purchase a cozy bed made especially for dogs and place it in a strategic location where their dog feels like part of the family while acting the role of watchdog.

WHY RESCUE VOLUNTEERS DEMAND DOG CRATES

Judy Marden, of the East Coast German Shorthaired Pointer Breed Rescue Network, explains why crating a newly adopted dog is so important:

"The period of adjustment with a newly adopted adult dog varies from dog to dog. Some dogs have a temperament that is very accepting of whatever fate life hands them. These dogs are quick to adapt to whatever lifestyle a new owner may offer. However, the majority of castoff dogs suffer separation anxiety. When out of the crate and alone in the house, they may be very fearful.

"Separation anxiety is often manifested through a variety of destructive behaviors. Instead of relaxing while home alone, the frightened dog may chew incessantly, bark, howl, or soil the rug. This is why we (the rescue network) insist on crate training. When properly introduced to a crate, the dog soon accepts it as home and happily enters it of his own volition. In the comfort of his own den, the dog feels more secure when left alone in new surroundings.

"Whether a dog has come from a neglectful, even abusive situation, it was theirs; they lost it, and they don't want to lose their family again. Believe me, they make this very evident. For this reason alone, we strongly stress the value of having a comfortable crate for the dog and crating him whenever none of the family is at home. If the dog is handled properly its fear of separation will subside, but there is no set time for the phenomenon to disappear. Normally it fades within a few days to a few months."

DOG-PROOFING YOUR HOME

To make your home safe for Prince, put all cleaning agents, antifreeze, pesticides, and other household chemicals out of his reach. If he is still in the chewing stage, coat any electrical wires he can reach with Bitter Apple, a safe, evil-tasting substance especially created to prevent chewing. Bitter Apple is also available in a leaf protector that can be safely sprayed on house plants, and it will soon teach Prince they are off limits. But if you have poisonous house plants, and some common varieties are deadly, they should be gone before Prince arrives. Simply

When adopting a racing Greyhound, most people, like the Furmans who you met in Chapter 4, visit Greyhound kennels and make their selection after meeting several dogs. Others tell an agency exactly what they want in a Greyhound (male or female, young or prime of life, medium sized or large, active or laid back) and whether or not they have young children or other pets. Then they let the agency choose a Greyhound for them. Still others, like Susan Evans of Houston, Texas, fall in love in the spur of the moment and make a lasting commitment. Susan never owned a dog before adopting her Greyhound, and didn't understand the importance of using the dog's crate to give it a sense of security and help it adjust to a new schedule. Consequently, she had a few problems . . .

Well behaved and content today, Chops, a retired racing Greyhound, created problems in his new home right after his adoption when he was given too much space before he learned to feel secure. Using a crate helps prevent such problems.

Civilizing Chops
by his owner, Susan Evans

"Five years ago, following a divorce, I moved into a quaint four-plex. Displaced and a bit shy, I didn't have a chance to meet my neighbors yet. One Saturday morning, I participated in an inner city festival that seemed to draw the homeless and the desperate in great numbers. That day filled me with great compassion. On my way back to the car, I passed a booth where retired racing Greyhounds seemed to be in a similar situation to the one I'd just witnessed. They were truly in a fight for

survival. I was on my way home to do the 'Ozzie and Harriet' thing;
cook a meat loaf and be thankful for the space that belonged to me.
Instead, I arrived home with no groceries, but with a new roommate—
a dog named Chops who was as tall as my furniture.

"I had never owned a dog before and was not prepared to find the
blinds, antique tables, and bedspreads chewed the first time I left him
alone. We spent the first six months adjusting, chewing up more furniture, barking all night (I got to know my neighbors quickly), and looking at each other longingly, wondering what was next. One neighbor,
who disliked dogs, reported to the police that the place where I lived
was too small for such a dog. At the brink of wanting to just give up, I
was given the opportunity to become a spokesperson for the Greyhound
Society and an article about Chops and adopting adult dogs appeared
in the local newspaper.

"Chops and I are now well adjusted. Although I don't have any general
insight into the problems of chewing and barking, in my situation the
chewing stopped as soon as Chops developed a routine and became
familiar with his surroundings. From the very start, racing Greyhounds
are crate trained and kept on a strict training routine at the kennel. My
mistake was giving Chops too much space too soon in unfamiliar surroundings, changing his feeding and exercise schedule, and then leaving
him alone. After some near disasters on favorite pieces of furniture, I
restricted his area to a space without any temptations and he quickly
adapted to his new schedule. The barking problems took a little more
effort. Chops is not a compulsive barker, but barks out of stress. The
longer you have a dog, the more sensitive you become to its personality
and you may find the dog's fears are similar to your own. Chops barks
when there is a thunderstorm (he hates to get wet), when strangers
threaten his territory, or when he feels a loss.

"I moved recently, and Chops was separated from a neighbor's dog
he'd bonded with. He barked in a low pitch (different from his usual
voice) for a couple of days at the loss of his buddy, but when he
discovered the dog next door to our new house, the barking stopped.
When it rains I always make sure he is indoors and dry, and when
those needs are met, he does not bark. Most Greyhounds almost
never bark and I know their owners feel blessed. But as far as the
threat of strangers goes, I welcome the notice and feel we are both
defending our space. Chops and I are now well adjusted. We have
become the best of friends and we just seemed to overcome the obstacles with trial and error. I feel if we can identify with our pets in their
particular needs, the solution to their problems is very close to how we
go about refining our own personalities. I have made wonderful friend-
ships through Chops, but none as valuable or as loyal as the one he
gives back to me."

hanging them out of his reach isn't good enough because they still shed leaves and berries. For example, Poinsettia leaves are so toxic that eating just one can kill a small child, and those pretty Mistletoe berries are also deadly poison. If you don't know whether a plant is safe or not, ask your local nursery.

A PLACE TO EXERCISE

Prince needs regular exercise, no matter what size he is. However, the frequency and duration necessary varies from breed to breed and even from dog to dog. One thing is certain. Dogs that get enough exercise always behave better than those that don't.

Fencing your yard will make exercising Prince easier on you. A well-installed chain-link fence is sufficient for most dogs. If yours likes to dig, check the condition around the bottom of the fence frequently. If Prince is going to spend several hours at a time outside, he'll need fresh water and shelter from heat, rain, and cold. Shade is especially important. When checking an outdoor area for shade, remember the section that looks so cool and inviting in the morning may be blistering under the summer sun by afternoon.

There are breeders who won't sell a dog to anyone who doesn't have a securely fenced yard or a chain link dog run. But unless they have an especially active breed, they may be eliminating some potentially fine owners. While a fenced outdoor area is safe, and handy too, it isn't always a realistic expectation. Urban apartment dwellers don't have outdoor facilities, yet most of them are excellent dog owners. They simply take their dogs for frequent walks on lead, or use the public dog runs available in some city parks.

A PLACE TO CALL HIS (OR HER) OWN

Prince should have a doghouse if he's going to spend more than a couple hours a day outdoors. Many pet supply stores have dog doghouses for sale, or you can easily make one yourself. The following are the attributes of good doghouses:

- The floor of Prince's house should be raised off the ground two or three inches. That protects it from rain, snow, morning dew, and general dampness.

- A removable roof or a hinged roof will make it easier to clean inside the house.

- The door should be near one side wall of the house (not in the middle) and partitioned off, with the sleeping space on the side away from the drafty door.

- Don't buy or build too big a house. To conserve body heat, the sleeping space should be cozy—just right for Prince to curl up comfortably.

- Cedar chips make great bedding for the inside of Prince's house. They smell wonderful, provide good insulation, and usually stay clean and dry for quite a while. If cedar bedding isn't available, wood shavings are a dependable second choice. Remember to always lay the bedding a half-inch to two or three inches deep, depending on winter weather conditions in your area.

SAFE TOYS

Toys aren't an extra, but an essential. Prince needs something safe to gnaw on, and should have a couple of toys available all the time. Whenever he is placed in his crate, he should be accompanied by a safe toy or two, and toys should also be handy when he is out and about, enjoying time with the family. Prince's toys should be purchased or created especially for him, so that he will learn the difference between his belongings and yours. For example, it isn't fair to give him an old shoe to gnaw on and then get angry when he destroys your bedroom slippers. A shoe is a shoe to a dog, and if he is encouraged to play with one, he won't understand that the others are off limits.

Even though Prince is an adult, not a teething puppy, he may still enjoy chewing. Encourage the habit because chewing is good for dogs. It helps remove plaque from their teeth, promotes healthy gums, and keeps them occupied and content.

Rawhide chew toys are a traditional favorite, but there have been rare accidents when a dog ripped a chunk from a rawhide, got it caught in its throat, and choked. So give Prince rawhide only when you're home and in the same room with him, and don't choose rawhide for his crate toy.

Squeaky toys (lightweight rubber or plastic with squeakers inside) are great fun for dogs, but they are easily torn apart and swallowed, dangerous squeaker and all. Get Prince a squeaky toy by all means, but keep it out of his reach unless you're watching or joining in the play. Some owners get the squeaky out every few days as a special reward and enjoy watching the playful pouncing.

Chew toys made of nylon are safe in Prince's mouth even when you aren't home, and small dogs prefer the softer, equally safe, gummy-type nylon chews. Solid, hard rubber toys are also safe and fun, but depending on his size and perseverance, Prince may eventually mangle even those labeled "indestructible." If he gouges pieces out of his rubber toys, don't leave him alone with them.

The *braided rope toys* sold at pet supply stores are fun for games of tug, and an aid in keeping Prince's teeth tartar free. If Prince starts unstringing his rope, don't leave him alone with it; swallowing the strings could cause intestinal problems.

For the ultimate crate treat, buy a *sterilized bone toy* (available at most pet shops), and stuff it with real cheese. That will keep Prince occupied for quite a while.

After Prince owns a few toys, don't let him have them all at once. Instead, rotate them every few days, putting different ones in his crate, and in the room where the family gathers. That way Prince will be less likely to become bored with his belongings.

PRACTICAL DOG DISHES

Practical food and water dishes are easy to clean and difficult to tip over. Many companies have designed dishes with these features in mind. Prince should have separate dishes for food and water. The food dish should be washed after each use, and the water dish should be refilled with fresh water frequently and washed thoroughly once a day. Position Prince's food dish so it won't slide across the floor while he is trying to eat. Placing it in a corner usually does the job.

It's always best to feed Prince indoors, but if you feed outside during the warm months, pick up the food dish within ten minutes. Otherwise, every bug in the neighborhood will be attracted to Prince's outdoor play area. When feeding outside during the winter, never use metal dishes. Prince's tongue could stick to the frozen metal. Constant access to fresh water (not snow) is critical, so purchase a self-warming dish if you won't be around to change the water frequently.

GROOMING GIZMOS

All dogs need some type of brush or comb, a nail clipper, a quality pH-balanced dog shampoo (sometimes you may need insecticide shampoo or dip), and a soft toothbrush. You may also want to purchase a dry shampoo (one that works on dry hair and doesn't need rinsing), for occasional spot cleaning. The rest of Prince's bathing needs are probably already in your medicine chest (see Chapter 8 for bathing and grooming details). Additional grooming equipment that will help you keep Prince healthy and beautiful depends on the texture and amount of his coat (see Chapter 8). When purchasing brushes, combs, nail clippers, trimming implements, and other grooming tools, always choose respected brands. Besides lasting longer, good grooming equipment makes the job easier and faster for you, and much more pleasant for Prince.

COLLAR AND LEAD (OR LEASH)

Prince's collar fits properly when it applies no pressure as it encircles his neck, but isn't loose enough to slip over his lowered head. The collar should be flat, made of nylon webbing or leather, with a buckle and ring for attaching the lead.

The lead should be four to six feet long and made of leather, nylon webbing, or some other strong, flexible fabric. Neither the collar nor the lead should be made of chain. You may want a chain training collar as a teaching aid, but Prince should wear it only during training, not in place of his regular collar. (See Chapter 7 for information on the proper fit and placement of chain training collars.)

CLEANING UP YOUR ACT

It's important to clean up after Prince when you take him for walks; in many places, it's the law. While there are various items on the market for this purpose, many dog owners simply carry a couple of plastic zip-lock bags. The bags fit in a pocket or purse, and may be turned inside out for the pick-up, then closed and tossed into the nearest garbage can. Or you may prefer the long handled poop scoops sold in

Not every dog has its own pool and shower like this American Staffordshire Terrier, but every dog needs a shady spot when it spends time outdoors.

Keeping a long-coated beauty like the Cavalier King Charles Spaniel free of tangles requires regular grooming.

Photo credit: Pets by Paulette.

pet supply stores. These are also convenient for cleaning up the yard, as are the fork-type versions.

EXTRA ATTENTION

Prince will need the reassurance of your presence when he is a disoriented stranger in your house, so try to launch your relationship when you can give him a little extra time. Dogs want someone to bond to, and being there for Prince will usually be all it takes to cement the tie.

AND IN ADDITION . . .

Before bringing Prince home, you should have nutritious dog food in the cupboard and the address and phone number of a trusted veterinarian. See Chapter 8 for more on feeding and veterinary care.

HUNTING WITH HARDY

Hardy, a fifteen-month-old Munsterland Pointer, was returned to his breeder by a disgruntled hunter who asked for his money back. According to the hunter, Hardy was no good. He chased birds instead of pointing them, and was uncontrollable.

The breeder placed Hardy with a friend who knew how to train pointing dogs. After working with Hardy for a few weeks, the friend described him as "a good hunter that only needed to be controlled." He would have kept Hardy, but he already had several dogs, so he offered Hardy to his friend, Gary McCready, of Roseville, Montana.

Gary and three buddies were scheduled to go to North Dakota on a hunting trip only six days after Hardy arrived. "I was afraid Hardy wouldn't bond with me by the time we left," Gary said. "So I kept him with me virtually night and day for the five days before the trip."

The extra attention worked. Hardy, who had lived with his breeder, his buyer, his breeder's friend, and now Gary during his first fifteen months of life, must have sensed that he had finally found a permanent home. The dog showed his gratitude as only a bird dog can.

"Hardy retrieved five pheasants to my hand," Gary said, "bypassing the other hunters to get to me. You know a dog is bonded when he won't deliver a bird to anyone else."

LEXY NEEDED LOVING

When Danny Lima of San Martin, California, decided to get a dog, he did his research well.

"I knew Danny had been to dog shows all over California looking for the 'perfect dog'," his wife Lori said. "But unknown to me, Danny had also made at least fifty trips to various animal shelters."

Lexy needed extra time and attention at first, but now she's steeled down and is a sweet and secure "big sister" to puppy Hans.

When Danny found Lexy at the San Martin pound he asked Lori to take a look at her. Lori liked the Weimaraner right away and described her as beautiful, underfed, and loud, with a mysterious past. A home-less woman who couldn't keep the dog any longer had given it to another woman, saying only that the animal's name was Lexy and she was good with children.

The Lima's took Lexy home, and made her feel welcome with affection and food. At bedtime, they put her in the roomy outdoor kennel they had prepared and went to sleep. But not for long. The "perfect dog" had an imperfection: separation anxiety. She barked all night.

Lori wasn't working during the adjustment period so she took Lexy everywhere with her. And that was exactly what Lexy wanted. "Lexy doesn't like to be outside when we're home," Lori said, "and if she has a downside, it's her verbal capabilities when expressing herself. She wants to be with us all the time."

Lexy's strong will made her almost "too much dog" when Danny trained her for hunting, but Danny was very persistent and it paid off. Today Lexy hunts well, holds a point, and works willingly. "Training is an ongoing process," Lori says, "but all in all, Lexy has arrived."

So has Hans. After two years of loving Lexy, the Limas decided to double their fun by getting a Weimaraner puppy. "Hans is also a handful," Lori says, "but he adores Lexy and she is a wonderful, accommodating 'big sister.' Our dogs may have brought us a little pain, but they give us lots of joy and hours of free entertainment."

CHAPTER SEVEN

THE PERIOD OF ADJUSTMENT

Whether you paid a high price for a dynamite dog or adopted a destitute dog, the period of adjustment will last for from four weeks to four months. You will need time to get to know your companion and become accustomed to performing the activities of a dog owner such as feeding, exercising, grooming, and training. Dogs are creatures of habit, so your new dog will also have to make adjustments. Even if living with you is paradise compared to his past, Prince will still be stressed by the sudden changes in his life.

THE FIRST FORTY-EIGHT HOURS

Being alone in a strange place can be quite frightening to a dog, so try to acquire Prince when you have a vacation or a long weekend so you can get to know each other slowly. Prince may not be ready to accept you just yet, but he does need your comforting presence. This isn't the time to do spring cleaning. Keep household activity to a minimum during Prince's first couple of days with you and give him time to adjust before inviting your friends over to meet him. Help him become familiar with his new home by going along as he investigates every nook and cranny, and don't hesitate to set the limits. For example, if Prince tries to play with a potted plant, tell him "No!" sharply and praise him softly when he turns away from it. Most new dogs begin testing the limits of your permissiveness during the first week in their new home. They want to please but don't know your expectations yet, so they are extremely receptive to education at that time.

During Prince's first few days at home, don't push him to relate to you. He needs time to watch, listen, and adjust. Invite him along as you go through your regular household routine but don't get your feelings hurt if he doesn't follow you from room to room right away. No matter how strong your urge to smother him with love, wait for him to come to you. Sit down and write a letter, or read, or watch television as long as the volume is low. Any activity where you're sitting in a fairly quiet part of the house with your dog in the same room is fine. Ignore Prince unless he asks for attention. If he does, welcome him quietly as if it was no big deal (even though it was!). Put your hand out toward him, and if he doesn't move away, stroke him casually, while continuing to concentrate on your book or T.V. program. If he shies away, don't apologize. You didn't do anything wrong. Just ignore Prince until he moves toward you again. Then let him get as close as he dares but don't try to pet him, until tomorrow. And if that doesn't work, try it again the next day, and the next. Depending upon Prince's past, it make take a while before he asks for and accepts your affection, but it's worth the wait. Forcing affection on him could crowd and frighten him, slowing down the physical and emotional process of his coming to you.

Older children, who can be trusted to take it easy and let Prince make the first move, may bring him out of his shell faster than you or your spouse can. Sometimes kids and dogs achieve a natural communication that eludes busy adults.

Dogs need time to get used to very young children and toddlers. Odie, a ten-year-old mixed bred, is relaxed around kids. He has known Gillian and Chloe Thornton since they were babies.

"Getting to know you" . . . Quiet communications works wonders when you and your new dog are adjusting to each other. This is Judith L. Gendron and her rescue Mastiff, Halcy, CD.

KIDS AND DOGS

Young children should never be left alone with a dog, but it's especially important that they be supervised when Prince first arrives and barely knows them. Babies and toddlers move erratically, have disparate body proportions, and smell different than adults. That's why dogs who haven't been around babies may not even realize they are human at first. Be especially vigilant if the children seem to want to tease Prince. Dogs perceive poking, prodding, and fingers or faces crowding right into their face as threatening. Some dogs simply walk away, but youngsters often follow. With no way out, Prince may growl, or even snap to make the teasing stop. Don't let it happen. Use positive teaching, not punishment, to show your children how to "make nice" to Prince. Supervise their play until they are old enough to be trustworthy, and when you need a break, put Prince in his crate.

Rowdy play, such as a ball game complete with tackling, pushing, shouting, and chasing, may over-excite Prince. Some dogs fear "their child" is getting hurt and try to protect him from his playmates. Others just want to join in the fun, but they may use their teeth—the only means they have for grabbing. Either way, someone could get hurt. Watch how Prince reacts to boisterous play and bring him inside if what you see worries you even a little. If the children are old enough to understand, explain that Prince can't handle rough games and they can have him back when that game is over and they play something quieter.

About the time they are in third or fourth grade, some children develop a real understanding of animals. If your children are eight or over, have patience, and want to work with Prince, show them how to teach him to sit, down, and come (training tips appear later in this chapter). Children often have a way with dogs and get the job done better and faster than grown-ups. Chapter 9 includes games that people and dogs can play together, as well as a few tricks your kids may enjoy teaching Prince.

DOG TO DOG

If you already have a dog, he and Prince should meet in a neutral place before Prince enters your house or yard. That way your dog is less likely to see Prince as a stranger invading his territory. Arrange for a friend or family member to take your original dog out for a ride or walk, on lead, to a designated place. Then meet them there with Prince also on lead. A park or a friend's yard is a good place, and walking distance is best because then you can walk the dogs home together.

When the dogs first meet, start a conversation with the other person and let the dogs do their thing. Keep plenty of slack in the leads so they can sniff noses, dance around each other, and perhaps growl a little, as they decide which of them is dominant. Keep talking through it all and avoid petting either dog. They will get to know each other better and faster if they do it on their own terms with as little human interference as possible. However, if the growling becomes so intense that a fight seems imminent, both of you should snap your leads hard enough to get your dogs' attention and head out in opposite directions. As soon as the dogs simmer down, try again.

Most dogs will live together peacefully and become good friends. These two even perform obedience jumps together.

After you bring both dogs home, don't leave them alone together until you're sure they get along well. Use their crates, or keep Prince in a crate and your already established dog in a different room when no one is home.

CATS AND OTHER CRITTERS

Cats and dogs can get along, and often become good friends, provided Prince doesn't have a history as a cat chaser or cat killer. Once a dog develops a prey drive toward cats, it can never be trusted with them. That's why "okay with cats" should be on your "Dream Dog Check List" if you have a cat or plan to get one.

Prince should be on lead when he meets Tabby, but she should be free to move at will. Correct Prince immediately if he barks or growls at Tabby or lunges toward her. A correction on lead entails snapping the lead, as you will learn later in this chapter. Just holding it tight and letting Prince pull won't do. In fact, it may tend to excite him even more.

If Prince isn't especially agitated at the sight of Tabby the cat may become curious and try to sniff noses with him. If Prince sniffs back gently, this is good. Just be careful because even a small dog can kill a cat in a heartbeat. Most won't try, unless Tabby runs. Then the instinct to chase moving prey is stronger than most dogs can deny. But that won't happen to you because Prince will be on lead and won't be able to chase Tabby even if she does run. If Tabby takes off and Prince tries to follow, correct him with a solid jerk on the lead and a firm "No!" He'll soon learn that this is Tabby's home too and will either ignore her or become her best friend. Until then, don't leave them alone together.

Almost every other popular pet appears to be prey to a dog and should be housed in a sturdy cage out of Prince's reach. Ferrets, birds, gerbils, hamsters, and rabbits are all creatures that a dog's instincts tell it to catch and kill. So keep Prince on lead when making introductions and correct everything, from too much interest to a menacing growl, with a lead snap and a firm "No!" You just want Prince to ignore your other pets, he doesn't have to love them. Very few dogs make friends with furry or feathered little critters (although some do become buddies with ferrets), but if Prince is supervised every time he is near these animals he will eventually learn to ignore them. Until then, don't take chances. Dogs have been predators for thousands of years, but

Whether you take a long walk together or play retrieving games, exercising your dog should be fun and relaxing for both of you.

millions of dogs live peacefully with other dogs, cats, and an array of other animals.

ROUTINE AND EXERCISE

Even before Prince accepts you as his best friend, a good routine will soothe him. Regular hours for food, exercise, training, and even affection will give him a sense of security and help him relax. It will also make housebreaking much easier.

Exercise is always essential, but it's especially important when a dog is adjusting to a new home. Tired dogs relax more easily and get into less trouble than hyper dogs, so use exercise to take the edge off Prince and help him calm down. Brisk walks are excellent for both of you. Retrieving games, keepaway, and catch are great fun, and help you become buddies—but only if your dog is ready to relate. If Prince doesn't know how to walk on a lead and won't play, read on.

YOUR DOG HAS A PAST

Prince may remember his original home and family with love and longing. Death, divorce, an allergic child, or a corporate move may have suddenly left him in the hands of strangers, and he may be in mourning—waiting, hoping that his beloved family will return. Your home is comfortable but still very strange, and its smells are similar but not the same. You talk to him nicely, but your voice, touch, scent, and appearance are different. Prince loved and trusted people in the past and will learn to love and trust again, but for a few weeks he may be bewildered and punchy; stunned by the sudden loss of everything familiar to him.

On the other hand, Prince's former owners may have made him view ordinary household activities with alarm. Newspapers, the rolled up magazine you carry in from the mail box, your hand reaching out to pet him, and anything that resembles a belt or stick may remind him of past pain.

If your Prince is a retired show champion or a wanna-be show dog that didn't win often enough, he may have lived in a comfortable kennel with heat, air-conditioning, affection, and good food, but still not be familiar with life inside a home. Household items will be strange, and perhaps somewhat scary, but he'll gradually get used to them. At least he won't have to contend with terrifying memories while adjusting to his new surroundings.

Maybe your Prince never had a home and had to find his own food. He never felt a carpet under his feet, walked up or down stairs, watched someone cook and salivated over the tempting aromas so new to him, heard a door bell, or encountered the frightening vacuum cleaner monster. No one ever gave him a hug. Tossing a ball for Prince in play may make him panic. Street dogs don't learn to play ball, but they do learn to dodge the rocks heaved at them when they raid garbage cans for a hasty meal.

PITY IS NOT THE POINT

Okay, life may have been unkind, even cruel to Prince, but just look how his luck has changed. He's with you now, and the rest of his life is still ahead of him. Although he may have been a victim, he isn't one now, so don't treat him like one. Save your pity for unwanted dogs that never get a break. Prince needs your help all right, but your pity will prevent progress, not encourage it. To blossom in his new home he has to become confident, and dogs gain self-confidence by learning how to please their owners. So the best thing you can do for Prince is train him, and the sooner, the better. Don't wait for him to adjust. Instead, help him adjust through gentle, but firm training. Prince especially needs direction when he first arrives. Letting him get away with actions you plan to correct later is confusing and unfair. Start him on the road to good manners and keep him from developing bad habits by teaching him the basics from day one. Praise every correct move he makes, and he will gradually develop the confidence you seek to instill.

Do you need a lot of specialized knowledge to train Prince? No. But you do need two attributes: common sense and consistency.

COMMON SENSE AND CONSISTENCY

Even before Prince enters your household, your family should discuss what a dog will and will not be allowed to do in your home. Except for the obvious, such as soiling the rug or stealing food from the dinner table, there is no right or wrong, just personal preferences. For example, some families may allow their dog to sleep in a bed, while others provide the dog with its own comfortable crate or doggie bed and teach it to sleep there. Some people invite their dog up on their lap or encourage it to sit on the sofa. Others don't permit their dog on the furniture. Don't worry about other people's rules. Set rules that suit you, and Prince will adjust to them provided they are upheld by the entire family. Common sense tells you how confused he will be if Dad doesn't allow him on the sofa, but Mom invites him up beside her the minute Dad leaves for his Elks meeting.

Children sometimes allow or even encourage their dog to break the house rules, believing this leniency will make the dog love them best. If you think this may be happening at your house, review the rules and the importance of consistency with the whole family. Then mention that if someone allows Prince to do something that gets him into trouble later, the dog will soon lose confidence in that person's leadership.

BECOMING A HOUSE DOG

Prince's understanding of human language will increase throughout his life with you. In the beginning, keep it simple.

Two Commands All Dogs Should Learn: "No!" and "Enough"

All dogs should learn to understand two words, "No!" and "Enough." "No!" means, "Stop that immediately and don't ever do it again." Use of the word "No!" should be reserved for really bad behavior such as

This lucky American Pit Bull Terrier is allowed to sleep on the sofa. However, if you don't want your dog on your furniture, make that clear right from the start, and create a comfortable place for her to sleep.

chewing the chair leg. Your sharp tone and intense attitude when you bark out the word "No!" will not be lost on Prince. However, if he ignores you and continues chomping the chair, go to him and repeat your sharp "No!" while shaking him mildly by the scruff of his neck with a slight downward pressure. He will understand this, because it's similar to what his own mamma might have done to teach him the limits of her tolerance. Before long, Prince will respect the "No!" word. When he responds to your "No!" by immediately stopping the undesirable activity, praise him with a sincere "Goood boy."

"Enough" means "What you are doing is just fine sometimes, but you have been doing it too long (or too hard), so stop now." Use "Enough" when you don't want to throw the tennis ball anymore but Prince is still depositing it on your lap. Say "Enough" when the game of tug gets too rowdy, or when your dog continues barking long after the meter reader leaves. Say "Enough" firmly, but without anger. "Enough" should work on dogs, as well as on the children that are playing with them.

Housebreaking

Dogs are basically clean creatures who try to avoid soiling their living, eating, and sleeping area. During housebreaking, take advantage of this fact by confining Prince to a small, safe area, such as a dog crate, or one room of the house (an easily cleaned room, such as the kitchen or bathroom) every time you are away and he is left unsupervised. As soon as you arrive home, take Prince outside and praise him for doing the right thing. Use the same door every time as that will help Prince learn where to wait to let you know he has to go outside. If Prince soils his crate or his playroom, clean it up immediately. Besides being dangerous to his health, putting Prince back into a wet or dirty crate teaches him to learn to live with his mess. That attitude will hinder, not help, the housebreaking process.

During this period of housebreaking, it is vital that Prince be on a regular feeding, watering, and exercise schedule.

MORNING

First thing in the morning, take him outside on lead for several minutes and always praise him for a job well done. Use a lead in the beginning even if you have a fenced yard. It works best because you can take him to the same area every time, you'll know if he relieved himself and you'll have the opportunity to praise him. Later, when he is reliably housebroken, you can simply open the door and let him out.

When you bring Prince in, offer him a drink and allow him to follow you around during your morning routine. Confine him when you leave the house, or even when you are at home but can't keep an eye on him. (If Prince is under a year old or a tiny adult, feed him twice a day; morning and evening and take him outside when you get up, and again after you feed him.)

AFTERNOON

Take Prince outdoors again at lunch time and give him a drink. Then confine him if you are leaving for the afternoon or are too busy to watch him.

EVENING

When you arrive home in the evening, take Prince outdoors and enjoy a nice long exercise period with him. Then let him watch as you prepare dinner or join you for the TV news. Prince should have access to fresh water while outside playing and for a couple hours after dinner. Feed him around 6:00 p.m., and by 8:00 p.m., remove his water bowl until morning. Take Prince outside when he finishes eating. Praise him after he relieves himself and let him spend the evening outside his crate and in the same room with you. Take him outside again just before you crate him for the night and go to bed.

Housebreaking Hints

Sometimes (especially when he is new and nervous), Prince may have to relieve himself more often than this schedule allows. When housebreaking, prevention usually works and correction usually doesn't, so watch him closely. Take him outside immediately if he begins walking in circles and sniffing the floor, if he starts panting when he hasn't been exercising, or if he suddenly leaves the room. Also, most dogs have to relieve themselves after heavy exercise, so if you played hard on the rug, get Prince off the rug and outdoors as soon as play time is over.

Most dogs, even housebroken ones, make a mistake or two in a new house. If you get home too late and Prince already had an accident, don't make a big deal over it. Never yell at Prince or punish him for anything unless you catch him in the act. Dogs don't relate punishment after the fact to something they did hours ago. Consequently, Prince won't understand why you are so angry at him when he was so glad to see you, and that will lead to far worse problems. So, if the dirty deed was done before you got home, take Prince outside anyway and he will eventually learn to expect the opportunity to go outside, and wait for it. Have patience and realize that Prince may still be too insecure or nervous in your absence to control himself for the amount of time you are away. Clean up the soiled spot as soon as you can, using an odor neutralizer or plain white vinegar. Never use anything containing ammonia, as the odor of ammonia causes dogs to seek out the same spot to go potty again.

If you catch Prince in the act, you may be able to stop him with a loud noise, like stamping your foot or clapping your hands. Then take him by the collar, snap on his lead, hurry him outside to right spot, and praise him if he finishes what he started. (If he's small enough, pick him up and secure his lead as you hasten outdoors.) Contrary to popular belief, spanking Prince with a rolled-up newspaper or rubbing his nose in his mess won't work. Such punishments only teach a dog to urinate or defecate where he thinks the evidence of his act will go undiscovered. Harsh physical punishments never accomplished anything in dog training and never will.

Once Prince is housebroken, keep him on a regular routine. Just because a dog is housebroken it doesn't mean he can "hold it" for unreasonable lengths of time. If Prince starts making mistakes after months, or even years of never soiling the house, have him checked by your veterinarian. Perhaps he has a kidney or bladder infection.

The keys to successful housebreaking are a regular routine and an alert trainer. A housebroken dog is simply a dog with a habit—the happy habit of eliminating outdoors.

Essential Education

Training makes the difference between whether your new dog becomes pure pleasure or a perpetual pain. It influences your dog's daily attitude and behavior.

The best thing you can do to increase Prince's confidence is let him know you approve of him. Conversely, the worst thing you can do is constantly berate him. That's why simple training is so essential. It teaches Prince how to earn your approval and makes living with him a pleasure. And, as a side benefit, it gets him accustomed to looking toward you for leadership; over and over, day after day. This develops his natural instinct to please and helps make his bad habits fade away.

OBEDIENCE SCHOOL

Obedience schools teach people how to train their dogs, so it would be ideal if every new dog owner and their pet signed up for an eight-week or ten-week course. Veterinarians often know where such classes are held or you can look them up in the yellow pages of your telephone directory or in the classified section of your newspaper. For more on obedience classes, see Chapter 9.

Of course, the ideal isn't always possible due to busy schedules, finances, and other considerations. If you can't attend classes, you can still teach your dog good manners by educating him on your own schedule. Here's how:

Reliable and Carefree: The "Come!" Command

The most important response Prince will ever learn is to come immediately when called. A reliable reaction to the "Come" command saves dogs' lives and makes life with a dog much easier.

OBEDIENCE HELPS ECO START OVER

Trained to bring honor to his owner as a stylish, productive Pointer, elegant Eco did his job well. He also lived the life many successful Pointers with wealthy owners experience—wintering in a southern state while perfecting his performance with the help of an expert professional trainer.

Aaron Knefelkamp doesn't mind having bald toys. After all, he can hug Eco when he wants to feel a fur coat.

At the start of spring when he was going on four, Eco arrived home from Texas with some problems. The pro said he lacked endurance. In fact, he got tired so quickly the trainer recommended a medical evaluation. Eco's owner complied, and the results showed that the dog had a sporadic heart beat during physical exercise or mental stress. His heart skipped a beat at times, and nothing could be done about it.

Eco's owner had no use for a Pointer that couldn't hunt, and wanted to find a new home for the dog. Michelle Knefelkamp, of Houlton, Wisconsin, an Obedience and Agility instructor, offered temporary foster care. With her many contacts in the dog world, she was sure she could find a good home for Eco. Michelle knew the Pointer well because she worked with horses on the same farm where he was kenneled. She had always admired handsome Eco, but she already had two Brittanies and didn't want a third dog.

That was four years ago and Michelle still has three dogs. "I couldn't give him up," she says, "And I'll probably never foster a dog again because I'm such a softie."

Bringing a four-year-old kennel dog into a home with a reluctant husband, a young son, two other dogs, and some cats wasn't easy. When the decision was made to keep Eco, the Knefelkamps had him neutered and worked on his house manners. Although the Pointer persisted in lifting his leg in the basement (where the cement floor probably

The other side of Eco is his intensity in the field. Here he freezes to a classic point during a training session.

reminded him of his kennel) for longer than the family would have liked, eventually he overcame it.

Surprisingly, Eco showed no evidence of his heart problem while living a house dog's life. He played outdoors, ran with his Brittany buddies, and hung out with Michelle when she worked in the garden, all with no signs of fatigue.

After they had Eco for six months, Ken Knefelkamp decided to try him in the field. That was the last time he was indifferent about the Pointer. "My husband almost dropped his jaw the first time he saw Eco on point," Michelle said. "Eco is so intense, so sure, and so truly awesome in a hunting situation, he took Ken's breath away." The first try was four years ago, and since then Ken has successfully hunted with Eco many times. He limits their time in the field to two hours and the Pointer has shown no signs of fatigue.

This was not so in obedience class. Being part of a class full of people and strange dogs seemed to stress Eco so much that he couldn't even focus. Insecure and irresponsive, he crept behind Michelle and couldn't be enticed to heel beside her, not even for bribes like hot dogs, cheese, or tennis balls. Meanwhile he did the whole lesson beautifully at home, heeling smartly and responding to praise, food, or toys.

Michelle solved the problem by taking Eco along to the obedience classes she taught and letting him lay down in the middle of the ring and watch the other dogs perform. Desensitizing him to crowds of strange dogs worked. By the time his own class was ready to graduate, he had overcome his lack of socialization and performed happily and accurately. Now Michelle occasionally uses him as a demo-dog when she teaches.

Eco has come a long way but he'll always have some idiosyncrasies. On the plus side, he's a superb watchdog, and Michelle says she feels quite safe with him waiting behind the front door at the end of their long driveway. But lack of early socialization still shows up in a few areas, and the Knefelkamps have adjusted by taking precautions in these areas. For example, Eco distrusts strangers and must be introduced to them gradually. The Knefelkamps accomplish this by putting the Pointer in the basement when company arrives. After fifteen minutes or so of getting used to the strange voices, the dog is allowed to join the party. By then he affectionately asks for his share of attention. Another idiosyncrasy that could stem from lack of puppy socialization is that while Eco is good with the Knefelkamp's son Aaron, they sense that he may not be trustworthy with other children. To be sure rather than sorry, they crate Eco when Aaron's friends visit. Aaron's toys also show evidence of an Eco peculiarity. All the stuffed animals are bald. While Eco never destroys them, he shreds out every single hair.

Are bald toys and a few adjustments worth the effort? "Yes," agree the Knefelkamps. "All in all, Eco is a success story," Michelle says. "I often catch Ken and Eco wrestling on the couch or taking a nap together. We're all glad Eco came into our lives."

Before Prince can learn to come when called, he has to learn what "Come" means. Decide how you want to call Prince and then always use the same word or words. If you use "Come" one time, "Here boy" the next and "Over here" after that, Prince may come in response to all these commands if your tone is inviting enough, but he won't learn the meaning of the command.

After you decide how to call Prince, use the command frequently. One of the reasons many grown dogs respond to the word "Sit" more readily than they do to the "Come" command, is because their owners use the "Sit" command much more often. Nowhere is the old saying, "practice makes perfect" more true than in dog training. So look for excuses to call Prince, and play calling games with him.

Bribery works best when teaching Prince what "Come" means. Introduce the command "Come" at feeding time, by saying his name, followed by "Come" in a happy voice—"Prince, Come!" Show Prince his dinner dish, and when he follows you and the dish a few steps, praise him and let him eat. Repeat this easy conditioning lesson every time you feed him.

Many dogs love to chase, and you can use that instinct to your advantage. Always move away from Prince when teaching him to come. In the beginning, call him only when you know he'll want to come—not when he's eating dinner, playing with a toy, or enjoying another person's company. Start by touching Prince playfully, then say "Prince, Come," and run away a few steps while bending, clapping, and talking happily to encourage him to reach you quickly. Let him catch you, play with him a few seconds, then call him and run off as before. Three or four times is enough. Always quit while Prince is still having fun. Too much practice will bore him.

Your whole family can have fun with "Come" games. Two of you can go to either end of a room and call him back and forth. When he arrives, reward him with praise and a tidbit. Dogs love to find people, so games of hide and seek work great. Children can hide behind a chair or a door and call Prince happily and often until he finds them. Then they should celebrate by petting and hugging him and possibly giving him a little treat for being such a splendid detective. The more places the children hide, the better time Prince will have, as long as the children are upbeat and patient.

Your new dog may be insecure in strange places unless he is close to you, at least for a couple of weeks. Use his insecurity to your advantage to help you instill the "Come" command. If you or one of your friends has a large, fenced yard, allow Prince to explore off lead. While he examines a flower, hide behind a tree or around the side of the house. Then call him cheerfully. Praise him enthusiastically as he heads in your direction and celebrate when he finds you.

Another conditioning trick that works well in a large, fenced area is to suddenly turn and walk in a different direction when Prince is investigating out ahead of you. After going a few steps, call him in a normal happy tone (not very excitedly as you aren't hiding), and don't miss a beat in continuing to walk away from him. The slower he responds, the faster you should move away. When he arrives by your side, welcome him casually and continue walking. The next time he moves away from you, do it all over again.

Wait until Prince is used to walking on a lead before practicing the "Come" command outdoors in a suburban or city neighborhood. Then, when Prince is walking beside you nicely on a loose lead, call him and start walking or running backward. Cheer Prince on as he chases you, and reward him with play, praise, and sometimes a treat, when you let him catch you.

The Bold and the Bashful

There is no way your dog can come and still be wrong, but some responses are more desirable than others. When you call Prince, if he comes bounding over eagerly, with his tail wagging his whole body, hug him and tell yourself how lucky you are.

If Prince saunters slowly toward you, vary your actions upon his arrival. Sometimes hug and praise him. Other times, give him a treat. About half the time, just give him a joyful pat, then turn and run away from him while calling him on the fly. Soon he'll join in the fun by coming to your call with more enthusiasm.

It's bashful Prince, the dog that lowers his body and kind of creeps toward you that needs more help. He may become even more submissive when he reaches you, keeping his head down and possibly rolling over and presenting his belly.

Don't rub that vulnerable belly to reassure Prince. Reassuring him is a mistake because it praises his submissive behavior. Instead, use the same happy talk you would use if he were an outgoing dog, but kneel down when he reaches you and cup his face in your hands. Tickle Prince under the chin. Get him to reach up for a treat. That encourages him to keep his head up and prevents him from lying down or rolling over. Don't despair over Prince's bashful behavior. Once he feels secure, bashful Prince may become bolder.

Don't Trash Your Training

After teaching Prince to come happily when called, don't erase your work by becoming lazy and calling him when you want to push a pill down his throat or chastise him for stealing your shoe. Always go to Prince for the unpleasantries, and keep his "Comes" carefree.

Lead Breaking Your New Dog

When lead breaking Prince, a flat buckle leather or nylon collar works best. While the collar should not feel tight against Prince's neck, it shouldn't be loose enough to slide off over his head either.

Besides teaching you how to train your dog, obedience classes will help you socialize your dog. Obedience instructor Amy Ammen demonstrates the technique for steadying a dog as a friendly stranger approaches.

These Border Collies demonstrate the Down-Stay and the Sit-Stay.
Photo credit: Pets by Paulette.

Chain training collars, also called choke chains, are useful when working with dogs six months of age or older, although they are seldom necessary for training tiny dogs of any age. They are the collars most frequently used by people who compete in Obedience competition. When purchasing a chain training collar, look for one that has small links and releases instantly. When tightened, it should have one-and-a-half to two-and-a-half inches of excess chain before the ring attaches to the lead. The best fitting ones are a little snug sliding over the dog's head. There is a right and a wrong way to put a choke chain on your dog. When worn correctly, the active ring (the one attached to the lead) will come across the top of the right side of your dog's neck.

For training Prince, you'll need a lead that is six feet long and as wide as feels comfortable in your hand. For just plain walks, you might be more comfortable using a shorter lead.

Most adult dogs are familiar with wearing a collar, but if Prince never had his own humans, let him get used to the feel of a collar before starting to train him. The first few times he wears one, play with him. If he's a chow hound, put the collar on just before feeding time. Let him wear it a little longer each session until he pays no attention to it.

When Prince is accustomed to the collar, attach the lead and let him drag it around. Keep your eye on him so he doesn't catch it on something and start struggling. When he becomes nonchalant about dragging the lead (or if he did not drag it at all because he was too busy playing with it), take him to an outdoor area with plenty of space. Then pick up your end of the lead and follow Prince wherever he takes you.

After Prince has enjoyed a couple sessions of leading you, attach his lead to the doorknob of a door that will remain shut when he pulls, and let him fight it out with a solid object instead of you. If Prince is a big, strong boy, you may have to take him outside and tie him to a tree. Stay in the room, or yard, but ignore Prince for five minutes. If Prince protests passionately, one minute may seem like five, so remember to time it instead of guessing. Be prepared for Prince to scream and struggle, but if there is nothing he can get tangled in, he won't hurt himself. Five minutes of this, once or twice a day for a few days, is usually enough. When Prince calms down and knows how to relieve the pressure on his collar, take him back to an open area with lots of space.

This time allow Prince to lead you for a minute, then begin putting gentle pressure on the lead and choosing the direction you both go. Walk toward, not away from, familiar surroundings, and encourage him with happy talk. Prince doesn't have to be in any particular position; out in front, behind, or beside you are all okay at this point.

Gradually, as Prince accepts your leadership and becomes confident enough to walk both toward and away from home with you, reel him in a little closer if he tries to pull you. When he walks near you on a loose lead, occasionally lean down and play with him or praise and pet him. If he still persists in pulling, put the lead in your right hand, place your right hand tightly against the front of your waist. Then put your left hand over your right to steady it. Pick a direction and start walking. Just as Prince is about to reach the end of the lead in front of you (an instant before he will pull), make a quarter turn to the right and continue walking at the same pace. Do not warn him, call him, or slow down for him, and wait until he catches up with you before talking to him. Then let him know you are delighted that he is by your side again by saying something like, "Oh, there you are," as you give him a quick, playful pat. Repeat the quarter turn to the right as often as necessary.

Some dogs lag behind instead of pulling. If yours is still way behind you after a few sessions, turn to face him and run backward while clapping and encouraging him with your voice. When he catches you, play with him. If he is shy or fearful, allow him to catch up to you as soon as you see him make the effort.

Ten minutes a day is enough when lead breaking, and more than fifteen minutes is too much.

Pulling on the Lead

If your dog pulls so hard that walking him is a battle of strength and wills instead of fun, there is a solution. Even if you are 4' 10" and weigh just 90 pounds, you can easily control any size dog. How? Stop talking. Then go the opposite of where your dog wants to go. Now you've begun sneakaway sessions.

Sneakaway Sessions

For sneakaway sessions, Prince should wear a snug buckle collar that he cannot back out of. In addition, make or buy a long line—a fifteen-foot nylon line with a swivel snap at one end and a loop handle at the other. Put your right thumb in the handle of the line and clasp your fingers around the remainder of the strap. Then place your left hand under your right so there's no slack between your hands, and hold both hands in front of you against your waist. The full fifteen feet of line should be dragging on the ground.

Modify your speed to fit the size of your dog. If your dog is short-legged or rather clumsy, walk more slowly than your normal pace. If your dog is scared or shy, and lags behind rather than pulling ahead, skip this section. Sneakaway sessions are not for him.

PART ONE: A LITTLE RESPECT

The first goal is to teach Prince to walk within five feet of you on a slack line, in spite of distractions. Distractions are anything Prince is interested in, such as cats, fire plugs, birds, food, children, other dogs, or the door to your house.

Imagine standing in the center of a large hula-hoop with a five-foot radius. When Prince steps outside this imaginary circle, silently and swiftly walk away from him, and keep walking until he comes back into a five-foot radius of you. If he passes you and continues out of your radius, turn and walk in the opposite direction. Prince will be jerked when the line tightens because he isn't attentive enough to realize you turned. Never move your arms to jerk him. The correction will be stronger and more meaningful when you keep your arms steady against your waist so that your full body weight powers into the line.

Even if you have an urge to warn Prince before the line tightens, don't do it. To achieve the goal, your dog's complete attention must be on you, not just one ear sort of cocked in your direction. When he can hear what you intend to do, he has no reason to watch you. Also, don't praise Prince when he comes into your radius. Staying near you on walks is not something you should have to ask for and reward. Instead, it should become a way of life; an act of respect.

Why have Prince on a slack fifteen-foot line when your goal is to keep him from pulling when he is on a regular four-foot to six-foot lead? Because holding him on a tight lead does nothing to teach him respect, attention, and a sense of commitment to you. In fact, some dogs think a tight lead is fun and games, and the harder you pull, the harder they pull. The long, slack line allows you to build momentum so that the tug will be stronger if Prince lunges away.

At first, the line may tangle in Prince's legs. Usually he can easily step out of his tangle if you continue walking slowly, but sometimes he may get hog-tied. When this happens, back up to put some slack in the line, take a step forward to tighten it and repeat until Prince moves forward to loosen the line. Avoid returning to rescue him or he may learn to tangle himself for sympathy and attention.

Some dogs think the line is a wonderfully wiggly chew toy. Discourage Prince from mouthing the line by having him wear it a few minutes a day in the house and commanding "No!" when he grabs it. If he won't drop it, spray Bitter Apple (mentioned earlier and available at pet supply shops) on the line.

Practice ten minutes a day for a week. With some dogs, you may speed results by training a half hour a day for two days before moving to Part Two. But don't rush. Dogs accustomed to pulling people down the street may need additional time to change their attitude.

PART TWO: DEALING WITH DISTRACTIONS

After Prince consistently succeeds at staying in the five foot radius, practice around distractions. They will teach him to ignore his impulses and remember his responsibilities. Use food dropped on the ground, animals, and children, and practice in new places, like parks, supermarket parking lots, or near a kennel of barking dogs. When Prince discovers he can't focus on other things and watch your movements at the same time, he'll become attentive to you.

Now, instead of walking, run away when Prince leaves your radius and stop dead when he corrects himself and the line goes slack. When he is in your radius and attentive to you, walk slowly or stand still. If Prince doesn't stop in your radius, turn and run in the opposite direction again. Running makes the correction stronger because you build more momentum. But don't try for track records when training small dogs.

After several ten-minute, or a few thirty-minute sessions, combining tempting distractions with running away, Prince should be watching your movements and staying close. If he lunges ahead, run straight in the exact opposite direction, so he won't be able to see your actions peripherally. With a strong, adult dog that has a bad pulling habit, build the maximum momentum by running away fast instead of gradually building speed. If there isn't enough space in some areas for you to sneak away effectively, avoid taking Prince to those places until he's ready for Part Three.

PART THREE: REAL LIFE

Once you have Prince's attention around a variety of exciting distractions, and he seems to want to stay next to you on a slack line, you are ready to enforce the "no pulling" rule on a six-foot lead. Hold the loop with your right thumb and grab up the slack in your right hand. There should be no tension on the lead when Prince is standing beside you at your left side. Straighten your right arm with your knuckles against the right seam of your trouser leg, so the lead runs in front of your legs. Now walk briskly with Prince on your left.

If Prince tries to lunge ahead, open and close your hand so you drop the slack, thus giving him more rope. Grip the loop end, turn halfway around to the right, and run as fast as you can until he is running behind you on a slack lead. Then fold the slack into your right hand again. If Prince passes you as you run, turn and go in the opposite direction until he is happy to stay near you. Don't jerk the lead at all. Your body will do that for you. If running is uncomfortable, walk with long, determined steps.

Prince may try to walk directly behind you. Correct that by shortening the slack in the lead, and be sure your right knuckles are against the outside seam of your pant leg. Then walk straight ahead briskly, and the force of your left thigh thrusting into the lead with every step, will bring him up beside you.

Now you have the know-how to teach Prince to take leisurely walks on a loose lead no matter who or what else is on the street, to stop rushing through gates and doors, and to remain attentive to you even if the neighbor's cat vies for his attention. Allowing Prince to drag you around tells him that he is the leader mentally and physically, so be ready to sneak away any time he forgets the "no pulling" rule.

From here on, your dog only has to learn to respond to the commands "Sit," "Down," and "Stay," and he will be a pleasure at home and away.

COMMANDS FOR DAILY LIVING

Every dog should respond to simple commands such as Sit, Down, and Stay. Ten minutes of training a day (twice a day if you are especially ambitious), is all the time it takes to give a dog of any age this essential education. Always end on the happy note of success and always stop after ten minutes. More is boring, not better, and does no good at all.

Sitting Is Super

If Prince is especially sensitive, use treats to teach the Sit. He will enjoy learning the meaning of the "Sit" command if you begin by holding a small piece of a yummy treat in front of his nose. Say "Sit," and move the treat over his head in such a way that his eyes follow it upward, his head tilts back and his rear reaches the floor. At that point, give him the goodie. Practice this five or ten times, twice a day, and Prince will soon know the meaning of the command "Sit." A soft treat, such as a nibble of cheese, is the best teaching aide. It's healthy and Prince can eat it fast so you can continue training.

No matter how good a "sitter" Prince becomes for treats, reinforce the command without showing him a goodie after he becomes more confident. Place your right hand on his chest and cup his rear in your left hand. Say "Sit," one time as if you mean it—short and firm, but not loud. Then push back slightly with your right hand and slide it upward to stop under Prince's jawbone. Tickle gently under his chin to keep his head up. At the same time, push down and forward lightly on his rear. When Prince sits, hold him in position for five or ten seconds using the least force necessary to get the job done. It's okay to give a goodie after time is up, but don't do it every time, and don't let him see it until after he has remained in position for at least a few seconds.

Use the "Sit" command several times a day, every day. Sit for a special treat. Sit for petting. Sit before receiving his dinner dish. Lots of practice and lots of praise means leadership for you and approval for Prince.

TEACHING BOLDER DOGS TO SIT

A more forceful method of teaching the Sit works on more confident dogs, as well as those that didn't respond to the milder method. With Prince wearing a chain training collar and lead (see "Lead Breaking Your New Dog" earlier in this chapter for fit and placement), place him beside you on your left. Take the active ring of the collar in your right hand, command "Sit," and pull mostly up but slightly forward while your left hand pushes down and slightly forward on his rear. Relax the pressure on the chain the instant Prince sits. If he tries to move, tighten the chain long enough to reposition him, then

Dogs who have learned to obey simple commands are a lot nicer to live with and a lot more fun. Imagine trying to get three untrained dogs to pose for a picture like these debonair Scottish Terriers.

Photo credit: Pets by Paulette.

Obedience instructor Amy Ammen demonstrates how to accomplish the Slide Down with a large dog that resists learning the Down.

immediately relax the pressure again. Keep Prince sitting in place for ten seconds. Kneeling beside him may make it easier for both of you.

Use only the amount of force necessary to get Prince to sit and remain in position for several seconds. Some dogs need only a slight pull on the chain and a light push on the rear. Others may need a quick, hard upward jerk on the chain, and if this describes your dog, you may have to practically sit on his rear to get compliance. Praise quietly when Prince succeeds. Loud praise can easily excite an exuberant dog, making sitting in place more difficult.

Teaching the Down

Teaching Prince to Down on command may be extremely easy, horrendously hard, or anything in between, depending on his attitude. Some dogs can hardly stand being placed in a submissive position. Because dogs react in so many different ways, there are several methods of teaching the Down. They are discussed here from the mildest to the most forceful. It's best to try them in order and give each method a chance before moving on to the next one. Then stick with the mildest method that works.

Some dogs will learn the Down with treat training. Begin with Prince in the Sit position, hold a tasty treat right in front of his nose and command "Down." Think of making a movement shaped like a capital L as you lower the treat straight down just in front of his paws and then slowly pull it outward. As Prince reaches for the goodie, the front half of his body will move downward. If it doesn't lower completely to the ground, use your free hand to push lightly on his shoulders, but don't mash him down. The instant his whole body is in down position, give him the treat.

A rather mild, but slightly more forceful method is the Slide Down. Start with Prince sitting beside you on lead. Reach over him with your left hand and grasp his left leg at elbow level (high up on the leg). At the same time, take his right elbow in your right hand. Command "Down," wait a second, and then lift both his legs up just enough to slide them forward into the Down position. If Prince resists, lean on him with your chest while sliding his front legs. When he's down, praise quietly while keeping him steady for a few seconds. Then tell him "okay," and play happily with him as you allow him to get up.

Always remember to wait a second between giving the "Down" command and starting the Slide. Otherwise you won't realize when Prince has learned to go down on command. Practice about ten times a day until you can easily keep him in the Down position for fifteen seconds.

If Prince doesn't cooperate after a week of practicing the Slide Down, try the Jerk Down. Use a chain training collar and sit him by your left side. Hold the lead in your right hand close to the snap and place your left index finger and thumb on either side of his spine just behind the top of his shoulders. Command "Down," and pause a second so you'll know if Prince responds. If he doesn't respond immediately, snap the lead down sharply at an angle so that your hand ends up by his elbow. Your left hand pushes down at the same time. Practice until you can easily keep Prince down for fifteen seconds, and praise happily when you give the "okay" signal allowing him to get up.

Now use the "Down" command daily. Down for petting. Down to receive a chew toy. Down to help Prince remember that he earns praise by responding to your commands.

THE ANXIOUS AND THE ANGRY

An occasional dog hysterically resists downing. If yours has this problem, practice Sneakaway Sessions (earlier in this chapter) first. If he still refuses frantically, or shows any signs of anger whatsoever, please do yourself the favor of getting help from an experienced trainer. (See "Aggression" later in this chapter.)

Staying in Place

When Prince knows how to Sit and Down on command, make your life easier by teaching him to stay in place. Use a chain training collar and lead (a nylon or leather buckle collar should do if he is tiny), and begin by having Prince either sit or down beside you. Then command "Stay" firmly, but not loud. At the same time, swing your arm just in front of his nose with your palm facing him. That's the Stay signal. If Prince moves from the Sit, reposition correct him immediately using the forceful method of teaching the Sit described earlier. If he moves from the Down, reposition him using the Jerk Down. Don't repeat the Stay command when correcting. The more you repeat commands, the more Prince learns to ignore them. If he doesn't listen the first time, let your hand and lead do the talking by using the forceful Sit and the Jerk Down.

Begin with a goal of ten seconds, then slowly increase the time by five-second increments. Practice several times a day until Prince will Sit or Down beside you for thirty seconds. Always pet and praise him when he achieves the goal.

Once Prince remains steady on the Sit and Down with you beside him, step in front of him, still holding the lead. Now do a little play acting. Tie your shoe. Pull a weed. Examine the carpet. But have one eye on Prince, and be ready to correct him the instant he moves. As Prince improves, slowly work your way further away from him but hurry back and reposition him right away if he moves.

Remember distractions? You need them here. A dog that holds a Stay only when it's bored won't make your life easier. You want Prince to stay where he was told even if your friend's toddler walks by dangling a hot dog. So practice Stays on lead around other animals, children, food, and friends, and continue to correct any movement immediately.

When Prince does steady stays on lead, replace his lead with a fifteen-foot long line and begin increasing your distance from him by tying him to a post or tree. Now you can move further away and use some new distractions. Just remember to return immediately to correct movement.

Eventually you will want Prince to stay even though you are out of sight. To teach this, find a corner outdoors, such as the corner of your house. Place Prince on one side, command "Stay," and walk around the corner. Hold the long line and toss out distractions such as treats or balls. Use a tiny mirror, or ask a friend to spy and to tell you what Prince is doing. Then return quickly and silently to correct any movement. Practice in new locations with tempting distractions and soon Prince will be so well behaved that you'll wish the same methods worked on kids.

Socialization

A friendly, easy-going attitude is very desirable in a dog, but no animal will have the confidence to take things in stride unless it is accustomed to going on outings and encountering many different sights and sounds. To become cheerful, reliable companions, dogs must be well socialized.

WHAT YOUR DOG MIGHT HAVE MISSED

Puppies go through critical periods of social development from birth to sixteen weeks of age. During the first six to seven weeks, they learn from their dam (mother) and their littermates. From their dam,

This puppy will grow up with a friendly, fearless personality because it's being socialized by a caring owner. Unfortunately, not every puppy is so lucky.

they learn respect for authority, which leads to a more trainable dog. Playing with their littermates teaches them social interaction and how to moderate aggression. In fact, the wrestling sessions enjoyed by young puppies make them less body and sound sensitive, resulting in dogs that are more tolerant of children, loud noises, and other dogs. The ideal time to take a puppy home is when it reaches seven weeks old. By then, it's mentally mature enough to adjust to leaving its dam and littermates and soon settles into its human family.

Dogs remember all their lives what they learned about the world when they were between seven and sixteen weeks of age. Those nine weeks play a major role in shaping their personality, making them fearless or fearful, outgoing or shy, eager to learn or resentful of training. The brevity of this time period is a throw back to the dog's wild ancestors. It correlates to when wild pups or cubs ventured out of the den for the first time to hastily learn the lessons of survival. Everything had to be instilled in a hurry, because young animals that made a mistake in the wild rarely got a second chance.

Although domesticated for centuries, dogs still arrive in the world programmed to learn how to handle their environment during their first four months of life. With or without their owner's help, they will form perceptions of what is safe and what is dangerous. With a good owner's help, they will be introduced to a friendly world and grow up

SUGAR NEEDED TIME

Jane Dillard and her husband Jim Greenlaw of Tacoma, Washington, researched several Pug kennels before calling one and inquiring about puppies. During the conversation, the kennel owner said a one-year-old adult was also available. The attractive female had a defect called lolly tongue (the tip of the tongue stays outside the mouth when it closes), so the kennel couldn't show her or use her for breeding.

Sugar appeared to be the perfect Pug, except for her tongue, and Jim and Jane decided to take her. Jane remembers being especially

impressed with the breeding kennel because all the dogs were kept in the house. She thought that practically guaranteed a socialized, trained dog with house manners, but she soon found out differently. In actuality, the kennel dogs were allowed only limited freedom in the house and were usually confined to their individual crates. If Sugar was any indication, they were bonded to each other instead of to people, and had no house training whatsoever.

Sugar was somewhat leery of her new home and especially upset to have only humans for company. She was lonesome for the other dogs, and since she didn't relate

Love and lots of attention from her new owners helped Sugar overcome her shyness.

to humans as friends, was not comforted by Jane and Jim's affectionate attention. It took several weeks for her to understand that she would not be chastised for walking from room to room. Housetraining also went slowly, as Sugar needed to become assertive enough to ask to go outside.

Sugar is three years old now and has become much more courageous. She goes outside on demand and enjoys her whole house. But she isn't the dog she might have been if she had been socialized from puppyhood. "She's so passive I grieve for her," Jane says. "But she's our special girl and we love her."

confident and outgoing. Without human help, they will have chance encounters with frightening noises, strangers, and scary objects, and may grow up defensive or shy.

Uh-oh. That's pretty scary stuff, especially if you don't have a clue about Prince's puppyhood. But a puppy can only be raised once, so there's no use fretting about what kind of dog Prince might have been with a different start. Instead, start now and help him become the best dog he can be.

Cram Course for Adult Dogs

Socializing Prince isn't a step-by-step regimen, like training. Instead, it's part of daily life. Every time Prince goes somewhere he's never been, does something he has never done, or meets a new person, he is being socialized. The process has only two rules. Rule one is never pet or talk to Prince when he's fearful. Rule two is always praise him for behaving bravely.

OVERCOMING FEARS

Is Prince leery of strangers, new places, or objects? If he is, remember the first rule of socialization whenever you have friends over or take him on an outing. When Prince looks fearful, don't reassure him by cajoling or petting, as he will interpret those actions as praise. Anything your dog is praised for he will repeat again and again, so a hesitant, fearful stance could become his learned response to the sight of a new object. Never yank him toward the feared object either. Treatment like that will turn a slight scare into full-blown terror.

Instead of feeding Prince's fear by babying him, or terrifying him by using force, just confidently approach the new object yourself. Touch it like it was long-lost treasure, and happily invite Prince over to see the wonderful thing. Sitting down by the feared object is an especially good way to encourage your dog to move toward it. Still scared, but curious too, Prince may crawl on his belly, nose outstretched, toward the frightful thing. After he approaches and examines the object, praise him for being a brave fellow. If the object is unbreakable and not too large, toss or roll it away from (never toward) him. This will arouse his natural chasing instinct, and before long he may play with the object himself.

Don't be surprised if Prince fears something as silly as a garbage bag or a fireplug. Before he is socialized, Prince may see the bogeyman everywhere. And don't expect instant results. Prince needs to be put in socializing situations again and again. Fears fade slowly, and those backed by bad memories may never disappear completely, but the following suggestions should help Prince learn to face each new situation with a bit more confidence.

SOCIALIZING YOUR DOG AT HOME

Educational toys for human babies sell well because parents know that while their children play, they are also learning how to manipulate and understand their world. Play learning works best for young adult and active middle-aged dogs too, and their games and toys aren't even expensive. For example, human babies learn about noise when they play with rattles and other toys that let them control the volume and duration of the noise. Dogs that learn how to create and stop a racket also become more confident around loud noises.

One toy that may help Prince overcome a fear of noise is an empty half gallon or gallon plastic milk container without a top. It doesn't matter if the container is as big as Prince, because a milk jug weighs practically nothing and can be pulled by the handle. Lay the jug on the floor, and ignoring Prince, turn on the TV or read the paper. Prince may have to overcome an initial fear of this strange object and might approach it and back off several times. Just ignore the whole scene and eventually he will become brave enough to drag the jug, then shake it, and finally bang it against walls and table legs. Like a child with a toy drum, Prince is learning that noise isn't so scary because it can be controlled. Later, he can graduate to a louder toy. Put a few pebbles inside a milk jug and screw the lid on to make a raucous rattle. Stay in the same room when Prince plays with this noisemaker, as you may have to stop him from chewing off and swallowing the lid.

NOISE SENSITIVITY

An occasional dog is especially sensitive to loud noises. This can be easily cured with patience and a bit of ingenuity. Simply think of every single thing Prince enjoys, and then think of what kind of noise you can make to continue the fun. For example, if Prince looks forward to feeding time, stir his dinner in a metal pan using a metal spoon, before giving it to him. Sometimes drop the pan (no closer than a few feet from him) before you fill it. If Prince can hardly wait for the children to come home from school, celebrate their arrival with applause and cheers. Tailor your noise-making to your own dog's delights, and soon he'll recover quickly when startled by a sudden sound.

SAVVY SIGHTS

Dogs sometimes spook at people who are wearing odd hats, big sunglasses, flapping rain gear, or other accessories that change the shape of the human body. To teach Prince that there is just a regular person inside those clothes, raid your closet for rain gear, a couple of hats, boots, and anything else that will change your appearance, including Halloween costumes. Get the children involved, they will enjoy the costume party, but be sure they are old enough to understand the purpose of the game and won't try to frighten Prince.

Begin with a single item, a wide-brimmed hat or a trench coat, and let Prince watch you put it on. Then call him to you for a pat or a treat. If Prince seems a bit wary of you in a trench coat or hat, get down to his level and pretend to tie your shoe. That gives him an opportunity to check out the scary item up close, without a word from you. Always let Prince reach you and make the first move. Then it's fine to pet him.

When Prince is used to seeing you and your family in silly clothes, have your children (or you) walk weirdly wearing a big coat or boots. Shuffle or hop and make funny noises, but sink to the floor and ignore Prince if he seems frightened. Wait to pet him until after he approaches and touches you (or your children) first. If Prince is a wary dog, add items gradually. Whatever you do, don't suddenly appear decked out like Dracula, with flapping arms and a swirling cape, or you could crush his confidence instead of cultivating it.

TOUCHING WITHOUT TENSION

Teaching Prince to enjoy being touched can lower your blood pressure (petting a dog does that) and help you bond to each other. It should be restful and pleasurable for you both.

After a tiring day, collapse in front of the TV with Prince on your lap, or on the floor beside you, and pet him while you unwind. This works best if Prince recently had exercise and is also ready to relax. When petting Prince, handle every square inch of him. Touch him from the tip of his nose to the pads of his toes.

If Prince shies away from being touched on some part of his body, don't pet that place continuously, but come back to it often with a quick caress. This is quiet time, a time of pleasant communication through touch, not a battle of wills or a wrestling match, so don't push any issue. Keep your mind on the TV program and your strokes gentle and lazy, and Prince may fall asleep. Now you can gently stroke the places that made him uncomfortable. Have you ever noticed that a new ring can be quite annoying, but after you wear it to sleep it feels more natural? This is the same principle.

OUT AND ABOUT

Prince should begin investigating the world beyond your walls as soon as he is lead-trained and vaccinated. Provided he has a gentle disposition, try to have him meet elderly folks and toddlers, gentle children and teenagers, young marrieds pushing strollers, bearded men, and women wearing big hats. While safely outside on lead, Prince will also get used to hearing motors, horns, sirens, and the rumble of the garbage truck. The more people Prince meets and the more sights he sees, the more confident he will become, and this will make him a better companion at home and away.

SHORT COURSES

If your house doesn't have stairs, find some elsewhere and see if Prince knows how to navigate them. If not, teach him patiently. To do this, deposit him on the third or fourth step, and encourage him to come down. When he is secure going down, sit on the third or fourth step and encourage him to climb to you. Soon navigating a flight of stairs will be a breeze. If Prince is too heavy to lift onto the stairs, you sit on the fourth or fifth step and encourage him to come up and join you.

Short car rides to the park, to visit a friend, or even to nowhere are also good for Prince. Once or twice a week is usually often enough to get him used to the scenery and the motion. Soon he will relax and even sleep peacefully in the car.

Preventing and Solving Problems

When dealing with problems, prevention always pays. Prevent Prince from making mistakes and correct slip-ups instantly, and undesirable behavior will never become a bad habit.

AGGRESSION

You should never, ever be afraid of your dog. Not for a minute. Not even for an instant. Don't ignore or excuse threatening behavior just because it was over quickly. Next time Prince's threat will be even stronger—and yes, there will be a next time.

A show of aggression sometimes occurs when a new dog tries to establish its position in the pack (that's the family to you). For example, Prince may know he isn't the leader because the person called Daddy obviously is, but he may try to dominate the person called Mom. Or maybe he knows Mom's the boss because she trained him, but he's jealous when she gives attention to anyone else and growls when Dad or the children try to get near her. This is the type of aggression that surprises people. The first time their dog growls a challenge at them they quickly explain that he never did that before. But he probably did. They just didn't recognize the signs.

The first sign that Prince is vying with his human family for dominance is when he simply ignores a command. You say "Down" and he walks into the other room. He's out of your way, which is what you wanted, so you don't bother to enforce and command and quickly forget the minor disobedience. But Prince doesn't. Another couple of unenforced commands, and he's ready to test you at a higher level. His opportunity comes up a few days later. In a rush to clean up, you bend to pick up his food dish before he licks the last morsel. He stands over it, body rigid, head cocked and eyes looking straight into yours. "Okay, hurry up and finish it," you say, never realizing that you just lost round two. When round three comes, it may be a growl. Surprised and momentarily fearful, you won't be able to deny that there's a problem, but you'll probably say he never did anything like that before.

SAVED FROM A CHAIN

Chances are that Samson was never socialized as a puppy. When the handsome Brittany was eighteen months old, his owners divorced and neither one wanted him. J. Kent and Jean Nelson of St. Mary, Montana, adopted him because he was related to their beloved Brittany who had recently died.

"Samson wasn't much of a dog when I got him," J. Kent said. "As a matter of fact, I'm not sure he knew he was a dog. He had been kept on a chain all his life, never allowed to run. I would let him out of his pen and he would just trot around with a blank stare on his face. He wouldn't respond to anything—not even his name."

Samson, a Brittany, spent his formative months on a chain. Today he is a good friend and superior hunting companion to his adopted family.

The Nelsons' gave Samson quality time every day, and after a month the dog's aspect improved. Gradually he responded to the attention and took an interest in his surroundings. In the Fall, J. Kent began training Samson for hunting and was pleasantly surprised. Samson learned much faster than any puppy he ever trained, plus the dog's obedience level was outstanding.

Samson became both a lovable companion and an exceptionally fine hunting dog. But he wouldn't tolerate other dogs or even other people. The Nelsons' believe Samson adopted his attitude because he spent his formative months on a chain. Dogs on chains are easy targets for sadistic people, youngsters who tease, and loose dogs that bully. Chained dogs also lack the crucial socialization that comes from being part of a family. They seldom get enough attention or affection, and miss out on learning to handle everyday events such as greeting guests and going for a walk.

The Nelsons overlook Samson's shortcomings because he behaves beautifully for them and is a superior hunting dog. J. Kent sums it up, "We love Samson, and I know he loves us. He will be hard to replace."

This type of escalating aggression is much easier to prevent than it is to correct. First, socialize Prince well. By meeting many people, your dog learns that almost everyone is a friend. When he needs to differentiate, he will. Don't push it. Never urge Prince to be aggressive toward humans.

Second, teach Prince a few basic commands and use them for everyday life. "Sit" for petting; "Down" for a biscuit; "Gimme Five," for fun. And don't allow Prince to yank you around when you walk him.

Third, and perhaps most important of all, never give a command you aren't prepared to enforce. For example, don't command Prince to "Come" when you're soaking in the bathtub unless you plan to make wet tracks to him immediately and enforce the command if he ignores you. Dominance is mental and has nothing to do with physical strength or physical punishment. It's as simple as this: When you train your dog and he obeys you, he is content. He knows how to please you, understands that you are dominant and doesn't try to test you.

CHEWING

Many dogs have a strong need to chew. Your home and your disposition will survive this stage if you give Prince lots of toys made especially for chewing, such as rawhide sticks or bones, nylon or gummy bones, and rope toys (see Chapter 6). These are all available at any pet store and some supermarkets.

Remember, dogs don't know the difference between a worn out shoe and your new leather boots, so don't give Prince anything to chomp on except chew toys made especially for dogs. If he picks up something he shouldn't, simply go to him and take it away. Then replace it with one of his own toys and praise him for chewing the right thing. After you do this enough times, Prince will get the idea. In the meantime, confine him when you can't watch him, and be sure he has a safe toy to gnaw on.

SUBMISSIVE URINATION

Between animals in the wild, such as wolves, submissive urination means, "You're the boss and I hope you're not angry at me, but if you are, I'm sorry." Dogs who greet their owners by submissively urinating (squatting and dribbling a few to several drops of urine while appearing happy but slightly shy), do not have a housebreaking problem. They have an anxiety problem that was caused either by heredity, abuse, or by corrections that were too frequent or too harsh.

Never correct submissive urination, because that only makes the problem worse. To help Prince overcome this behavior, toss him a treat when you arrive home instead of talking to him, hugging him, or leaning over him to pet him. Once inside, ignore Prince until he comes to you for petting, then tickle his chest and under his chin instead of reaching over his head.

Teach Prince something easy, such as "Sit," as soon as possible so you have reason to praise him. Then use the "Sit" command immediately when you and Prince greet each other at the door. That will give Prince a positive and praiseworthy way of expressing his submission to you. Besides, praise is confidence building, and confidence is exactly what Prince needs to conquer submissive urination.

JUMPING UP ON PEOPLE

Some people enjoy having their dog joyfully jump on them the instant they come home. If you're one of those people, there is nothing wrong with that as long as Prince's buoyant greeting will always be welcome; no matter what you are wearing. Don't allow Prince to do something one day that you won't want him to do another day. He doesn't know the difference between jeans and a tuxedo. In the case of jumping up, simply condition him to change his greeting. Teach him to sit as explained earlier, then happily tell him to sit the instant you come in the door. When he does, (whether you have to put him in position or not), meet him at his level and happily praise and pet him. Prince jumps on you for instant attention, but if you withhold your affection until after he is sitting, and then kneel down to pat and praise him, he'll soon adjust to the more well-mannered method of gaining your attention.

POSSESSIVE OVER FOOD

Puppies compete with their brothers and sisters for food. Homeless dogs must steal food to survive. No wonder some dogs have to be deprogrammed when they join a human family. The good news is deprogramming your dog is usually easy. Just mix up these three actions, doing one during one meal and a different one during the next meal, and after a couple of weeks, Prince should be much more relaxed around his dinner dish.

1. Pet Prince for a second or two as he begins eating dinner, then walk away and let him eat the rest of his meal alone.

2. Give Prince only one-fourth of his dinner. Then, just as he finishes the tiny portion, put the rest of his meal in his bowl.

3. When Prince is nearly finished eating, place a small but very special treat in his dish. A slice of hot dog, a bit of hamburger, or a sliver of cheese will make him glad you put your hand in his bowl.

If Prince is still growly over his dinner dish after two weeks of alternating the choices above, use the strongest "No!" you can muster at the first sign of a rumble. If that doesn't calm him, seek help from a professional trainer.

NOISE STOPPERS

Most dogs bark and whine the first few times they are confined in a new home. That's why you and your neighbors will be much happier if you condition Prince during the daytime to accept confinement, instead of training him at night. There are several ways to squelch screaming, so begin with the least forceful and move ahead from there.

- The first time you confine Prince and leave him alone, try to put up with the noise for ten minutes without doing anything. Some dogs simply quit when they find themselves dramatizing to an empty theater.

- A radio playing softly relaxes some dogs. In fact, they even seem to have musical preferences. Just be sure to keep both the radio and the cord out of Prince's reach.

- If a little time and a radio doesn't help, make a sudden loud noise from another room such as stamping your foot or slapping the wall. Be sure not to say anything. It's best if Prince thinks that his own racket, not you, caused the noise. As soon as he becomes noisy again, make the loud noise again. Repeat as often as necessary.

- From the room next to the one where Prince is confined, bang two metal pans together every time he barks, whines, or screams.

- Fill an inexpensive water pistol, not a high powered one, and every time Prince makes a racket, walk in silently and squirt him one time, directly in the face. Then walk out again. When Prince is quiet for a couple of minutes, go to him without the water pistol and praise him. Repeat as necessary.

Never take Prince out of his place of confinement to stop his protest. That's exactly what he wants, so he will feel rewarded for complaining loudly. Wait until he is silent for at least a minute before going to him and letting him out.

Always be sure Prince has a chew toy with him in his area of confinement. Nothing will keep him occupied longer than a sterilized bone stuffed with processed cheese (a long, rather thick, hollow bone that won't shatter, available at pet stores—you supply the filling).

MOVING ALONG RIGHT

No matter what kind of past Prince had, you and he will need a period of adjustment to live comfortably with each other. During this period, give Prince enough attention so he feels loved and secure, keep him safely confined until he learns house manners, and patiently train and socialize him. Praise everything Prince does right, and never reward fear or noise tantrums, and the period of adjustment will soon pass, leaving fun and companionship in its place.

Now that you have the mental part down pat, let's get on with the physical. The next chapter will tell you how to help Prince have a long and healthy life.

DOG TRAINING DO'S AND DON'TS

Do:

- Be consistent
- Be patient
- Be fair
- Praise often
- Give commands firmly, but in a normal tone of voice
- Keep your sense of humor
- Train at least five times a week
- Keep training sessions short and upbeat

Don't:

- Train when you're in a bad mood
- Train if you recently had a beer or a cocktail (not even one)
- Yell at or strike your dog
- Forget to praise
- Repeat commands over and over; instead, enforce them
- Give a command you can't enforce
- Train too long at a time
- Take minor setbacks seriously

SOME ADJUSTMENTS ARE FOREVER

When Judith L. Gendron of Frankenmuth, Missouri, adopted Halcy from Mastiff Rescue, she and her husband were warned that the dog had a serious problem. Halcy had been allowed to develop an almost uncontrollable prey drive, and her 150 pounds of speed and power could be lethal to smaller animals.

Aside from her problem, Halcy was lovely. She was young, healthy, attractive, confident, and very friendly to people. Retired and with no small pets, the Gendrons were the ideal adoptive owners for her.

With help from a professional trainer and lots of practice, Judith handled Halcy to her Companion Dog title in AKC Obedience Competition. Today Halcy is a therapy dog who is greatly appreciated at her favorite nursing home. Best of all, she is a responsive, devoted companion and a lot of fun. Even so, Judith is too knowl-

At 150 pounds with an uncontrollable prey drive, Halcy the Mastiff was a danger to other animals. Her new owners gave her the gift of training, and today she has an obedience title and is a therapy dog at a nursing home.

edgeable about dogs to become careless, and knows that some adjustments are forever.

"To prevent a possible reversion to her former behavior, Halcy is not allowed to run free outdoors," Judith says. "She is always on a leash in public places and is expected to mind her manners at all times."

A healthy dogs sparkles from the inside out, like this perky Jack Russell Terrier.

CHAPTER EIGHT

IN SICKNESS AND IN HEALTH

Prince will soon be part of your family—happy and hardy in health, and nursed through sickness. Health is easier. Mostly it's just prevention and maintenance. Here's how to keep Prince at his best.

DAILY DOG CARE

Making Prince look and feel like royalty may be easier than you think. Nutrition, exercise, and grooming are the big three in daily dog care.

Nutrition

Good nutrition prevents dietary deficiency diseases. It also helps ward off infections and reduces Prince's susceptibility to organic diseases.

USING COMMERCIAL DOG FOOD

It's human nature to believe that if a given quantity of a substance is good for building bones, calming nerves, or increasing appetite, then a lot more will probably be better. But this isn't true, and in some cases, more is actually toxic. The scientists who develop high-quality commercial dog foods know the proper amount of each nutrient a dog needs and how each ingredient in a specific formula interacts with the other ingredients. That's why most brand-name dog foods are far healthier than anything you could create at home for twice the price. So let the experts create the combination of nutrients that make up Prince's diet. The proper balance of vitamins, minerals, proteins, and fats is too complicated and too important for speculation, and is better left to the test kitchens of the major dog food companies.

Nutrition, exercise, and grooming are the keys to good daily dog care. It's obvious that the owners of this beautiful Boston Terrier provide all three.

Photo credit: Pets by Paulette.

The three major categories of commercial dog foods are dry, canned, and soft-moist:

1. *Dry.* Dry dog foods come in a variety of shapes, sizes, and colors. Some brands are in meal form, with the various ingredients simply mixed together. Pelleted dog food is meal pressed into pellets. Food labeled "biscuit" may be made up of whole or crumbled biscuits and is formed by adding flour to the dry ingredients and baking the mixture. Always read the directions on the bag of feed, because some dry foods are meant to be fed dry, others form gravy when moistened and are meant to be fed slightly wet, and some may be fed dry or moistened. Many adult dogs are routinely fed dry food exclusively and live healthy, active lives. Other wholesome and popular ways to feed are two-thirds dry and one-third canned food mixed together, or almost all dry with a tablespoon or two of canned food mixed in for added flavor.

2. *Canned.* Read the label carefully if you plan to use canned food exclusively. Some canned foods provide total nutrition while others are meant to be mixed with dry food. Canned food capable of standing alone will be labeled "100% complete," "complete dinner," or something similar. Several brands of canned dinners are available either "chopped" or "chunky." Their nutritional values are equal, but most medium-sized and large

dogs prefer their food "chunky," while small dogs often find that it's easier to eat the chopped variety.

3. *Soft-moist.* Soft-moist food is conveniently portion-packed, but has high contents of salt, sugars, and preservatives. While its simplicity is tempting, especially if you do a lot of traveling, you can enjoy the same ease of feeding by portion-packing high-quality dry food into self-sealing plastic bags. Quality dry food is better for Prince and will even help clean his teeth.

WHY BARGAIN HUNTING DOESN'T PAY

Bargain dog food is seldom a bargain. The nutritional analysis on an inexpensive brand may read similar to the name brands but deliver something far inferior. For example, even though the percentages of protein on a bargain brand and a name brand appear to be identical, it's the amount of usable (digestible) protein that's important. Even shoe leather is protein when analyzed, but it has no nutritional value at all.

FOOD FOR ALL AGES

A fine selection of dog foods is available for all stages of Prince's life. If he is under a year old, feed him a reputable brand of puppy food according to label directions. When changing brands, mix the old with the new, gradually increasing the new and decreasing the old until the changeover is complete. When Prince reaches a year old and is ready for adult dog food, make that change gradually too.

If Prince is still a growing boy (any dog under twelve months old is still considered a puppy), remember to gradually increase the size of his meals as he gets bigger. Between the ages of five months and a year, he should eat two meals a day (younger puppies must eat more often). As an adult (over twelve months old for most dogs, but 18-20 months for giant breeds), Prince will probably eat slightly less than he did as a growing puppy and will only have to be fed once a day (exceptions are the tiny breeds, which do better on two daily feedings at any age). Look at your dog to tell whether or not his food keeps him in top condition. Prince's coat should shine, his eyes should be bright, and he should be in good, solid flesh. Whatever you do, don't let him get fat. Many serious health problems in dogs begin with obesity.

Poor nutrition almost always shows up first in the quality of the coat. During adolescence (five to eighteen months or more of age), Prince may appear long and lanky, but as long as he has boundless energy and a gleaming coat, his nutritive requirements are probably being met. But if Prince's coat is dry or dull, consider it an early warning signal that something's wrong and have your veterinarian examine him. The quality and quantity of his food may be fine, but he might need to be wormed, or treated for a condition unrelated to nutrition. If Prince's nutritional needs are not being met, your veterinarian may recommend that you change brands of dog food. Always do this gradually, and wait patiently for improvements. It takes three months for a new dog food to make a noticeable difference. If you want to supplement Prince's diet with a vitamin-mineral preparation, give it according to your veterinarian's directions. Over-supplementation is dangerous and has been linked to a variety of ills.

Don't be surprised if Prince shows less interest in his food during the warm months and turns into a chow hound by November. Many adult dogs retain their proper weight when fed a little extra during the winter and a little less during the heat of summer.

When Prince grows old, he may have less interest in food. If sore teeth are the culprit, your veterinarian can make feeding time a pleasure again. If age is dulling Prince's senses, warming his food will give it a more appetizing aroma. Offering much smaller amounts of food several times a day, instead of one big dinner, may also pique an aging dog's appetite.

TREATS

A wide variety of dog treats are available at any supermarket or pet supply store. Try different types until you discover which ones Prince prefers, but don't overuse any of them or Prince may become overweight.

Use good judgment when feeding treats. Small dogs have only so much room in their tiny tummy. Too many treats, or treats just before dinner, especially those with high sugar content, could spoil Prince's appetite for the nutritious food he needs.

Prince may also enjoy low-calorie treats right out of the vegetable bin in your refrigerator. Carrots delight many dogs, and some of them also like celery stalks and apple slices. Offer Prince tidbits of various fruits

NUTRITIONAL NO-NO'S

- Don't give Prince any bones other than cooked knuckle bones. Chicken, turkey, fish, beef, and pork bones, among others, can shatter and catch in his throat, or slice open his intestines with their sharp points.

- Don't believe ads that encourage you to vary Prince's diet. Dogs do best when they are fed the same brand of food daily at a regular hour, and they don't need their kibble to come in the latest colors and shapes. If you want to add something to Prince's dish, mix a few tablespoons of canned dog food with his dry dinner. But don't start unless you plan to do it every day, because Prince will surely come to expect it.

- Don't fill Prince up with table scraps. No matter how nutritious your dinner is for humans, chances are his own food is better for him. Also, dogs that eat table scraps usually lose their taste for dog food completely. That doesn't mean Prince can never have a taste of your dinner. If the leftover beef and barley soup is too yummy to waste, mix it with Prince's regular dinner. The water from steamed or boiled vegetables also makes a healthy addition to dry dog food.

- Never feed Prince chocolate as it is deadly to some dogs. He should also stay away from highly spiced, greasy, and salty foods, as well as all junk foods. They lead to upset stomachs.

> • Don't let Prince's dinner dish sit untouched for hours. Pick it up after ten minutes, empty or not. That helps Prince learn to eat on a regular schedule.

and vegetables occasionally, but don't overdo it even though they are healthy. Receiving a treat should be a special part of Prince's day, not an hourly occurrence.

Exercise

The muscles rippling beneath Prince's coat are not the only ones that are toned and strengthened by regular exercise. His heart is almost entirely muscle, and even his intestine contains muscle tissue. Regular exercise keeps a healthy supply of blood circulating through these muscles. If Prince leads an active life he will look nicer, live longer, and behave better. Countless so-called behavior problems have been corrected through giving an energetic dog more exercise.

A brisk walk through the neighborhood is good exercise. This is 14-year-old Darcy Peterson and her Papillon, Peppy, CDX.

There are many ways to exercise Prince. Consider his size, age, and fitness, your fitness and time limitations, available space, and even the weather when deciding which forms you will use. Brisk walks are good for both of you, but you can also teach Prince to play ball (or Frisbee if he is big enough) and exercise him while sitting or standing in place. Small dogs can get plenty of exercise playing indoor games. Variety is good, so walking briskly for several blocks or playing a rousing game of fetch are equally desirable. If Prince is a lively dog, another choice is giving him a securely fenced play area and a couple of his favorite toys, and letting him exercise himself.

Getting Prince ready for Obedience or Agility competition is also good exercise and challenging fun for both of you. No, he doesn't have to be a purebred to compete (see Chapter 9). The form Prince's exercise takes isn't important, but it is important that he get regular exercise in some form all his life. When he's young, Prince will help you discover games that will exercise both of you. He will still need exercise when he is old, but you may have to initiate it.

Grooming

Just a few minutes of daily grooming will keep Prince clean and beautiful, but its benefits go far beyond that. Grooming also makes him more loving and more lovable. If Prince shies away from handling because of bad experiences in his past, your gentle brush strokes and kindness will eventually override his fears. One day he'll even realize that your touch makes him feel good. How will you know when you've crossed that mental barrier? When he leans into your hand for more!

Prince becomes more lovable after a brief brushing because it cleans his coat and makes him feel silky, or fluffy, or luxurious, depending on what type of coat he has. And no matter what type of coat he has, it's mighty inviting for petting and hugging when it's clean. That's why a regularly groomed dog looks great, and just naturally attracts your attention and affection. On the other hand, no one likes to pet a smelly, matted dog that is busily scratching and biting at itself. Unfortunately, cleaning up such a sorry dog is a big job, one that often gets put off again and again, until the poor dog is banished to the basement or yard because it isn't clean enough for house dog status. This sad scenario is completely preventable. Just set aside a few minutes a day for grooming Prince, perhaps while watching the news or just after the kids go to bed. Soon he will look forward to his grooming sessions with happy anticipation.

Some circumstances may keep you from grooming Prince for weeks at a time. If your Prince is long-coated and it ever gets out of hand, don't expel him from your affections. Instead, take him to a grooming shop

The abundant coat of this appealing Keeshond needs regular care to remain in good condition and free of mats.

Photo credit: Pets by Paulette.

and let the professionals decide if he can be brushed out without pain, or if the mats are too far along and have to be clipped. Sure, he'll look a little weird when he comes home, but he'll be clean and sweet-smelling again. Clipped coats grow back quickly, so go back to your daily brushing routine even if there isn't much to brush. Before long Prince will be wearing his regal robes again.

COAT AND SKIN CARE

Read a book about your breed to learn how it is groomed and which grooming implements are recommended. Then buy top-quality grooming tools. They last longer than cheap ones and help you do a

All-white dogs, and predominately white dogs like this Dalmatian, don't need baths any more often than darker dogs. Regular brushing will keep them shiny and clean.
Photo credit: Pets by Paulette.

faster, better job. If Prince isn't a purebred, consult a book with pictures of all the breeds at your local library. When you find a breed with a coat much like Prince's in length, thickness, and texture, check out a book on that breed if possible and read the grooming section. Don't settle for guessing. The right way is almost always the fastest and most efficient. It cleans all the way to the skin and stops problems before they start.

Prince's daily brushing or combing keeps his skin and coat healthy because grooming stimulates circulation and the secretion of natural oils. It also removes dirt, dead hair, loose skin particles, and dandruff. While brushing or combing, check for ticks. Although easy to spot on short-coated or lighter-colored dogs, sometimes they hide in the ears, between the toes, in the slightly thicker hair of the neck, or in the rump area just before the tail. Fleas are also easier to find on smooth-coated breeds than on long-haired and profusely coated dogs. To uncover them, rough Prince's coat the opposite direction from the way it grows and be sure you can see all the way down to the skin. Although you may not see any of the little pests move, tiny black specks on the skin are a sign that fleas are using Prince for a bed-and-breakfast. Purchase insecticide shampoos and dips on your veterinarian's recommendation, and always use them exactly as directed on the label.

TOENAILS

Prince's toenails are too long if they make clicking noises on the floor when he walks, or touch the ground when he is standing still. Dogs with very long nails tend to walk on the back of their feet, leading to splayed (separated) toes and an unattractive gait. Besides making the dog uncomfortable, there is an additional danger. When left untrimmed, toenails and dewclaw nails eventually curl under the foot, circling back to puncture the pads. This last is every bit as painful as it sounds.

Clip Prince's nails by lifting his foot up and forward. Then hold it securely in your left hand so your right hand can do the trimming. (Reverse this if you are left-handed.) If Prince's nails are white, your job is easier than if they are dark. A blood vessel called the "quick" in the bottom stem of the nail is clearly seen through white nails. Trim the nail just outside the quick. You won't be able to see the quick in dark nails, so make the cut just outside the hook-like projection on the underside of the nail.

When you cut his nails properly, Prince will feel only the same slight pressure you feel when cutting your own toenails. But if you accidentally cut the quick, Prince will yelp because his nail will hurt and bleed. Work in good lighting so you can cut his nails without mishap. Most dogs forgive an occasional severed quick, but Prince will resist work on his feet if you slip up too often. Everyone makes an occasional mistake, so keep a styptic pencil or styptic powder nearby to stop the bleeding and some soothing words to hasten Prince's forgiveness.

TEETH

Hold Prince's head firmly and lift his lips upward to check his teeth for tartar. If you find discolorations, remove them with a damp washcloth or soft toothbrush dipped in baking soda. Prince should visit the veterinarian for a professional cleaning if the stains are not easily removed. You can also help Prince's teeth stay strong and white by giving him hard dog biscuits as treats and nylon chew bones for toys.

BATHING

Since daily grooming cleans the coat and reduces body odors, Prince will rarely need a bath if he's brushed or combed daily. Shampooing dries the coat by washing away natural oils, so bathe him only when necessary.

Equipment for a bath includes old clothes (when Prince shakes, you'll be as wet as he is); a tub, preferably with a drain so Prince won't be standing in soapy water; a rubber mat for traction in the tub; a spray-nozzle hose attachment or a pail for dipping water; pH-balanced dog shampoo or insecticide shampoo if necessary; cotton balls; a wash-cloth; mineral oil; and a large towel or several towels, depending on Prince's size. Coat conditioner or detangler following the shampoo is optional, but recommended for long coats. If Prince is a tiny fellow, bathing him in the sink will be easier on your back. Just be careful that he doesn't fall when he is slippery with soap. You might want to use a sink-size rubber mat to improve his footing.

Give Prince some exercise outdoors before bathing him. Then he won't have to dash outside to go potty (and probably roll in the loose garden dirt) immediately after his bath.

Prince's bathwater should be warm but not hot, and the drain should remain open so he isn't standing in a puddle of dirty water. Before putting him in the sink or tub, place a cotton ball inside each of his ears to keep the water out. Next, spray or pour water over Prince's whole body, with the exception of his face and head, and use your hands to separate the hair, working the water all the way to the skin. Then put a small amount of shampoo on his back and massage the lather into his coat. Add more shampoo as needed to clean his legs, neck, tail, and underbelly. Cleaning down to the skin is easy if Prince has a short coat, but it will take a mighty good massage if his coat is profuse.

Use the hose or pail to thoroughly rinse off the lather. Don't rush this step. Shampoo that dries in the coat makes it dull and can cause intense itching. If you accidentally get soap in Prince's eyes, put a few drops of mineral oil in the inner corner of each eye to relieve the sting. When using insecticide shampoo or dip to kill fleas and ticks, follow the label directions carefully. Coat conditioner or detangler goes on last and is used according to label directions. It may or may not have to be rinsed out.

Finish by wiping Prince's face and head with a warm, well-wrung washcloth. Remove the cotton from his ears and wipe each ear out with a dry cotton ball dipped in a smidgen of mineral oil. Then wrap Prince in a towel, lift him from the tub, and towel-dry him well, especially his chest and underbelly.

PREVENTION PAYS

Most well-kept adult dogs enjoy good health and seldom show signs of sickness. Dogs don't fake illnesses either, so if Prince ever appears to be sick or in pain, it's a good idea to visit your veterinarian immediately. While dogs have different tolerances for pain, and some scream over a stubbed toe while others suffer a broken leg in silence, you will soon know your own dog well enough to trust your instincts. And your instincts are exactly what you should trust when deciding if Prince needs to visit his veterinarian. If something seems wrong (even though you can't pinpoint it), make the visit. Early treatment is always better for your dog and easier on your wallet than the aftermath of a wait-and-see attitude.

Many of the most dangerous dog diseases are preventable through vaccinations, while other problems can be avoided through adequate housing, good grooming practices, proper nutrition, and regular exercise. Next to you and your family, your veterinarian is your dog's best friend. Take Prince to the vet for a complete physical examination within two days of acquiring him, whether his next vaccination is due or not.

Visiting the Veterinarian

Prince's reaction to riding in the car and visiting the veterinarian will depend upon his previous experiences. He may jump in the car and greet the vet with a happy slurp, or he may get carsick on the way and sink to the floor of the clinic, shaking in terror. While something in between the extremes is most likely, the following suggestions should help:

- Feed Prince two or three hard dog biscuits an hour or more before driving him to the veterinarian, as that may keep him from getting carsick. But just in case, pack a roll of paper towels and a container of those wonderful wet wipes used on human babies. They clean up almost anything. Bring along Prince's health record if you have it, and a stool sample in a small plastic bag. While waiting in the vet's office, keep Prince on your lap, in his crate, or sitting quietly by your side. Don't allow him to play on the floor or sniff strange dogs. He might pick up something contagious.

● Even if thinking about Prince getting a shot makes you nervous, don't let him know that. Be friendly with the veterinarian, not apprehensive, or Prince will feel your tension and become fearful himself. Some veterinarians have a nurse or technician hold your dog while they administer medication. Others expect you to handle your dog. When holding Prince on the examination table, use as much physical firmness (without roughness) as necessary to keep him in place while talking to him in a happy, upbeat way. Don't console or coddle him or he'll be certain something terrible is happening. Prince will take his cues from you. If he senses that you like the vet, he'll learn to like his vet too.

VACCINATIONS ARE VITAL

When you acquire Prince, you should receive a list of his inoculations and his worming schedule, complete with dates. Give a copy of this health record to your veterinarian so he or she can plan future treatments. If you have no record, your veterinarian should administer protective vaccines immediately. These vaccinations are Prince's best protection against a variety of potentially fatal diseases. The number and type of inoculations your veterinarian recommends may depend upon your locale. Tell your veterinarian if you plan to travel a lot with Prince, as exposure to new places and strange dogs may demand extra precautions. Don't take Prince on any outings until his inoculations are complete, and bring him back to the clinic for booster shots every year.

Combination shots have various names depending upon the company that made them, but many of their names are made up of letters, such as DHLPP. The following sections tell you what the letters stand for, and why those preventative shots are so essential for your dog.

D IS FOR DISTEMPER

Distemper virus is the number-one killer of unvaccinated dogs and spreads rapidly from one dog to another. Its victims are usually puppies, but adult dogs contact it too. Because distemper shows up in various forms, it is sometimes difficult for veterinarians to diagnose. While dogs with distemper occasionally recover, they often suffer permanent damage to the brain or nervous system. Symptoms of distemper include diarrhea, vomiting, reduced appetite, cough, nasal discharge, inflamed eyes, fever, exhaustion, and lack of interest in toys or games. If you ever think Prince has come down with distemper (even though he has been vaccinated), take him to the veterinarian immediately. The earlier treatment begins, the better his chance of survival.

H IS FOR HEPATITIS

Infectious canine hepatitis spreads through contact with an infected dog's stool, urine, or saliva. Hepatitis in dogs is not transmissible to man, although it affects the liver just as it does in the human form. One specific symptom is intense thirst, but all the other symptoms are similar to those of distemper. The disease progresses rapidly and is often fatal, so prompt veterinary treatment is critical.

L IS FOR LEPTOSPIROSIS

Leptospirosis is caused by a spirochete, a microorganism that's often carried by rats. It can infect a dog that has contact with a rat, or eats something contaminated by rats. Symptoms include bloody diarrhea or urine, fever, depression, red and congested eyes and mouth membranes, painful mouth ulcers, vomiting, increased thirst, loss of appetite, pain when moving, and sometimes, reddish or jaundiced eyes. The dog's kidneys and liver can be permanently damaged by this disease, so quick veterinary treatment is essential. Since humans can contact Leptospirosis, it's important to prevent infecting yourself when caring for a sick dog. Your veterinarian will explain the proper precautions.

P IS FOR PARVOVIRUS

Parvovirus is a deadly killer that was unknown in dogs until 1977. It is believed to be a type of feline distemper that mutated to infect dogs. The virus attacks the stomach lining, bone marrow, and lymph nodes, and in young puppies, the heart. It spreads rapidly from dog to dog through contaminated stools, easily carried and spread via dog paws or shoes. Beginning with depression and loss of appetite, symptoms soon progress to vomiting, diarrhea (sometimes bloody), and fever.

Puppies with infected hearts (myocardial Parvovirus) often die suddenly or within one or two days of contacting the disease. Those few that recover may develop chronic heart problems later. How severely adult dogs are affected depends upon the individual dog. Some become violently ill, while others just lose their appetite for a day or two.

P IS ALSO FOR PARAINFLUENZA

Parainfluenza is also known by a couple of other names. Veterinarians often refer to it as Infectious Canine Tracheobronchitis, while its common name is kennel cough. Highly contagious from dog to dog, Parainfluenza is caused by several different viruses, as well as a bacterium. Symptoms are a frequent dry, hacking cough and sometimes a nasal discharge. Other than that, the dog usually appears to feel fine, and many dogs infected with kennel cough don't even miss a meal. Dogs vaccinated against Parainfluenza sometimes come down with it anyway, but generally have milder symptoms than unvaccinated dogs. While the disease is seldom dangerous as it runs its course in mature dogs, it can be perilous in puppies. Don't panic if Prince gets Parainfluenza, but do take him to the veterinarian. Many vets prescribe medication to control coughing and antibiotics to prevent complications.

RABIES

Rabies is always fatal, and a dog with rabies is a danger to humans and animals. The disease is a virus which can infect dogs that come in contact with squirrels, skunks, foxes, bats, cats, raccoons, or other animals that already have the virus. Rabies affects the nervous system and is generally passed from animal to animal, or animal to man, by infected saliva—usually from a bite. However, it may also infect a victim through cuts or scratches that come in contact with a rabid animal's saliva.

One of the first signs of rabies is a difference in disposition. A gentle dog may become aggressive, or an independent dog may suddenly crave affection. Soon the dog's pupils may become dilated and light may appear to cause him pain. Eventually the dog will want no attention or petting at all, and may show signs of stomach trouble and a fever. Later symptoms can include lack of coordination, random biting, bared teeth, twitching facial muscles, and loss of control of the facial muscles, resulting in an open mouth with the tongue hanging out. The dog's voice may change and he may drool, paw at his mouth, and cough. Eventually he slips into a coma and dies. All warm-blooded animals are subject to the disease, so anyone bitten by a dog (or any other animal) should see a doctor right away.

Rabies vaccine prevents this dread disease. Your veterinarian will give the rabies shot separately, not in combination with the other vaccines. Some rabies shots are good for longer than a year, so ask your vet when Prince's vaccination should be renewed.

SAY NO TO DEADLY DISEASES

After that list of gloom and doom, how about a cheerful reminder? Preventative medicine will keep Prince safe from all of those deadly diseases. Just follow the vaccination schedule your veterinarian recommends.

Spaying and Neutering for a Happier, Healthier Dog

The nicest thing you can do for yourself and your dog is to have it spayed or neutered. Spayed females don't have unwanted pregnancies and won't bleed all over your carpet for a week or more twice a year. And since spaying removes the female's reproductive organs, spayed females never suffer cancers or infections of the ovaries or uterus.

Spayed females are a lot nicer to live with, too. They won't tantalize males into serenading them on your front lawn, and they won't develop a sudden urge to roam. Spaying helps your female's disposition remain stable, and lets her take part in performance events, such as Obedience or Agility, without a three-week break every six months. In short, spaying your Princess gives you fewer hassles, gives her a healthier life, and doesn't add to the unwanted pet population.

Male hormones make a dog crave every female in season whose scent wafts by on the wind, and some dogs break windows and fences to search for that female with the provocative perfume. Male hormones also make a dog more aggressive toward other dogs and are often implicated in housebreaking problems, such as scent marking (when the male lifts his leg and urinates on objects inside the home to stake out his territory). Frustration (caused by male hormones) is what makes a dog embarrass everyone by making love to Granny's leg during the family picnic. While neutering won't immediately cure a frustrated, dog-aggressive, escape artist with a housebreaking problem, it eliminates the production of male hormones, which almost always starts the dog on the road to improvement.

DON'T BELIEVE IT!

Did you ever hear that spaying or neutering makes a dog fat and lazy? Well, that's just not true. Overfeeding and lack of exercise do that. In fact, spayed and neutered pets are often the best performers in Obedience, Agility, and other competitive events. Neutered males are better able to keep their mind on their work, and spayed females can perform all year, without losing six weeks due to being in season. That's why nearly all service dogs (guide dogs for the blind, hearing dogs, and dogs that help the physically handicapped) are spayed or neutered.

It is also untrue that neutered males don't make good watchdogs. Not only will they protect their home and family, but they concentrate on their job better than males who have the scent of a female on their mind. Spayed females are also reliable guardians.

Cartoonists and comedians often get laughs by implying that male dogs think as people do and are resentful or depressed over being "castrated." These skits are hilarious at the comedy club, but the notion is ridiculous in real life. Dogs don't have human feelings about romantic love and sex. Dogs simply have drives and feel frustration when they can't fulfill them. They don't miss the hormones that made them feel frustrated and drove them into trouble. In fact, after they are neutered, most dogs become more affectionate and closer to their family. And that's where dogs really want to be.

Defeating Parasites

Besides vaccinating to prevent contagious diseases, your veterinarian should also check Prince for internal parasites such as intestinal worms and heartworms. Roundworms, whipworms, tapeworms, and hookworms can be detected though a sample of Prince's stool, while a blood test is necessary to detect heartworms. No matter how carefully you care for Prince, he can still become infested with all of the worms except heartworm. As a well-kept dog he shouldn't get heartworm, because preventative medication is available through your veterinarian.

The symptoms of roundworms, whipworms, tapeworms, and hookworms are all similar, and include a rough, dry coat, dull eyes, a

CARING FOR KIPPER

Gee Weaver, of Kalispell, Montana, gives foster care to dogs as part of her volunteer work with the local humane shelter. She also educates new dog owners on the importance of spaying and neutering. Not everyone listens. This is Gee's story:

"When my neighbor bought Kipper, a Cocker Spaniel pup, I taught her how to groom and showed her how to teach the puppy some tricks. Kipper had the nicest personality, and eyelashes to match. Her favorite things were her ball, and making us laugh when she howled to the chorus of her favorite song. I really liked Kipper and she really liked me. Her owners gave her lots of attention and she was a very good girl.

Receiving this photo of freshly groomed Kipper made Gee Weaver's day.

"Kipper came into season at seven months old and her owner had her bred. She thought it was an easy way to make money. Kipper was still a puppy herself, and when she started labor she became a wreck. My neighbor called and asked me to come over and handle the delivery. From the time I got there Kipper wouldn't leave my feet and she didn't want anything to do with her puppies.

"For three weeks, Kipper had to be forced to feed the puppies. When they started getting around they were a pain for the owner, and Kipper was held accountable for everything they did. During that time, Kipper picked up fleas and an ear infection. Her owner thought fleas were the worst disease in the world, but I helped out and got rid of the flea problem. Kipper wouldn't let anyone but me treat her painful ears, and eventually they healed too. With everything back to normal, I tried to explain why Kipper should be spayed, but my neighbor decided against it. Eventually they moved about seventeen miles away but we still visited each other occasionally.

"When Kipper was eighteen months old, she had puppies again. This time both ears became badly infected, and because of the ear smell and the pups, she was exiled from the house and became an outside dog. She also got fleas again and hadn't been groomed in such a long time that her coat was horribly matted. Still, Kipper remembered the good times and greeted me with her ball in her mouth. I felt so sorry for her that I treated her ears. Before I left I told my friends that if they ever wanted to get rid of Kipper, I'd be willing to keep her until I could place her in a loving home. They didn't accept my offer.

"The third time Kipper came in season, my old neighbors called me up and asked if my offer still stood. Kipper came to me with fleas, infected ears, and an infected neck. I had her spayed, shaved, and defleaed, and treated her ears and neck. Three months later, with no fleas, no infections and a healthy coat, I found her a home with an older woman.

"Kipper has been a much-loved house dog for over four years now and I receive a Christmas card with her picture on it every year. In this year's photo she was freshly groomed and her ball was at her feet. It sure brought back some memories."

generally unsound appearance, weakness, weight loss despite an enormous appetite, coughing, vomiting, diarrhea, and sometimes, bloody stools. Few dogs have all of those symptoms and some dogs lose their appetite entirely when infested with worms. Other dogs show no symptoms at all until they become seriously anemic from a heavy infestation.

Don't be surprised or embarrassed if Prince gets worms. Many puppies are born with roundworms, and dogs can become infested with worms while out for a walk or from biting at a flea. Treatment is effective and safe. Just have your veterinarian check Prince's stool at least twice a year, and if medication is prescribed, give it exactly as instructed.

Heartworms are a different story. They are transmitted from dog to dog by the bite of a mosquito, and eight months or more may go by from the time a dog is bitten until the worms mature. Heartworms interfere with the action of a dog's heart, and symptoms of infestation

Even a beautifully cared for dog, like this Rottweiler, could pick up worms while out for a walk.

Photo credit: Pets by Paulette.

include a chronic cough, weight loss, exhaustion, and eventually, death. Prevention is the only defense, and it should start as soon as you acquire Prince and continue throughout his life. The first step is having your veterinarian test Prince for heartworms. Mature dogs must be free of adult heartworms before taking preventative medication or they can become critically ill. If Prince is unlucky enough to have heartworms, he'll need immediate treatment. Procedures to rid a dog of heartworm are dangerous (although less dangerous than the deadly worm), but crucial. Once Prince is heartworm-free, prevention will keep him that way.

EXTERNAL PARASITES

Fleas, ticks, and ear mites are all looking for a free lunch and a cozy condo, compliments of Prince. Deer ticks are especially dangerous as they could carry Lyme disease, while other ticks may carry diseases such as Rocky Mountain Spotted Fever. Don't attempt to pull attached ticks off your dog by hand. Instead, remove them safely with a preparation recommended by your veterinarian. If you are camping in the woods far from a veterinary clinic and didn't pack a tick preparation, separate Prince's hair so you can see where the tick embedded itself in the skin. The embedded part is the tick's head. Use a tweezers to clamp down as close to the head as possible and pull it out. If you have alcohol with you, drop a bit right on the tick and it will release its hold. If part of the head remains in Prince's skin, apply an antiseptic.

Ear mites live in the ear canal, irritating Prince's sensitive ears and producing a dry, rusty-brown to black discharge. The condition is easily treatable when caught early, so if you suspect ear mites, see your veterinarian.

Lice seldom infect dogs, and are easily destroyed with modern preparations. Fleas, on the other hand, are never easy to get rid of. They quickly become resistant, or actually adapt to insecticides. That's why new flea dips, powders, and sprays appear on the market every year. For tips on how to discover if Prince has these pests, read the section on grooming earlier in this chapter. Have fleas already invaded your home? For an easy way to find out, read "Dog Care for All Seasons," later in this chapter. Your veterinarian knows which preparations work best in your locale, so if your dog and your home are harboring creepy crawlies, ask for professional help.

Potential Problems

Prince may never have any of the following problems, but it's sensible and safe to be aware of them.

SARACOPTIC MANGE

Saracoptic mange is caused by mites. It will make Prince itch, and you will see tiny red bumps and patchy, crusty areas on his body, legs, and/or stomach. Take Prince to the veterinarian. The condition is treatable and will respond to topical medication.

FOLLICULAR MANGE

Follicular mange is caused by a different type of mite. It's also called demodectic mange or red mange, and it may or may not make Prince itch. Whether it bothers him or not, you'll notice small, circular, moth-eaten-appearing patches, usually on his head and along his back, sides, and neck. Juvenile cases, involving a young dog with only a few patches, might be stress-related. Perhaps Prince recently was in a boarding kennel for the first time. Some females, for example, get a patch or two of mange when they come into season for the first time. Your veterinarian has medication to clear this condition, but if Prince ever gets a generalized case of mange (covering much of his body), be sure to have him neutered (if he isn't already). Dogs with generalized cases of mange should never be used for breeding as they can pass the misery on to their young.

RINGWORM

In spite of its name, ringworm is a fungus infection, not a worm. Carried more often by cats than dogs, ringworm causes small, round, itchy, bald patches, which are often inflamed because Prince can't help but scratch them. They are easily cured by the fungicide your veterinarian will recommend.

Just as these skin problems have similar symptoms, so do several others that Prince might encounter. Since it's difficult to determine which condition is making Prince itch, and each one requires a different medication, leave diagnosis and treatment to your veterinarian.

CLOGGED ANAL GLANDS

If Prince is scooting along the floor on his haunches, he probably has clogged anal glands. His anal glands are located on each side of his anus and they secrete a substance that enables him to pass his stool. When clogged, they are extremely uncomfortable, smell bad, and could become infected. Your veterinarian can quickly unclog Prince's anal glands, or you can do it yourself. Use one hand to hold his tail up and hold a soft cloth in your other hand. Take the skin on either side of the anus, just below the middle, between your cloth-covered thumb and forefinger. Then push in slightly and squeeze gently. If you succeed, a brownish, nasty-smelling substance will be on your cloth and Prince will stop scooting. Blood or pus in the secretion is a sign of infection, so if either one is present, take Prince to the veterinarian.

HIP DYSPLASIA

Hip dysplasia is caused by an abnormality of one or both hip joints. If Prince has a borderline case, it may never be noticeable to him or to you, and only a hip X-ray would tell for sure. In more severe cases, HD causes lameness in the hindquarters, ranging in severity from a slightly odd gait to barely being able to stand. Hip dysplasia is incurable, but there are several ways to lessen its pain, including surgery in some cases. If Prince is lame and HD is suspected, your veterinarian will X-ray him before determining the best treatment.

LYME DISEASE

Transmitted by the deer tick, Lyme disease attacks humans as well as dogs. Symptoms include fatigue, loss of appetite, fever, and sometimes swollen glands in the neck. In areas where the deer tick is prevalent, avoid those wonderful walks in the woods, keep your own lawn well trimmed, and take precautions to keep field mice from nesting in your home. A vaccine is available for Lyme disease prevention. Since it's a must in some parts of the country and unnecessary in others, discuss it with your veterinarian. Don't forget to mention any trips you and Prince will be taking to other locales.

HEAT STROKE

A dog suffering from heat stroke must have immediate attention. Sometimes only a cold water enema, applied by a veterinarian, will save him. Symptoms include some, but usually not all, of the following:

- Rapid or heavy breathing with the mouth and tongue a very bright red

- Thick saliva

- Vomiting

- Bloody diarrhea

- Unsteadiness on the feet, and possibly falling

- A hot, dry nose with legs and ears hot to the touch

- In extreme cases the dog may be glassy-eyed and his lips may appear gray

When a dog's rectal temperature is 104° or more, he is in serious trouble. If you suspect heat stroke, immediately take Prince somewhere cooler, and wet him down gradually with cool (not ice cold) water. Give him cool water to drink, but in small amounts at a time, never all at once. Apply cold compresses to his belly and groin area, but do not suddenly place your overheated dog in extremely cold water. While cooling Prince, make preparations to get him to the veterinarian.

Be especially cautious if Prince has already suffered a heat stroke and survived. After a dog has one heat stroke, he's prone to getting another.

All dogs need shade when they are outdoors, but some breeds, like this smooth-coated Chow Chow, are especially prone to overheating.

Photo credit: Pets by Paulette.

SNAKE BITE

Symptoms of snake bite include swelling, labored breathing, glazed eyes, and drooling. The best first aid you can give while rushing your dog to the veterinarian, is to keep him warm, and as calm and inactive as possible.

DOG CARE FOR ALL SEASONS

From sniffing dewy daffodils to scampering through snow, each season brings a special brand of fun for you and Prince. But changes in temperature, and even holiday celebrations, can have a dangerous side too. The following guide will help you keep Prince happy and healthy all year.

Spring

Along with the flowers and showers come pests. Of these, the mosquito, carrier of heartworm larvae, is one of the most dangerous. Since mosquitoes are most abundant between April and October (except in the deep south where there is no respite from their bite), every dog should be blood-tested in the early spring. If Prince tests free of heartworm, your veterinarian will start him on another season of preventative medication. But if he tests positive, he will need immediate treatment.

Since you're visiting your veterinarian anyway, spring is an appropriate time to update Prince's vaccinations. So-called "permanent shots" are only permanent in the sense that Prince doesn't need a series of puppy shots. But all dogs need booster shots once a year. Don't forget to bring along a stool sample for the fecal exam. That's how the veterinarian finds out whether Prince has any worms in his body tissue or intestines.

Are fleas a problem in your area? Then ask your veterinarian's advice on prevention or treatment, because some dogs (especially sighthounds) are dangerously sensitive to flea products. Dogs react to fleas in various ways. A dog with a flea-bite allergy may become miserable over one or two fleas, while another dog may be quite infested without giving any indication. Your veterinarian can treat the allergies, but Prince will itch again in no time unless you get rid of the fleas.

With flea prevention, earlier is better. Fleas are capable of producing another generation every twenty-one days and one female can produce thousands of eggs in her lifetime. Once Prince is infested, your house probably is too. One way to check for fleas in your house is to take a large, shallow pan, fill it with water and add some liquid dish soap. Before retiring for the night, put the pan on the floor and place a desk lamp next to it with the light aimed at the water. After you go to bed and the lamp is the only light in the house, fleas will jump at it, fall in the water, and sink immediately because the dish soap made the water soft. Drowned fleas in the pan the next morning means there are fleas in your home. If you aren't in a hurry, you may choose to use the water-and-lamp method of flea control. Just repeat every night until there are no fleas in the pan three nights in a row. The "bombs" sold in pet supply stores and supermarkets are faster, but check with your veterinarian before using any pesticides. If you do use a "bomb," remember to protect small pets, and always follow the label directions.

Beware of red ants (fire ants) anywhere Prince plays. Since you shouldn't put poison in your dog's yard, try pouring boiling water on the nest several times. Just be careful where you stand while pouring, or ants near the nest will attack your feet. Taking a shovel full of red ants from one nest and placing them on another nest is also effective. Maybe they hate each other as much as we detest them, because it often makes them leave the area. Once your yard has been infested by red ants, check it frequently because long after you think they are gone, they often reappear in a different place.

Dangerous chemicals are commonly used in the springtime and include the pesticides and herbicides used in gardening, radiator coolant (which tastes wonderful to dogs and cats but kills them), swimming pool conditioners, and even suntan lotion (not meant to be swallowed, so don't let Prince lick you when you have it on). Everything is blooming in the spring and some attractive plants are exceedingly poisonous when chewed or eaten. If Prince is a walking vacuum cleaner, keep the number of your nearest poison control center where you can find it in an emergency.

If Prince has a lot of loose hair, more than you can remove with daily brushing, a bath will help you get rid of most of it. Are you proud of Prince's glossy dark coat? If you want it to stay that way, let him play outside for extended periods only during the early morning, late afternoon, and evening hours. Otherwise the sun may bleach his hair and make it dry and brittle.

If Prince is outside during the evening, an electric bug zapper in the yardwill get rid of most biting bugs, but not flies. Be extremely careful when using fly bait because it can be fatal if Prince eats it.

Summer

Fresh, clean water must always be available, especially when Prince is outdoors. If he plays in his water and regularly upsets his dish, try one that is weighted, or attach a galvanized steel bucket to the fence or the side of the dog house. Should Prince topple those, go to a livestock supply store and purchase the type of bucket-holder used in stables.

If Prince is lethargic, depressed, or lacks appetite after upsetting his water, he may be in danger from dehydration. To check, pinch up a fold of skin from his back and release it. The fold will flatten into place immediately unless Prince is dehydrated. This is an extremely serious condition that requires prompt medical attention. If dehydration is diagnosed, your veterinarian may have to administer fluids subcutaneously (under the skin) or intravenously (into the vein).

When Prince is outside during the summer, make sure he has shade in some section of his exercise area all the time. Natural shade from trees and shrubs is best because regular evaporation of moisture from the leaves cools the air, but be careful not to plant anything that is poisonous when chewed. When building a dog run, use shade screen over the top and down a side or two. A doghouse alone can become dangerously hot unless it's in a permanently shaded area. Prince will survive as best he can, so if you don't give him a spot of shade, he may have to dig himself a cool bed in your flower garden.

If Prince spends most of his time in your air-conditioned home, don't put him out in the heat of the day for prolonged periods. Instead, give him most of his outdoor exercise in the early morning and evening, with just a quick trip to the yard to relieve himself, if necessary, at midday. No matter where Prince spends most of his time, avoid strenuous play during extreme heat.

The temperature inside a car or truck, even one parked in the shade, is usually twenty-five degrees hotter than outside the vehicle. Every year hundreds of pets die from being left in closed vehicles for just a few minutes. Try not to leave Prince alone inside your car at all, but if you must, make sure the car is in the shade. The windows should be partially open on both sides to provide plenty of ventilation, but shouldn't be down so low that Prince can squeeze out.

Don't overfeed Prince in the summer. Obese dogs suffer from the heat more than dogs of normal weight, and dogs need fewer calories during the summer than they do the rest of the year. Also, try to schedule Prince's feeding for the cooler part of the day.

To keep Prince's summer coat beautiful, brush or comb it regularly. Grooming stimulates the skin and promotes air circulation.

A wire crate is best during the summer because it has ventilation all the way around. Heat can build up inside a plastic crate. Put Prince's crate in a cool part of the house, not where the sun will shine on it through a window. When crating Prince outdoors, put the crate in the shade and provide water.

Keep Prince indoors and safely confined on the 4th of July. Some dogs become so frightened by fireworks that they break loose and run away—usually into the street.

Veterinarians constantly patch up the tragedies caused by pets riding in the back of pickup trucks. Many dogs do it without mishap for years, until one abrupt stop or quick swerve tumbles them out on the highway. Dogs who ride inside the car with their head hanging out the window are also in danger. They often suffer serious eye injuries when hit at high speed by flying bugs or seeds.

Fall

Fall is a good time to take a stool sample to your veterinarian for a fecal exam and ask if any booster shots are recommended in your locale.

Temperatures can fluctuate rapidly during the fall, so be ready for sudden changes. It may be freezing cold for several days and then hit eighty degrees for Indian summer. When frigid weather comes suddenly, it's smart to have Prince wear a sweater outdoors if he is short-coated or small.

Prince may start scratching soon after you start heating your house. This is usually caused by low humidity, which makes his outer layer of skin lose much of its moisture. Complications of dry skin are bacterial infections, which can be caused by Prince scratching and biting himself. A humidifier often helps prevent dry skin in dogs and humans.

Keep Prince away from the good tasting, sweet-smelling, deadly antifreeze you put in your vehicles during the fall, and clean up all spills completely. Just a little on the paws can kill a dog when he licks them clean. Signs of antifreeze poisoning are depression, lethargy, loss of coordination, and liver failure.

While every dog deserves a Thanksgiving treat, too much turkey, turkey skin, mashed potatoes, and rich gravy can give Prince a tummy ache or worse. You may already know this, but your guests probably don't. If some of your guests are children, and Prince eats gently from young hands, portion-pack a sandwich bag with the amount of goodies you know Prince can handle. Then let your young visitors feed Prince his holiday treats either before or after you serve dinner.

Winter

Watch Prince's weight during the winter. His coat will grow thicker and may make him appear heavier, but underneath he might be losing weight. An active dog, especially an outside dog, needs to take in more calories during cold weather. Prince also needs fresh drinking water in the winter just as much as he did in the summer. The dry,  heated air in our homes causes water loss.

Purchase a warm sweater for short-coated Prince so he can be bundled up on frigid days, and you can both enjoy invigorating wintry walks. A canine coat may look more stylish than a sweater, but seldom provides the underbelly protection that a bald-bellied breed appreciates.

VACATIONING WITH AND WITHOUT YOUR DOG

Camping, fishing and hiking vacations are often more fun when the family dog goes along. The following tips should help you to smooth sailing on land or water:

- When vacationing with your dog, pack easy, efficient clean-up items, like a poop scoop or heavy plastic baggies. It's important that you walk Prince in the designated areas and clean up after him. Each year more and more motels and campgrounds refuse to accommodate dogs because of the dirt and destruction left behind by a few irresponsible owners.

- Unfamiliar water causes diarrhea in some dogs, so it's smart to carry water from home or buy bottled water along the way. Also bring dog food from home, portion-packed for easy use. Sometimes it's difficult to find Prince's brand on the road and a sudden switch to a different food could cause an upset stomach.

- When driving with your windows closed, your air-conditioner on, and Prince crated in the back of the vehicle, check occasionally to be sure cool air is reaching him.

- High humidity makes a day feel hotter than it actually is and could cause Prince to breathe noisily or appear to have difficulty breathing. Don't over-exercise him when the humidity is high. If you're driving, carry ice, water, and towels even on short trips because you may get into a traffic jam or have car problems. Even if you're stuck on the side of the road for hours without air conditioning, Prince will stay cool by laying on a wet towel and licking ice cubes.

- Be wary of undertows (strong currents) when allowing Prince to swim in rivers and in the ocean. After he swims in salt water or chlorine, wash him with fresh water. Doggie life preservers are available in all sizes and are excellent for fishermen and boaters who take their dogs out to sea with them. It is extremely difficult to rescue a dog that has fallen from a boat in heavy seas, and even a dog of a top swimming breed can eventually become exhausted and drown. A life vest will help Prince maintain buoyancy, and the convenient handle will make water rescue easier.

- Vacationing without Prince may necessitate putting him in a boarding kennel. Plan ahead so you can get references from friends, and tour the facility before deciding to leave him there. Ask what medical records you will need to bring along, and beware of any boarding kennel that doesn't demand that your dog be up to date with his inoculations. Also, find out what brand of dog food the boarding kennel uses, and buy some about a week before leaving. Then get Prince used to the brand by mixing it with his regular food, adding a little more each day. If he dislikes it, or if it changes his stool, ask if you may supply pre-measured servings of his regular dinner.

Just as senior citizens mind the cold more than younger folks, so do senior dogs—and they can't pack up and retire to Florida. Keep your old dog's bed away from drafts, raised a little off the floor, and cushion-soft. Younger dogs will also enjoy the same treatment.

Prince may love to lay down close to a source of heat, but that can present several dangers. Although humans feel a spark on their skin immediately, dogs don't realize one has landed on them until it burns through their hair and reaches their skin. A cozy fireplace will be Prince's favorite winter resting place, so protect him by always having a firescreen in place. Sometimes the warmth from a wood-burning stove feels so inviting that dogs fall asleep too close to the heat and suffer burns, so use a firescreen there too. Space heaters pose a triple threat. Dogs may chew the cord, burn themselves on the heater, or knock the unit over and cause a fire.

Many dogs enjoy playing in snow. Just provide water afterwards (snow is not a substitute for drinking water), take normal precautions against frostbite, and watch for cracked pads or tiny cuts on the feet. If Prince is usually your couch companion, winter sports should be introduced gradually and enjoyed in moderation.

If you must leave Prince unattended in your car during the winter, don't shut all the windows no matter how cold it is outside. Your dog still needs some ventilation, so open opposite windows about two inches.

The always-hazardous practice of allowing a dog to ride in the back of a pickup truck is most dangerous during the winter. Besides the potential for Prince to go flying in the event of a skid or an accident, winter adds the threat of frostbite.

Walking in winter also has hazards, one of which is road salt. Unlike ordinary salt, road salt can burn Prince's feet and mouth, and he can kick it up onto his belly and burn himself there too. Road sand, used mainly for traction, also contains chemicals for melting ice that can burn your dog. So keep a towel and an old throw rug by the door, and after a walk, towel Prince's chest, underbelly, and feet, in that order. Besides warming him and increasing circulation, it will get rid of snow and chemical accumulations and keep your floors clean and dry. If Prince's hair still feels gritty, assume it is road salt or sand, and wash it off with warm water and a gentle pH-balanced dog shampoo.

Christmas cheer presents its own doggie dangers. Pretty poinsettia plants and merry mistletoe are both poisonous if chewed, and those glittery balls, so appealing to a playful dog, may be made of glass or easily shattered plastic. Every year dogs are shocked by mouthing the electric cords attached to Christmas tree lights and poisoned by getting into chocolate goodies (chocolate is fatal to some dogs). Also, reliably housebroken Prince may think the natural Christmas tree with its woods-like aroma makes part of your home an appropriate potty spot, so be prepared with an immediate correction. If children are on your visitors list for Christmas dinner, prepare a portion for Prince just as you did at Thanksgiving.

If Prince lives outside during the winter, he needs a well-insulated dog-house with deep, clean bedding and a main room free from drafts. Metal water dishes are taboo in winter because a dog's tongue can get painfully stuck to the frozen surface. Constant access to fresh water is vital, so if you can't remove the ice from Prince's dish frequently, purchase a self-warming water dish.

It takes commitment and dedication to safely maintain a dog outside during the winter. Inviting Prince indoors is often easier, and surely more fun for both of you.

MOVING ALONG RIGHT

What do you do with a well-adjusted, healthy dog? Have fun, of course. The next chapter is all about fun and games and will take you on a tour of available activities.

EXPENSIVE, BUT WORTH IT

When Tom and Jean Hoag of Phoenix, Arizona adopted their dog Joe from Mastiff Rescue, he tested positive for Valley Fever. That was two years ago and Joe has been on medication ever since. Today he shows no symptoms and has gained forty needed pounds. His blood tests have improved at each testing and the Hoags are anticipating a gradual withdrawal from medication. Tom says, "We are sure Joe is in the running for the most expensive dog in the universe, and I might add, worth every cent."

He's the picture of health right now, but Joe the Mastiff needed medication for the first two years after his rescue and adoption.

THE HEALING IS MUTUAL

Mary Lewis, a veterinarian from Glenview, Illinois, received a call from a colleague asking if she and her family would be willing to let a Labrador Retriever named Sandy recuperate at their house for a couple months. The young dog needed a place to live until her plated femur healed and she could be placed in a permanent home. Mary's friend explained that Sandy's original owners had elected euthanasia when they heard it would cost nearly $800 to repair the dog's mangled leg. But the veterinarian saw a special sweetness in Sandy and asked her owners for permission to repair her leg and place her.

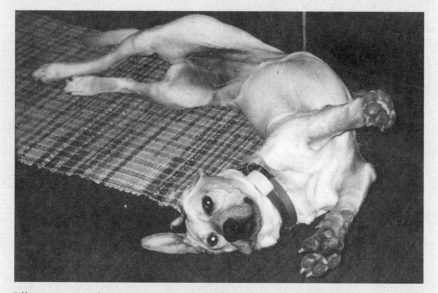

Silly, sweet Sandy was in pain and needed a home just when the Lewis family was grieving and needed a dog.

Sandy arrived at the Lewis home depressed and in pain. Coincidentally, the Lewises were also suffering. Only a few days earlier their beloved family dog had died prematurely. "We took Sandy with hurting hearts," Mary Lewis said. "We didn't have any intention of keeping her. I really hoped to start with another Lab pup."

Even though she was so sore from surgery that it took her a few minutes just to figure out how to lie down, Sandy never had an accident in the house, was quiet and comfortable in a crate, and didn't get upset by the constant activity in a family with three youngsters under four years old. The Lewises were smitten in spite of themselves. Mary says, "The same sweet face and big heart that saved Sandy's life won a permanent place in our home. The demands of our three children dictated that we didn't have time to start a seven-week-old puppy. This fifteen-month-old dog was perfect."

Today Sandy performs a wide variety of tricks, has become an accomplished Frisbee catcher, and provides cheer as a pet therapy dog. She also helps her owner save other dogs' lives by serving as a donor dog for blood transfusions in Mary's veterinary practice. "Most importantly, every day Sandy tests my shadow," Mary says. "She's always there with her unconditional love. I'm thankful this silly, sweet Lab came into our family."

CHAPTER NINE

LET THE FUN BEGIN

One of the reasons people love dogs is because dogs love to please people. Making you smile will put a thump in Prince's tail and a sparkle in his eye. And the more he learns, the more he will be able to learn. Neither a pathetic past nor advanced age will stop Prince from learning if the motivation is there. What is the motivation? The motivation is you. Learning even a simple trick, such as shaking hands, will give Prince a sense of accomplishment, and your praise will be his standing ovation. So praise every small step along the way as Prince learns how to learn, and soon he will perform a few tricks, play a variety of games, and be ready for higher education. The possibilities are limitless.

OLD DOGS SURE CAN LEARN NEW TRICKS!

Lacer, a six-year-old Labrador Retriever, was adored by her original owner, Bob Adams. An obedience judge and writer from Southern California, Bob often played retrieving games with his energetic dog, and she spent her quiet time relaxing by his desk. When Bob was struck down by inoperable cancer, he immediately began looking for a good home for Lacer. A mutual friend put him in touch with Kurt and Kristine Litke of Rice, Minnesota and they got to know each other through a series of letters. Bob said he was worried that Lacer would be too active for someone living in a small space and told the couple he wanted her to have a permanent home with people who would take good care of her and love her. The Litkes said they had the space and the love.

Six-year-old Lacer (left), finally stopped grieving for her original owner and likes participating in new activities with her adoptive family and her new friend, Lucy.

Two days after Bob's death, Lacer was shipped to Kurt and Kristine. Mourning for her owner, and shaken by so many sudden changes, the once active Labrador retreated to her shipping crate, making a bee-line for it whenever she felt insecure. A man's dog, she responded a little to Kurt, but she wouldn't even make friends with Lucy, the Litkes' friendly young Labrador.

As time passed, Lacer gradually emerged from mourning and began to relax in her new home. Kurt remembered Bob saying that Lacer loved retrieving balls and sticks, but had never had an opportunity to hunt. He knew that a job can do wonders for a dog's confidence, so he took Lacer to training sessions at his retriever club. When the middle-aged Lab jumped in the lake and swam out to retrieve her first duck, it was the real beginning of her second start. "She's been doing great ever since," Kurt says. "Besides enjoying life again, she has a new career. This past fall was her first hunt and she performed well. She hunts with an intense amount of energy and enthusiasm."

FOR P.J., LIFE BEGAN AT FIVE

Socialized as a puppy, P.J. had been banished to a 10' by 10' kennel run during adolescence. From then on, the Golden Retriever was fed and watered and that was all. He had no companionship, no toys, and no opportunity to exercise. Completely bored, and with no outlet for his energy, P.J. pulled all the hair from his legs and belly and chewed rocks until his teeth were worn down to the gum line.

Neglected for five years, P.J. received obedience training after he was rescued and now has a Companion Dog title.

P.J. had survived his personal prison for five years when his breeder heard about his situation and bought him back. Starved for attention, the rescued Golden was barely controllable. It was as if he were trying to make up for all the affection and exercise he had missed, and didn't knew where to start or which way to turn. His breeder, however, did know which way to turn. She turned to her friend, Dave Wedum, owner of Grizzly Dog Obedience School in Whitefish, Montana, and offered to give P.J. to him.

When Dave saw the exuberant dog, he accepted the offer and took it a step further. He said he would put an obedience title on the high energy animal just to prove it could still be done.

Dave trained P.J., and several months later they competed at an Obedience Trial in Spokane, Washington. All attention was focused on the team when it was their turn to perform, and it proved too much for the excitable Golden. In his glee, he visited the judge and kissed the stewards, and when Dave gave the recall command, P.J. bounded in so eagerly that Dave was knocked backward.

"You're an awfully brave man," the judge commented, but he didn't give P.J. a qualifying score.

Dave kept trying, and by the time P.J. turned six, he earned his Companion Dog (CD) title in obedience. He's eight now, and Dave says he's ready to earn a CDX (Companion Dog Excellent). Has he calmed down a little?

"No," says Dave. "He's still gets so exuberant about being the center of attention that sometimes he's on the edge of out of control. But he sure enjoys training sessions and he's a loving and well-behaved dog at home."

Why Tricks Are Terrific

You don't have to lead Prince into a whole new career unless you want to, but you can add laughter to his life by teaching him a few tricks. Dogs love making people laugh. Just give Prince the opportunity to make you laugh and see how he sparkles. He'll want to do it again and again. So, why are tricks terrific?

- Teaching them makes you smile.

- Prince feels warm and happy inside when he makes you smile.

- Prince correlates learning tricks with making you smile and feeling warm and happy.

- When other people see a dog doing tricks, they smile too. Some even laugh, and from Prince's viewpoint, that's even better.

- Knowing a trick or two will make it much easier to socialize Prince, because he'll have something to focus on that always earns approval from friendly strangers. But first, he'll have to be appealing enough to attract their eye. Some dogs are magnets for attention but others are likely to be ignored or feared. How do people react to Prince?

Is socializing Prince somewhat difficult because he's so big or tough-looking that strangers fear him? Do some people even go out of their way to avoid walking near him on the sidewalk? Prince probably feels their distrust and responds in kind. You don't want him to feel uneasy around people, but how can you make a formidable mug like his look lovable? Easily. Just tie a bright bandanna around his neck before you take him for a walk. Or attach a big fake flower to his collar. Buy a few seasonal flowers. A silk poinsettia for December. A daffodil to herald spring. You get the picture. Now Prince can't possibly look frightening. In fact, he's kind of funny, and funny makes people feel friendly.

Is Prince so plain no one notices him? Or so tiny that people who know nothing about dogs believe he's brainless? Go for the bandanna (cut it down to fit, of course), or the flower, or a doggie tee shirt that says "Hi, I'm Prince." Now Prince isn't scary or plain. Now people won't think he's too small to have personality. Now all but confirmed dog-haters (or those with unreasonable fears) will pass Prince with a smile, and some will actually stop and talk to him. Aha! There's his chance to shine. When someone asks to pet Prince (and someone will), have Prince sit politely for petting (he learned that in Chapter 7). Then tell the person to ask Prince to "shake hands," or "gimme five," or whatever cue you taught him. After that, tell Prince to "say hi" (one bark). By then the stranger is laughing and you are smiling. And Prince feels warm and happy inside and correlates his good feelings with obeying his cues and making a new friend.

Three Entertaining Tricks

When teaching these tricks (or any tricks), use praise and treats or toys to motivate Prince. When he does something right, he is rewarded. When he does something wrong, or does nothing at all, he

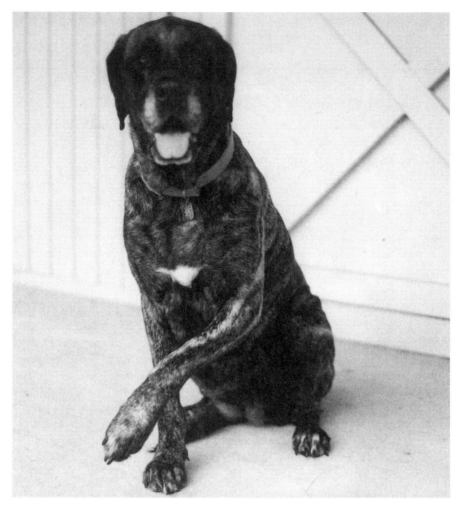

Pokey, a well-mannered six-year-old mastiff, likes to shake hands and play with toys. She belongs to Walter Tice of Southern Pines, North Carolina, who obtained her through Mastiff Rescue.

is not rewarded. It's as simple as that. No force or punishment should ever be involved.

SHAKING HANDS

As soon as the "Sit" command is second nature to Prince, you can teach him to "shake hands" or "gimme five" (use the same cue words every time). Kneel down to his level after he sits and say whatever the cue will be. Then pick up one of his forelegs, by lifting it from

underneath, and shake it gently a couple of times. Praise Prince as soon as you drop the leg, and give him a tiny treat. Repeat five times. Then try it again later, or tomorrow. One day Prince will lift his fore leg as soon as you say the cue word and move your hand toward him. Let him know how tickled you are. Gradually wean Prince off expecting a treat every time he performs, but always tell him what a *gooood boy* he is. And once, every five times or so, surprise him with a goodie when he gives you five. Once Prince has this trick down pat, have family and friends practice it with him (but not more than five tries at a time). Eventually he will happily perform it for anyone who asks.

SAYING "HI"

You'll have to get silly to teach Prince to "say hi" or "speak." Show Prince his favorite treat or special toy but don't let him have it. Instead, get him all wound up by teasing him with it. As he dances around, say the cue word excitedly, over and over. The object is to get Prince to make a sound. When he does (even if the sound is a squeak instead of a full-fledged bark), give him the toy or treat and praise him. After he eats the treat or parades the toy, try it again. Five times in a row is plenty.

Soon Prince will make the connection, and bark when you say the cue words and show him the treat. That's a good start. Continue using the treat or toy until you only have to say the cue words once. Then gradually wean Prince off the treat, just as you did when teaching him to shake hands.

Some dogs anticipate this trick and begin barking before you give the cue. Every time Prince tries that, tell him "Shhhh," and don't say the cue words until he quiets down and remains quiet for several seconds.

SITTING UP

Start with Prince sitting in a corner, facing out, as the walls will brace his back as he learns to hold this new position. Tell him to "Sit up," or whatever cue words you like, show him one of his favorite treats and slowly move it upward to just above his muzzle. As Prince watches and stretches toward it, keep moving your hand backwards toward his eyes. As soon as he sits up on his haunches, give him the treat and praise him (if he stands on his hind legs instead of sitting up, you probably held the treat too high above his muzzle). Gradually increase the length of time Prince sits up before you reward him. When he's no longer wobbly, he won't need the corner. Five tries in a row is plenty when teaching this trick, and there's really no need to wean Prince off the treat.

Activities for You and Your Dog

From shaking hands with your friends to earning an Obedience title; from hide-and-seek in the living room to Agility competition in a coliseum; a multitude of exciting a activities await you and your dog. Many events welcome all dogs, purebred or mixed. Others allow only registered purebreds, while some showcase dogs which were bred to do specialized work, such as herding or coursing. Most dogs are suited for several fun and functional activities, and doing them together builds an even stronger bond between you and Prince.

Physical and Educational Games for Dogs

Just as children learn through playing with educational toys, play conditioning is a great way to educate dogs. Most healthy, well-adjusted dogs learn physical games in a jiffy. In fact, if Prince has a high activity level and you don't teach him a few games, he may create his own and invite you to join in. Dogs also like to play mental games and the whole family can participate in the fun. Mental games will develop Prince's memory, making all types of training come easier.

Keep the mood light when playing games with Prince, but always appoint yourself, not him, team captain. No matter which one of you starts the game, you should be the one to end it. Fun becomes work if you play until Prince is bored or tired, so call it quits while he is still avidly engaged in the game. Calling time out if the sport becomes too rowdy is also the captain's duty. Be consistent, and Prince will soon learn the rules and limits of each game.

Dogs that were never socialized or were abused or neglected may not play games for several months. But don't conclude that Prince must have been deprived in the past just because he won't play right away. Prince probably won't feel like playing until he adjusts to his new home. He may be in mourning, or insecure in his new surroundings, and just needs more time. If fun and games don't interest Prince after his first few weeks in your home, don't despair. First, check your attitude. Maybe you're trying too hard and making it look like work instead of fun. Next, check your timing. Was Prince full from dinner, or even sleeping, when you invited him to play? If a change of attitude or timing doesn't help, the following suggestions might.

Help for Serious and Sullen Dogs

While some dogs change owners with ease, others fret and grieve and need time to relax and accept their new family. Only then will they be secure enough to enjoy games. Other dogs don't play because no one ever played with them and they simply don't know how. Their progress may be frustratingly slow at first, but once they catch on they often make up for lost time. A few dogs are too timid to play, but once they accept affection without fear, their sense of humor may suddenly surface. An occasional dog suffers shock from its sojourn in the animal shelter and is unable to relate to its new surroundings. Your love and patience will eventually bring it out of its apparent apathy, and into a world full of fun and games.

Making Prince Charming

No matter what caused Prince's problem, one thing is certain. If he's still a solemn dog after he trusts you, you're going to have to get silly first and encourage him to follow suit. Choose exciting toys, like a squeaky rat made of fake fur or a bouncy latex hedgehog, then play with a toy yourself while Prince watches. Throw it, catch it, drop it, and chase it. Have a great time playing with the toy, and occasionally tease Prince with it, but don't give it to him. Family and friends can join in the fun, tossing the toy to each other and rolling it across the floor, but don't let the game get wild enough to frighten an insecure dog. After two or three minutes of continuous (but not rough) fun, "accidentally" drop the toy near Prince and see if he mouths it. If he ignores it, pick it up and continue playing for another minute or two. Then put the toy away until another day.

The first time Prince takes the toy, allow him to play with it without interference for about thirty seconds. Then trade it for a treat, play with it yourself for a few seconds, and put it away. Don't use any command when taking the toy away from Prince. Your first objective is developing his desire to play. Once the desire surfaces, you can start teaching the rules of the game.

The following games are fun for dogs of all sizes and ages. When rough-housing with Prince, take his age, size, temperament, and coordination into consideration. Treat him like the healthy animal he is (or is becoming), but don't overwhelm him with your physical superiority.

HIDE-AND-SEEK

Besides being fun, games of hide-and-seek may enhance Prince's memory and scenting ability. Since food is one of the rewards, play these games before Prince eats dinner.

Start playing hide-and-seek by putting Prince in a room and closing the door. Then hide a treat in a different room, perhaps beside a table leg or under a chair. Open the door, and when Prince comes into the room say "Find it" in an excited voice. Of course Prince won't know what the words mean at first, so keep repeating them while encouraging him toward the treat. Help him locate the goodie, but let him make the actual find. He should pick up the treat from the floor, not your hand. When he does, tell him "Gooood" and let him eat it—a double reward.

Now put Prince back in the other room and place another treat exactly where the first one was. Open the door, say "Find it," and watch what he does. You will probably have to help Prince find the treat a few times before he goes directly to it on his own. When he succeeds by himself, repeat it one more time and quit for the day.

Use the same hiding place for the next few days and soon Prince will find it all by himself on the first try. When he goes directly to the spot without hesitation, throw him a curve. Put the treat in a new hiding place and start over.

Don't tell Prince "No!" when he goes back to the original spot. He's learning to use his memory and that's good. In fact, have a treat waiting in the old hiding place(s) ever so often. Eventually Prince will learn to remember several rewarding locations. Continue adding hiding places as long as he keeps enjoying the game, and soon he may exercise his sense of smell as well as his memory.

It's easy to create variations of this game. For example, try using more than one room, or even the entire house, with your spouse or child in hiding. Instead of saying "Find it," say "Find Tom." Meanwhile Tom is hiding behind the drapes, or in a closet with the door slightly ajar, ready to reward Prince with a hug and a treat.

LITTLE LEAGUE

For this game you need a lightweight, bouncy ball. It should be a size that Prince can easily pick up and hold in his mouth, but can't swallow. Tennis balls are just right for most medium-sized dogs, but Prince may need something bigger or smaller. Use this particular ball only for playing games together and put it away, out of your dog's reach, when playtime is over. Soon Prince will quiver with happy anticipation as soon as he sees you holding his "special" ball, and he won't ruin it by using it for a chew toy.

To play "Little League," toss the ball against a wall and compete with Prince to catch it on the rebound, before or after the first bounce. Throw it softly at first, adding a little more speed when your dog gains confidence. As Prince becomes good at catching, start gently pitching the ball underhand to him from a short distance, and encourage him to catch it before it hits the ground. Lengthen the distance gradually. Experiment to see what else Prince likes to do. He may be a natural

Frisbee snatcher. For indoor fun, many dogs love to catch popcorn, one delicious kernel at a time. Prince may enjoy all these games, plus others that you create especially for him.

If Prince refuses to give up a ball or Frisbee after he catches it, he should learn to respond to the word "Out." Many dogs are willing to trade the ball for a treat. Say "Out," as you remove the ball from Prince's mouth and replace it with a goodie, and he may soon learn to open his mouth on command. But if Prince clamps down harder when you try to take the ball, drape your hand over the top of his muzzle, thumb on one side, fingers on the other. Curl his upper lip inward and upward until it's pressing against the tips of his large canine teeth while you say the word "Out," firmly (but not loudly). Praise Prince when he lets go of the ball and resume playing the game.

DOGGIE IN THE MIDDLE

For this game you need two or more people and a lightweight ball that's big enough so Prince can't swallow it. The ball used for "Little League" (above) will work just fine. To play "Doggie in the Middle," one person rolls the ball across the ground to the other person with the dog in the middle trying to intercept. When Prince captures the ball, clap and cheer him on for a few seconds while he parades with his prize. Then say "Out," take the ball back, and begin playing again. Later, you can advance to bouncing the ball across the ground. If Prince is big enough, and already knows how to catch the ball, try tossing it underhand to each other, but never so hard that it would hurt if it hit him. No matter how good a ball player you are, let your dog catch the ball and parade it ever so often. It's a real confidence booster.

TUG TOY

Many dogs of all sizes love playing tug and would gladly jerk and shake their tug toy long after you are exhausted. Rubber figure-eight shaped tugs, and tug toy balls attached to ropes, are available in different sizes at animal supply stores, or you can make a tug toy out of scrap leather or an old tee shirt or towel. Put Prince's tug toy away after use, or he will probably use it for a chew toy. After all, it's his and he knows he's allowed to put it in his mouth.

When playing tug with Prince, begin by telling him "Take it," so he knows when it's okay to grab the toy. Then let him win sometimes. In his mind, he's tugging to gain possession of the toy, so an occasional victory will keep him interested. While he parades around with the tug toy, make a few obvious, but fake, attempts to take it from him. That will make him even prouder of his prize. Eventually call Prince to you, say "Out," and take the tug toy from his mouth. (If he hasn't been taught to come when called, keep a long, lightweight lead on him during play sessions and use it, if necessary, to bring him back to you). At first, trade him a treat for the tug toy. If he won't give up the toy that easily, use the method described in the "Little League" section. A few dogs are so stubborn about keeping their prize that almost all methods fail. If that describes Prince, put one drop of Bitter Apple on your finger and touch your finger to his tongue as you say "Out." Keep the Bitter Apple from touching the tug toy, and as soon as Prince releases his grip, tell him "Take it" and play tug with him again.

Play as roughly as you want, as long as Prince responds to the "Out" command and never grabs at anything in your hand until he is told to "Take it." Remember, you are the captain. As long as you can always stop the game at will, it's fine to intensify it by pushing your dog around with your hands and feet while he's tugging. That may make him growl up a storm, all in good fun.

Occasionally a dog becomes so excited playing tug that he grabs fingers by mistake, instead of the toy. If this happens to you, yell "No! Ouch!" (and whatever else comes to mind if no children are near), and stop the game instantly. Put away the tug toy and ignore Prince for several minutes. He'll soon learn to be more discriminating, no matter how rousing the game.

To speed up teaching "Out" and "Take it," occasionally practice them three times in a row before starting the game, and a time or two during the game. But don't practice every time you play. Always try to finish each game on a high note. For a grand finale, let Prince capture the tug toy, parade for applause, and trade it for a treat and a hug.

FETCH

Fetching (retrieving) games are favorites with some dogs, while others have no interest in them whatsoever. Any number of objects, from sticks to tennis balls, are suitable for fetching, as long as the diameter and weight of the object is compatible with your dog's size. Make your throws short at first, and increase the distance as Prince catches

Wheee!

Shake

Splat

Here it comes!

Got it!

Let's do it again, please, please!

Ten-year-old Yog loves retrieving sticks from the water. In fact, the bigger the stick, the better she likes it. Her friends call her favorites Yog's logs. Her owner, Jerry O'Neil, taught her to shake as soon as she reaches the bank and he stays far enough away to remain dry. Yog is a mixed-bred, spayed female.

on. When tossing something for Prince to fetch, it's important that he see it leave your hand, especially when he's new to the game. If he chases the object and brings it all the way back, trade it for a really special treat, like a tiny piece of bologna or cheese, and lay on the praise.

Some dogs will chase an object, then parade it in triumph without bringing it back. If this describes Prince, put him on a long leash before the game begins, and reel him in gently after he picks up the object. If he keeps holding the object and carries it all the way to you, give him a treat. If he drops it long before he reaches you, don't give him anything and don't be upset. Many dogs don't have a strong retrieving instinct. Keep trying occasionally even if Prince initially shows no desire to retrieve. He wouldn't be the first dog to change his mind.

If Prince likes retrieving, keep him interested by limiting the number of retrieves you do at a time. Five in a row is plenty. After that, play something else and do another set of retrieves later. Never bore or exhaust your dog. Always quit while he is still having fun.

WRESTLING

Getting down on the floor and wrestling or rough-housing with Prince may be fun for both of you. When you push or shake him, he may play-growl and take an arm or leg in his mouth, but he should never squeeze with his teeth. Dogs of all sizes enjoy rough-housing, as long as their owners take their size into consideration and don't overwhelm the little ones.

Generations of dog owners have played this game with nary a mark on them, but they were always captain of the wrestling team, and their dogs knew it. When wrestling, the captain starts the game and stops the game. And if Prince ever gets overexcited and mouths you so hard it hurts, say "No!" sharply, quit playing immediately, and ignore him for the next half hour.

CERTIFICATION PROGRAMS

Two non-competitive certification programs test canine behavior during simulated everyday activities, such as a walking around the block or meeting a new person. While similar in structure, the two tests are quite different. The Canine Good Citizen (CGC) Test evaluates learned behavior, while the Temperament Test (TT) evaluates untrained responses to various stimuli. Both programs help fight the ongoing battle against anti-dog legislation, so dog owners are encouraged to support them. Besides, they're fun, and passing either one means earning a certificate and the satisfaction of coming so far with Prince. Both tests are available to all dogs, whether purebred or not.

Qualifying for the CGC

"A Canine Good Citizen is a dog that makes its owner happy without making someone else unhappy," according to the American Kennel

Club's Canine Good Citizen program booklet. That means Canine Good Citizens have learned to behave at home, are good neighbors, and have good manners in public. Dogs that pass the ten-part test earn a certificate proclaiming them a Canine Good Citizen, and their owners proudly add the letters CGC to their dog's name.

The CGC test evaluates practical training (not formal obedience), so dogs are tested on how they behave during everyday situations such as being touched by a friendly stranger, walking on a crowded street, and meeting another dog while out for a stroll. They are also evaluated on their reaction to distractions, coming when called, and their attitude when their handler is out of sight (separation anxiety). In addition, they must obey simple commands such as "Sit" and "Down," but not with the precision of competitive Obedience dogs. All tests are performed on lead.

While preparing for the CGC test, owners learn how to train and control their dogs and the dogs become better companions. Many dog clubs and private obedience schools offer short courses in CGC training, and some of them give the test as their graduation exercise. In addition, the American Kennel Club offers free material to help people train their dogs for the test. Write or call: The American Kennel Club, Attention: CGC, 5580 Centerview Drive, Suite 200, Raleigh, North Carolina 27606. Their phone number is (919) 233-9780. Ask for Canine Good Citizen training information and how to find a test near you.

Qualifying for the TT

"A sound mind in a sound body," is the motto of the American Temperament Test Society, Inc. (ATTS). Dogs that pass the ATTS's ten-part test earn a certificate, and their owners proudly display the letters TT (Temperament Tested) behind the dog's name.

In its flyer, ATTS describes the test as follows:

"The ATTS test focuses on and measures different aspects of temperament such as stability, shyness, aggressiveness, and friendliness, as well as the dog's instinct for protectiveness toward its handler and or self-preservation in the face of a threat . . .

"The test simulates a casual walk through the park or neighborhood where everyday-life situations are encountered. During this walk, the dog experiences visual, auditory, and tactile stimuli. Neutral, friendly, and threatening situations are encountered, calling into play the dog's ability to distinguish between non-threatening situations and those calling for watchful and protective reactions."

Your dog needs no special training or preparation to take the ATTS test. Well-socialized family dogs usually earn their letters (TT) with ease.

For additional information and to find out where Prince can be tested, write or call: American Temperament Test Society, Inc., P.O. Box 397, Fenton, Missouri 63026. PH: (314) 225-5346. Request a flyer describing the test and a test schedule.

CARING AND SHARING AS A PET THERAPY VOLUNTEER

Science has proven that interacting with animals is therapeutic for people of all ages. Even traumatized children sometimes respond to animals long before communicating with people. That's why thousands of dog owners thrill disabled children and warm aging hearts by visiting institutions and inviting residents to play with their friendly pets. Some volunteer independently at a nearby institution and make weekly visits on a regular schedule. Others join one of the hundreds of Therapy Dog clubs across the nation. These dedicated groups, with names like Compassionate Canines and Sirius Angels, prepare their members to visit children's homes, nursing homes, hospitals, schools for the physically or mentally challenged, cancer wards, rehabilitation centers, hospices for AIDS victims, and even prisons. While the results are almost always positive, occasionally they are astonishing. Minor miracles have been documented. For example, when a mute four-year-old finally whispered her first word, it was the Therapy Dog's name. And when the tiny victim of a drunk driver finally moved her injured arms, she reached out toward a Therapy Dog.

While you and Prince may not create miracles while performing pet therapy, you will surely enliven drab, depressing lives. When bored eyes brighten and pinched mouths relax into smiles, you'll understand that you and Prince are giving a great gift, and receiving wondrous rewards, by just being there.

SHADOW'S SECOND START

Hugo James had been looking for the right black Labrador Retriever for several months when a volunteer at Labrador Retriever Rescue of Southern Connecticut told him about one at an animal shelter whose time was running out. At the shelter, Hugo was introduced to a listless, bedraggled three-year-old, the bottom dog in a pen of three. The spiritless dog has been in the shelter three months and Hugo could easily understand why no one had adopted him. But Hugo made an effort anyway. He talked, he walked, he spent time with the dog trying to elicit a response. When everything failed he drove home alone. He wanted a dog, but not this joyless, lifeless creature.

That night Hugo couldn't sleep. His thoughts kept returning to the sad sack, soon-to-be-euthanized dog. In the morning he returned to the shelter, paid the adoption fee, and named his new dog Shadow. On the way home, Shadow broke a car window, tripling his cost.

Within hours of adoption, it became evident that Shadow did indeed have intelligence. Within days, the dog asked to go potty outdoors with a soft whine at the back door. Within a month, Hugo and Shadow started attending training classes and discovered that obedience exercises were fun for both of them and elevated Shadow's personality. Within a year, they progressed to showing at local matches. "The thrill of winning a blue ribbon in a Pre-Novice competition at a local match is still with me," Hugo says. "No win has ever been so sweet or so exciting since."

Soon Hugo began thinking about entering AKC Obedience Trials so Shadow could earn Obedience titles. But there were two obstacles. One was that Shadow, although obviously a purebred, had no AKC registration papers. The American Kennel Club allows obvious purebreds to compete in obedience (and several other events) provided they meet the requirements for an Indefinite Listing Privilege (ILP) number, so Hugo obtained the forms and read the requirements. Shadow met all but one, and that was the second obstacle. Before dogs are issued an ILP number they must be spayed or neutered.

Hugo admits, "Like many a male pet owner, I had resisted Shadow's castration, but I knew if I were ever to enter an AKC event, I had to agree to the neutering. Thus, I reluctantly had Shadow neutered. My fears of his getting fat, of losing his spirit, or changing for the worse in some other way were all groundless. As soon as the incision healed Shadow was the same frisky, happy, and well-proportioned dog that he had been. With the neutering accomplished, AKC issued Shadow his ILP number and we were off to the Obedience Trials."

Well, almost. Actually Shadow was more than obedient enough for a pet, but he wasn't attentive enough to compete in trials. At a practice match, Hugo was impressed at how well a female Labrador worked and asked her owner where they trained. He was soon introduced to a new instructor and attended a series of classes. The new school's methods worked so well that within a few months Shadow was ready to compete. When he entered the ring, he did much more than just qualify for

titles. In his first two shows alone, he averaged 197 out of a possible 200, and won first place in his class.

"I can't overemphasize the importance of having the correct teacher for person and dog," Hugo says. "Our choice changed our lives. Working hard on a regular basis in an effort to attain the highest possible scores is both fun and rewarding."

Today Shadow has a Companion Dog (CD) and a Companion Dog Excellent (CDX) title and is well on his way to earning the Utility Dog (UD) title. For Hugo, a retired college professor and former administrator, competing in dog events adds a new dimension to

Shelter dog Shadow has come a long way with the help of his owner, Hugo James. In this photo he's shown winning first place at an obedience trial.

Photo credit: Chuck Tatham.

his life. Through Shadow, he has become actively involved in a variety of dog activities including stewarding at matches and shows, and serving as his club's Obedience Match Chairman.

Hugo says, "Friends tell me how lucky Shadow is to have found such an ideal home as mine, but I think I'm fortunate in having found such a wonderful dog as Shadow. He has become my steady, constant companion. He rides on my backhoe when I work, picks up and carries the newspaper to the house, plays catch, and loves to ride in the boat and the car. To dwell further on his virtues is unnecessary. My rescue dog Shadow may not be perfect, but he is certainly the best dog I have ever known."

All dogs, purebred or mixed, are welcome in pet-assisted therapy programs. Requirements vary from one Therapy Dog organization to another, and sometimes from institution to institution, but generally Prince will have to pass one or more tests before being allowed to participate. That's because dogs working in therapy situations are very special. They must be completely confident, and have temperaments stable enough to withstand petting with jerky motions that may resemble hitting; hugs that may be too hard and too confining: and accidental bumps from hospital equipment such as walkers and wheelchairs. Tests for Therapy Dogs evaluate temperament, as well as training, because these animals must have dependable dispositions and impeccable manners. They must also obey basic commands in the midst of major distractions, including institutional odors, hospital equipment, crowds, and noise.

At least three national organizations, Therapy Dogs International, Therapy Dogs Incorporated, and the Delta Society, have certification programs and tests for potential therapy dogs. They require that dogs pass the therapy version of the Canine Good Citizen Test (the AKC's original test with the addition of service equipment) and in addition, each organization has requirements of its own. For information on how Prince can become a therapy dog, contact Therapy Dogs International (201) 543-0888, Therapy Dogs Incorporated (307) 638-3223, or the Delta Society (206) 226-7357.

COMPETITIVE EVENTS FOR ALL DOGS

Eager to please and quick to learn, some adult dogs become top performers in spite of a late start. Prince may excel at one or more competitive events and love showing off on center stage.

Obedience

The best way for a dog to learn to obey, despite such distractions as strangers and other dogs, is to attend obedience school. Obedience training that's upbeat and creative will provide a fine outlet for Prince's enthusiasm and spirit. It will also stimulate his innate intelligence, by making demands on his trainability, memory, and dexterity. When properly presented, obedience will enhance Prince's inborn desire to please by teaching him exactly how to please you. Best of all, it will educate him in self control without dimming his sparkle.

But what if Prince's personality doesn't sparkle because he's too insecure or shy to express himself? Then obedience training may be especially useful since it gives apprehensive animals exactly what they need—a fool proof way of doing something right and being rewarded for it. If Prince lacks confidence, make progress slowly and reward even his most hesitant efforts to please. When he discovers that every time he sits on command, or walks proudly beside you, he is rewarded with praise, he'll gradually gain self-assurance. The next reward will be yours. Prince's hidden sparkle will emerge and you'll savor its reflection for the rest of his life. That's exactly what happened when Hugo A. James of Trumbull, Connecticut, brought out the best in his adopted dog, Shadow.

Attending Training Classes

Obedience classes may be offered by dog clubs or private instructors, and may be advertised in the yellow pages or the newspaper. Shop around to find the best school for you and Prince. Good obedience instructors are not prejudiced against any type of dog, and they do more than just call out commands. They encourage the use of praise and take the time to solve individual problems, offering alternative training methods when necessary.

Prince may revel in the additional attention and praise, prompting you to showcase his talents by competing for Obedience titles. Depending on whether he is a registered purebred or a mixed-bred, you may earn titles through the American Kennel Club (AKC), the United Kennel Club (UKC), or the American Mixed Breed Obedience Registry (AMBOR) (see Appendix). With knowledge of Prince's background, your obedience instructor will guide you to the correct organization. It's always important to know the rules of the game, so write for a copy of the obedience regulations.

Obedience titles are awarded at three levels of difficulty. While sound dogs of all shapes, sizes, and ages are physically capable of earning the Companion Dog title, the advanced titles are more demanding because they include jumping obstacles. You are the best judge of whether or not Prince is a candidate for the rigors of advanced work. While it's excellent exercise for most dogs, it may be too physically demanding for an oldster.

Whether or not you compete in Obedience Trials, schooling will give Prince direction and stability. Obedience is often called "companion

Jackie Clemens praises her Shetland Sheepdog for a good retrieve. Besides making dogs better companions, training is fun for owners and dogs.

There are myriad activities for those with trained dogs. This group formed a K-9 drill team. They participate in parades and give demonstrations in schools on request.

dog training" because it teaches dogs to be responsive partners while teaching handlers how to train and understand their dogs. The result is enhanced companionship. Learning to be attentive to you, to heel smartly by your side, to come immediately when called, and to obey a variety of commands makes Prince a far more responsive pet. Obedience enthusiasts often say, "A trained dog is a happy dog," and they are right. Since trained dogs are such good companions, they get to go along on more outings, are welcome in more places, and generally have fuller lives. Earning an Obedience title is nice, but the ultimate goal of every trainer should be a happily working dog with a trustworthy temperament. Use encouraging methods, combine firmness with fairness, and incorporate fun and games into every practice session, and you will end up with more than a well-trained companion. You and Prince will be partners.

Agility instructor Virginia Isaac demonstrates on a practice course. Notice the other obstacles in the background.

Agility

Agility is the canine version of a challenging obstacle course. Thrilling to participants and spectators, this sport epitomizes the ultimate in exciting teamwork. At Agility trials, dogs sprint up A-frames, crawl through brightly decorated tunnels, stride across balance beams, soar over jumps, and maneuver see-saws. And they do it all at high speed,

CURING KEGGER

Two-year-old Kegger had a barking problem. Kenneled near a public walkway and starved for human attention, the Brittany barked his hello whenever someone walked by. Naturally the neighbors complained. To keep peace in the neighborhood, Kegger's owner offered the dog "free to a good home."

Once a problem dog, today Kegger is a demo-dog when his owner teaches obedience. Most important, the Brittany is marvelous with children.

When Michelle Knefelkamp, of Houlton, Wisconsin, heard an adult Brittany was available, she visited the dog with her husband, her toddler son, and their aging Brittany, Rastus. Kegger liked them and they liked him, so they took him home for his second start.

Trouble started immediately. Kegger had seemed so happy during the half hour ride to the Knefelkamp's rural home that Michelle just knew he'd go from the car to the house with the rest of the family. Wrong. Instead, he dashed off across the countryside. The Knefelkamps searched and called fruitlessly for a long time, then were amazed when the dog's sensitive nose eventually brought him back. His return wasn't the only thing that surprised Michelle. "I'm still amazed I made that stupid mistake," she says. "Kegger only knew me for half an hour and here I thought he'd be gratefully doting on me for his second chance at life."

Sweet and sociable, but utterly untrained and totally out of control after being confined to a kennel for two years, all Kegger wanted to do was run. The Knefelkamps had him neutered and spent many months on his training. Their effort paid off. Eventually he became a reliable companion, and more.

Today Michelle teaches dog obedience classes and Kegger is her demo-dog; proudly displaying how an educated and trustworthy partner should behave. Besides his outstanding obedience work, he participates in Agility and Flyball. Even more important, he's always been marvelous with children.

What does Michelle say about Kegger seven years after giving him a second start? "He's an ideal Brittany; happy, energetic, enthusiastic, and friendly. I know I'll never have another dog like him. Every dog is unique, but sometimes those who are the most work turn out to be the truest companions."

while taking direction from their handlers. The object of the sport is for the handler to direct the dog through the obstacle course without the dog making a mistake such as touching a jump or missing a weave pole. Scoring is based on faults and time, and the course is never the same twice.

Dogs of all shapes and sizes are capable of earning Agility titles provided they are healthy and physically fit. Big dogs don't have an advantage over little dogs either. Agility classes are divided into height divisions for judging, so Prince will compete with dogs that are similar to him in size, and the height of the jumps will correlate to the size of the dogs.

An especially good sport for high energy dogs, Agility training will help Prince learn how to be under control and in high spirits at the same time. It will also turn you and Prince into teammates. The best place for you to learn Agility together is at a dog training school or an Agility training club that has all the necessary equipment. Good

Agility instructors move ahead slowly and safely, taking each obstacle one step at a time. They are patient, upbeat, and keep the dogs motivated through rewards such as toys, treats, and praise.

Several organizations offer Agility programs where dogs can earn titles for excellence in the sport. For Agility regulations and additional information, contact the United States Dog Agility Association, Inc. (USDAA), the American Kennel Club (AKC), the United Kennel Club (UKC), or the American Mixed Breed Obedience Registry (AMBOR). While dogs must be AKC registered to participate in AKC Agility, non-registered and mixed-bred dogs are welcome in the other three programs (see Appendix).

Tracking

If Prince is AKC-registered, he's eligible to earn a variety of American Kennel Club tracking titles through participation in non-competitive tests. The American Mixed Breed Obedience Registry (AMBOR) offers similar tests for mixed-bred dogs.

Tracking combines training with instinct, and results in a dog that is able to follow the path of a person who is minutes or hours ahead of him. The training can be viewed as either good exercise or hard work, but watching your dog learn to use his incredible sense of smell in a beneficial way is both fascinating and fun. Nine and ten-year-old dogs have started this sport as beginners and earned titles. For more information contact AKC or AMBOR (see Appendix).

Dog Shows (Conformation)

The purpose of dog shows is to preserve the best qualities of the breeds. Every breed of dog has its own Standard of excellence. This Standard is a word picture of what constitutes a perfect specimen of that breed. Dogs competing in conformation are registered purebreds, and they are judged on how closely their physical attributes conform to the written Standard. The winner is the dog that, in the judge's opinion, of those competing that day, comes closest to the faultless animal described in the Standard.

Most dogs destined for the show ring are bred by dedicated breeders and sold as potential show prospects.

The vast majority are acquired as puppies or young adults, but in rare cases a mature show dog may be sold provided the new owner agrees in writing to show it. Don't sign any contracts or make any promises to show a dog until you attend a show or two as a spectator to see if the sport appeals to you. If it does, buy a show catalog and stay awhile. Watching the judging is the best way to learn ring procedure. While procedure may differ slightly under different judges, there will be more similarities than differences, and knowing what to expect will be mighty helpful the first time you compete.

You and your dog will need special training in preparation for conformation competition plus your dog will need grooming and conditioning. Check the yellow pages or newspaper for conformation classes (also called handling classes), or ask your veterinarian if he or she knows where show training is available. Spayed and neutered dogs, blind, deaf, or lame dogs, and male dogs which are missing one or both testicles are not eligible to compete in conformation. For complete show rules, including the point system by which dogs earn conformation championships, write to the American Kennel Club and the United Kennel Club. (see Appendix).

While show dogs in their prime competitive and breeding years are seldom sold as pets, retired show dogs sometimes become available because their owners may need room for the next generation and want to retire the older dog to a loving home. It's showing days may be over, but the benefits an ex-show dog gained from performing in the show ring linger forever, and make it an engaging companion. Crate-trained, super-socialized, a placid traveler, and a confident companion, a retired show dog is usually a pleasure to have as a pet. And if your Prince or Princess is a retired champion, you may want to learn a bit about dog shows and participate in a national Specialty. Your pet could strut his stuff in the Parade of Champions or even compete in the Veterans Class when he is old enough (even if he or she is neutered or spayed).

BREED-RELATED EVENTS

A variety of exciting events evaluate inherited and trained abilities and award titles to qualifying dogs. These activities are available to registered purebreds through the American Kennel Club (AKC) and some of them are available to non-registered purebreds and mixed-bred dogs through the American Mixed-Breed Obedience Registration (AMBOR).

Hunting Tests

If Prince is an AKC-registered dog of any breed in the Sporting Group, he is eligible to participate in non-competitive Hunting Tests. These tests evaluate a dog's ability to serve as a hunting companion by assessing its natural hunting instincts, as well as its training. Judging is based on how closely your dog's work meets an acceptable standard of performance.

Spaniels, retrievers, and pointing dogs each have their own type of Hunting Test to match their specific hunting style. The Test setting is as close to natural hunting conditions as possible, and Tests are offered at three levels of difficulty. Most of the handlers who enter their dogs at Hunting Tests are not competitive hunters. They simply enjoy outdoor sports and believe dogs should still be capable of performing the work for which they were originally bred. There are many Hunting Test clubs across the United States where you and Prince can learn the skills necessary to earn a Hunting Test title. To find one near you, contact the American Kennel Club (see Appendix).

Lure Coursing

Sighthounds were originally bred for coursing live game thousands of years ago. In fact, murals on 4,000-year-old Egyptian tombs show sleek hounds in full gallop chasing fleet-footed hares and antelopes. Today, the sport of lure coursing gives sighthounds an opportunity to participate in a humane sport that simulates their ancient purpose. Instead of chasing live game, the hounds dash after a mechanical lure with flapping white plastic bags as surrogate prey. The lure is created by running a string through a set of pulleys, and laid out so the bags seem to run away and make turns with an action similar to live game. Exhilarating to the eye and great fun for the hounds, lure coursing is gaining popularity yearly.

If Prince is a registered sighthound (a hound bred to hunt wild game by sight and speed), he's eligible for lure coursing tests and trials. Breeds participating in lure coursing include Afghan Hounds, Basenjis, Borzois, Greyhounds, Ibizan Hounds, Irish Wolfhounds, Pharaoh Hounds, Rhodesian Ridgebacks, Salukis, Scottish Deerhounds, and Whippets.

Tally ho! Lure coursing is exciting for sighthounds and their owners.

If Prince was formerly a racing Greyhound, he will be registered with the National Greyhound Association (NGA) instead of the AKC, but will still be eligible for coursing events. Sometimes the owner of a retired racer can't get the dog's NGA volume and certificate number. If you have that problem, contact AKC and request an application for an Indefinite Listing Privilege (ILP) number. Fill out the form as directed, return it with the required fee and requested photos, and in a few weeks your dog will have an ILP number and be eligible for coursing competition.

Coursing events are held under the rules of the American Kennel Club (AKC) or the American Sighthound Field Association (ASFA).

Herding

AKC's herding program develops and preserves the skills instinctive to the traditional herding breeds, and gives modern dogs an opportunity to perform the work their ancestors were originally bred for. Tests and trials at a variety of levels evaluate a dog's basic instinct and trainability. Eligible AKC recognized breeds include the Australian Cattle Dog, Bearded Collie, Belgian Malinois, Belgian Sheepdog, Belgian Tervuren, Border Collie, Bouvier des Flandres, Briard, Collie, German Shepherd Dog, Old English Sheepdog, Puli, Samoyed, Shetland Sheepdog, Cardigan Welsh Corgi, and Pembroke Welsh Corgi.

Only a few of the handlers at AKC herding events actually use their dogs to work livestock. The majority are people who love outdoor sports, enjoy dog training, and love watching their dogs' incredible herding instincts in action. Tests and trials are offered at six levels of difficulty, from beginner to extremely advanced. Contact AKC for additional information and a list of herding clubs (see Appendix).

Earthdog Events

The small terrier breeds and all varieties of Dachshunds were originally bred to hunt and kill vermin. In fact, the word "terrier," comes from the Latin "terra," which means "earth" or "ground," and terriers earned their name by digging into the ground after their prey. Their job was to keep homes and farms free of mice, rats, foxes, and other pests that contaminate grain or kill poultry.

Today these dogs are cherished mainly as companions, but AKC's Earthdog Tests give them a chance to prove they still have the instincts of old. If Prince is an AKC-registered Dachshund, Australian Terrier, Bedlington Terrier, Border Terrier, Cairn Terrier, Dandie Dinmont Terrier, Smooth or Wire Fox Terrier, Lakeland Terrier, Manchester Terrier, Norfolk Terrier, Norwich Terrier, Scottish Terrier, Sealyham Terrier, Skye Terrier, Welsh Terrier, or West Highland White Terrier, then he is eligible to participate.

At Earthdog tests, dogs enter a tunnel, find their quarry (securely caged laboratory rats), and work the quarry by barking, digging, growling, lunging, or any other action indicating their eagerness to finish off their prey. Don't worry, they never do! The rats are safe and the dogs relish the test. Four levels of non-competitive tests are offered. For more information and a list of Earthdog Clubs, contact the American Kennel Club (see Appendix).

MAKING THE FUN LAST FOREVER

Make fun and games part of your lifestyle with Prince whether or not you participate in organized events. Your dog will always be young at heart and will keep you that way, if you let him. Remember the basics of daily care and use your dog's training during everyday living, and life with Prince will always be charming.

Author's note:

You just read the "real" ending of this book. I hope you use the preceding chapters to find your own Prince or Princess and that you will have many wonderful years together. Yes, there is one more chapter, but I hope you never need to read it. It deals with finding a good home for Prince if you ever have to let him go.

PART THREE

LOVE TO
SPARE

Companion dogs, like this faithful Pug, are sensitive and compassionate when their owners have problems. Keep your friend if you can, but if you can't, place her in a secure home.

Photo credit: Pets by Paulette.

CHAPTER TEN

WHEN YOU HAVE TO LET GO

Acquiring a dog with the attitude that you'll get rid of it if it doesn't work out is like contemplating divorce while sending out the wedding invitations. Reasonable people know adjustments have to be made on both sides, and they feel good about cementing a strong relationship. So why include a chapter on letting go? Because lives change. Because not every match is made in heaven. Because taking action is better than living a lie or wallowing in guilt.

TRANSITIONS

Psychologists not only believe that pets are good for people, but that they can be buffers against stress and depression. Although the purpose of this chapter is to help you find a good home for Prince if you can no longer keep him, please think long and hard before giving him up. Getting rid of your dog to simplify a life suddenly thrown into turmoil could backfire, as missing the dog's comforting company may only make you feel worse. Dr. Mary Burch of Tallahassee, Florida, a Certified Behavior Analyst and behavior researcher, explains:

"In the course of our lives, there are times when our status as family members or companions may change. These changing times are referred to by psychologists and counselors as 'transition periods.'

"Significant transitions occur when a loved one dies, when there is a divorce, when a relationship is terminated, or during a major lifestyle change. Changes in lifestyle can result from job transfers or loss of a job, selling the family home, moving into a new family situation such as remarriage, or moving into a retirement community or home.

"The logistics of keeping a dog during a difficult transition proves too complicated for some dog owners. In an attempt to simplify things or put everything from the past behind them, they find new homes for their pets. In times when they are grief- stricken or upset, many people feel the practical details of keeping a dog in a new life situation are just too hard to work out. Yet, keeping their dog would make them feel better in the long run. Transitions are high stress times for most people and medical evidence shows that having a dog to stroke reduces stress and lowers blood pressure.

"Giving up a dog that has been a devoted, beloved companion may be the worst thing you can do for your mental health, besides being a bad thing to do to the dog. In the case of a death of a loved one, depression may occur after the initial grieving period is over. Dogs can alleviate depression by evoking pleasant memories of happy times. And something as simple as keeping up your daily dog routine reminds you, even when you are depressed, that life goes on.

"In the case of a divorce or relationship change, having a dog means there is a friend in your life giving you unconditional love. Dogs need us, and at a time when we feel alone in the world, unloved, or unwanted, being needed fills an important emotional role."

This chapter will help you find a home for Prince if you must, but if you have always enjoyed his company, do yourself a favor. Slow down and think twice before denying yourself the comfort of keeping your dog.

WHEN THE DREAM IS IMPOSSIBLE

Does Prince make you smile? Help you relax? Add new dimensions to your outings? Or, does Prince frustrate you? Make you tense? Disappoint you almost daily?

No matter how hard we try to make a good match, sometimes mismatches occur. Assuming you honestly tried to do right by Prince— used a crate, gave him attention, took him to obedience school, had him checked by the veterinarian to make sure his problems weren't rooted in something physical—and his responses are still disagreeable, he probably isn't the right dog for you. Letting a dog go is painful. Even if the love was lost long ago, giving up still feels like failure. But, if you've tried everything, what's the alternative? Is it ignoring your

CORRECTING A MISMATCH

Service dog agencies, such as those that pair blind people with guide dogs, habitually create great relationships. But even partnerships hand-picked by professionals can go wrong occasionally. That's what happened to Ed Eames and his guide dog Jake. As Ed tells it:

"From the time I began my partnership with Jake, he became somewhat distracted in the presence of dogs and cats while guiding me. He pulled so hard in harness, I frequently felt off-balance and uncomfortable. Unlike most Golden Retrievers, he did not enjoy being groomed, and daily obedience training sessions were a chore. And unlike most guide dogs, he resisted having his harness put on."

Toni and Ed Eames, with guide dogs, Escort and Jake.

In spite of these problems, Jake had redeeming qualities and Ed wanted to make the relationship work. During this period, Brad Scott, the Director of Training at Michigan-based Leader Dogs for the Blind, visited Ed in California and tried to salvage Ed and Jake as a team. But Jake was breaking down. Noises such as the slamming of a car door or sirens made him pull even harder in his harness, and when he was extremely nervous he forgot his role as a guide altogether. Unwilling to call it quits, Ed continued working with Jake for eight more months, until he totally lost confidence in him as a guide. Then he accepted Scott's offer of a different dog. Scott wrote about the situation for the Leader Dog newsletter. This is an excerpt:

"We tried both positive reinforcement and negative reinforcement blended with multiple doses of psychology. We encouraged, coaxed, praised, and generally tried to out-think the dog—he just wouldn't budge. He simply refused to cooperate.

"The handler and I have recently reached the conclusion that the dog should be retired from the work. Although the dog adjusted well to the new home, the park schedule, and was generally a pleasure to be around, when in harness he was inconsistent and therefore unreliable.

"The graduate's first reaction was to blame himself and to comment that he felt frustrated because he couldn't correct the problem. He questioned whether he had done enough. Subjectively he felt like he had failed; objectively, he realized he had done everything possible. The scales tip when you realize the enormous emotional investment that both undertook when the relationship began.

"It's difficult to know when it's not going to work and find the strength to move on. But the reality is that sometimes it doesn't work. Training a dog to lead a blind person is not a perfected science. Due to the fact that half of the equation is a living, breathing, thinking, feeling, emotional four-legged furry ball of potential—there may be some facets of the dog's personality that won't surface until confronted with the real world . . ."

Ed says he grieved at the thought of breaking the bond but everything worked out for the best. The Eames' friend adopted Jake and often takes the well-mannered dog to work with her. She has a big yard and a Lhasa Apso, so Jake has plenty of space and a new friend.

"With the arrival of my new guide dog Echo, my emotions shifted from sadness to anticipation," Ed said. "Echo promises to be an outstanding guide and Jake has made a wonderful adjustment to his new lifestyle."

dog the same way you overlook the ill-fitting suit in the back of your closet? Your dog (if it isn't people-aggressive) deserves better than that and so do you. Both of you deserve the opportunity to make a good match. When there is no love left, and banishment to the backyard seems imminent, finding Prince another home is probably best for you both. Prince may be an entirely different dog when living in different circumstances. Or he may be exactly the same dog, which may be exactly the dog someone else is looking for.

If Prince isn't the right dog for you and you know it, all the problems in your relationship will come to a head one day and you'll want him out of your life immediately. Instead, start now, so you don't make the move in haste. Use the suggestions in this chapter to match Prince up with a new owner and prepare him to recycle successfully. Then take your time and try again, this time armed with your "My Kind of Dog List," that great crate, and all the ammo you need to break through the period of adjustment. The right dog is worth the effort. Believe it!

RIP RATES A FAMILY OF HIS OWN

Stan Lieberman of Rapid City, South Dakota, has been training retrievers, judging field trials, and running trials for over forty years. Five years ago he was planning to retire Rip, his eight-year-old black Labrador Retriever, from running trials. He had a new field trial prospect on hand and limited kennel space, but he wanted to make sure Rip got a good home. A mutual friend told him about a twelve-year-old boy named Thad Johnson who would love to have Rip, and the transfer was made.

Thad and his family enjoyed Rip for five years before the dog died at the age of thirteen. By then Thad was seventeen, and Stan received this letter from him:

"I'm writing to tell you that after five years Rip has passed on. I can't tell you what a great dog he was, he really was one of a kind. I want you to know how much I appreciate you giving him to me. Last year he was still hunting, he was a little slower but you could tell there was nothing he would rather be doing. He was our house dog and he loved being with everyone. I can't thank you enough for letting us have him. He was an all-around great dog."

Stan says he feels doubly fortunate. First he had a terrific dog like Rip, then he was able to share him with a wonderful family.

GIVING THE GIFT OF TIME

Dogs are social animals, so they are happiest when they get lots of attention from their special humans. Of course there are times in every dog owner's life when they are unable to give their dog enough attention, and since most dogs learned Guilt 101 at their mother's breast, they repay the lapse with wounded expressions that silently plead, "Why don't you love me anymore?" But dogs are incredibly forgiving, and when things get back to normal the relationship is as strong as ever.

But sometimes things never get back to normal. Sometimes the nicest thing you can do for your dog is place it in another home, one where it gets plenty of individual attention.

SHOW DOG AND FIELD TRIAL KENNELS

If you breed show or field dogs, you may have a retired brood bitch. In her heyday, Princess was your pride and joy. Maybe she finished her championship at the National Specialty and became the dam of several successful show dogs. Or she might have won her breed's national field trial and produced pups that grew up to be field champions. Now she's six years old and two of her champion daughters have replaced her in your breeding program. There are new puppies to socialize and young dogs to train. You still love Princess dearly, but now the love is tinged with guilt because you never find enough time for her. She gets good food and responsible medical care in your kennel, but she's a charity case when it comes to affection. Her melancholy expression when you leave for a dog show or field trial without her haunts you on the highway. You keep telling yourself you'll give Princess some quality time tomorrow, but the most tomorrow brings is a quick hug and the promise of a private hour for just the two of you, well, maybe tomorrow. Now, too many tomorrows later, you believe Princess deserves better than you will ever have time to give her. She deserves to be someone's cherished companion, not a has-been waiting for a handout of your precious time. It was hard to face the fact that Princess might be better off with someone else, but now that you've admitted it to yourself, what's next?

MAKING SURE YOUR DOG WILL RECYCLE SUCCESSFULLY

You want Princess to have a home where she will be treated like royalty for the rest of her life, so making her as pleasant to live with as possible is the first step. As a former show or field dog, she was probably crate-trained, but how long has she been living in a kennel situation? Don't offer Princess to a home straight from the kennel. Instead, bring her inside your home for a few weeks first, and make sure she is still crate-trained and has a good start on housebreaking. While she adjusts to living in your home, walk her on lead for exercise instead of putting her in a run or yard. The daily walks will serve two purposes. They will get her accustomed to going potty during a walk like most pet dogs do, and they will resocialize her if it has been a long time since she was out and about. If Princess forgot her manners on lead, or shies away from friendly people, work on these problems before placing her. Her new owners may mean well, but you are the dog expert. Help Princess over the rough spots so her transition from kennel to home will be smooth and successful.

Before sending Princess off on her second start, give her the gift of a complete veterinary examination. Be sure all her vaccinations are current and she is free of all internal and external parasites and on a heartworm prevention program. Then turn her health record over to her new owner.

Upon her retirement from breeding, Princess should be spayed. It's just good preventative medicine. A spay is a simple operation that removes a female dog's reproductive organs. Besides preventing unwanted pregnancies, spaying prevents the heat cycle that arrives for three weeks twice a year, complete with bloody spots on the carpet and stray dogs howling at the door. Spaying also prevents cancers and other infections of the ovaries or uterus.

The last thing you want is for someone to decide your aging Princess should "earn her keep" by having a litter or two. The only absolutely foolproof way to prevent that possibility is by having her spayed before you offer her for sale or adoption. Some kennels write a spay clause into their adoption contract, stipulating that the new owners will have Princess spayed within a certain period of time. While usually effective, the contract may be difficult to enforce if the owners move away and leave no forwarding address. Another viable method is holding the registration papers until the new owners provide proof that they had Princess spayed. While this works in most cases, some owners aren't concerned about obtaining registration papers.

When David and Kimberly Richards of Pheasant Run Kennels decided to breed English Springer Spaniels exclusively, they had to find a home for River Road Helga, a sweet, six-year-old Labrador Retriever. It was hard for Kimberly to give away her "Big Yellow Girl," but the adoptive family enjoyed her so much that it eased her pain.

River Road Helga used to be one of several dogs at a fine breeding kennel. Today she's Marco's best buddy and has a whole human family all to herself.

The transition was surprisingly easy for Helga. Instead of sharing with other dogs, she was suddenly the only dog in the family of Mark, Miriam, and Marco Ondrusek. Helga loved having her family all to herself, and even though she wasn't raised around children, she became especially attached to Marco, the Ondrusek's adopted son from South America. And what does Marco think about being shadowed by Helga? "She's my best friend," he grins.

In the final analysis, if you want to make sure a bitch is spayed, have it done yourself. Neither contracts nor promises prevent accidental pregnancies 100 percent of the time, and they may not stop a new owner from intentionally breeding Princess and selling the puppies as purebreds without registration papers. Besides, the type of owner you want for Princess will prefer a spayed female or a neutered male.

If the dog you want to put into blissful retirement is a male, especially a male you used as a stud dog, he should be neutered before he becomes someone's pet. This is for his sake, as well as the new owners, and is also good preventative medicine. Neutered males have less incidence of certain cancers than intact males, and usually have longer attention spans and more stable dispositions. In addition, neutered males don't suffer from frustration every time they catch the scent of a female in season, are less likely to urinate on household furnishings to mark their territory, become aggressive around other dogs, or feel the urge to roam. In short, neutered dogs are happier, healthier, and easier to live with than frustrated wannabe studs.

SEARCHING FOR SUPEROWNER

After your dog is spayed or neutered, had its physical, and brushed up on its manners, its time to start searching for superowner. Where can you find a fabulous family or a super single who just happens to want a dog? And how will you know if they are the right people for your Prince or Princess?

Contact the Breeder

If Prince was purchased from a breeder, contact that person first when you have to place him. Many dedicated breeders accept their "puppies" back no matter how old they are, or may have a waiting list of families looking for a nice adult dog.

Finding a 4-H Family

If Prince adores young people, your local 4-H club is a good place to start searching for superowner. The children and teenagers who participate in 4-H dog projects learn daily dog care and the fundamentals of training, and soon become responsible dog owners and effective trainers. In addition, some projects offer a variety of activities, such as Obedience, Junior Showmanship, Agility, and the Canine Good Citizen program. Parents of 4-H kids are generally both proud and supportive, so a home with a 4-H family may be an ideal placement for Prince. Most 4-H dog project members already have a dog, but sometimes a child's dog dies due to age or illness and the parents don't want to start over with a puppy. The offer of a mature, settled dog might just save the day.

To locate your local Dog Project Leader, call your state Extension Service or simply 4-H. One or the other is listed under County Government Agencies in most phone books. The Extension Service can put you in touch with the 4-H Dog Project Leader, if there is one in your area. Tell the Leader all about Prince—his breed, age, health record, training or lack of training, and his idiosyncrasies. Depending

4-H youngsters do marvelous things with their dogs. This is Darcy Peterson of Opheim, Illinois and her Papillio, Peppy. Darcy is wearing her 4-H shirt and giving pet therapy at a nursing home. She has trained Peppy to a CDX title in Obedience.

on age, strength, and years of experience with dogs, some children need a dog that is extremely easy to handle, while others need an exceptionally active dog to keep their interest high. If the 4-H Leader knows of a child in need of a dog like Prince, he or she can put you in contact with each other. No matter how much you want to make this match, meet the family and ask all the right questions (which appear later in this chapter) before sending Prince off on his second start.

Networking

Networking works best when searching for superowner. To begin networking, always tell your veterinarian that Prince is available, and don't forget to mention it to the receptionist and staff. No one knows more about who takes good care of their dog, and who needs a dog, than the people at your veterinary hospital. Also, tell your relatives and friends that you're willing to place Prince in a good home, and let those people pass the word if they happen to hear of a nice family looking for a dog. That's how Dave and Kimberly Richard of Pheasant Run Kennels do it.

Kimberly explains, "We are emotionally attached to all our dogs so it's difficult to place one of our family in a new home. We are very particular and cautious in this process and never advertise a dog as 'free to a good home' or sell it at a significantly reduced price. Instead, we network through our friends and relatives for potential adoptive families. Our standards are high and we interview the entire family, usually twice, and visit the future home to verify the living conditions. Once we are convinced and in total agreement, we give the new family time to make preparations for a smooth and pleasant transition— not only for them, but for the dog. Meanwhile, we prepare a contract between both parties stipulating the conditions necessary for this transaction. The contract is notarized after it's signed, and each party gets a copy. Thus, the dog is adopted, not purchased. Although every item in the contract is important, I consider item number three paramount. Simply put, it says the dog must be returned to us if the adoptive family no longer wants it."

Sample Contract

On the following page is a sample contract, similar to one used by Pheasant Run Kennels. Notice that it's personalized to reflect the dog and the situation, and stipulates that the dog must be spayed. If you use it as a model, make any changes necessary to fit your dog and situation.

Advertising

Whether you want to sell your dog or give it away, be cautious if you decide to advertise in the classified section of your local newspaper. It's especially important that your dog be spayed or neutered before your ad appears. In fact, make that part of your ad. Many unscrupulous people, pretending they want a pet, purchase registered purebreds cheap through newspaper ads and use them for breeding, over and over again. The dogs are treated as disposable property and live in tiny, filthy cages without love, attention, exercise, or medical care. Honest breeders call these horrid facilities "puppy mills," and try very hard to make sure no puppy they produce ever ends up in one. Spaying or neutering your dog guarantees it will never be purchased or "adopted" by the owner of a puppy mill. Other pretenders may also know all the "right" answers to your screening questions, but actually collect cheap or free dogs and sell them to a laboratory for experimentation purposes. This practice isn't as prevalent as in the past, because today many of the major labs raise their own stock, but it still occurs often enough that you should be aware of it.

May 10, 1997
Article of agreement between:
KEN L. KAIR
and I. M. AND EMMA GUDHOLME

The Gudholmes will take possession of one white female Miniature Poodle named "Snow City Sue," (tattoo number or microchip number, and rabies tag number and state) at no financial charge, but under the following conditions:

1. Sue will not be bred at any time in the future.

2. Sue will be spayed as soon as recommended by the Gudholme's veterinarian.

3. At any time in the future, if the Gudholmes decide they do not wish to keep Sue, she must be returned to Ken L. Kair, at no charge to him. At no time will the dog be sold or given to a third party not mentioned in this agreement.

4. Sue's AKC registration papers will be assigned to the Gudholmes upon submission of her spay verification.

5. It is agreed that Sue will be a house pet, although she may spend a portion of her day in a securely fenced yard. She will be fed and exercised daily, professionally groomed on a regular schedule, and always handled with affection and understanding.

WE, THE UNDERSIGNED, AGREE ON THE ABOVE CONDITIONS:

_____

I. M. Gudholme   Ken L. Kair
_____

Emma Gudholme
Address_____
_____
Phone_____
NOTARY:_____
TERM EXPIRES:_____

Saucy, a loving long-coated Chihuahua, spent her first three years in a puppy mill but was lucky enough not to produce puppies, so the facility sold her. Now she belongs to Liz Moore of Newman Lake, Washington. For Saucy, it was quite a transition. Instead of living in a tiny wire pen with a dishrag bed, she goes everywhere with Liz and has her own spot under the covers.

Animal Shelters

Because there is never enough space to accommodate all the unwanted dogs, most shelters have to euthanize dogs a week or two after they arrive in order to make room for the constant influx of new ones. However, there are no-kill shelters in many communities, so if you must get rid of Prince so fast you don't have time to network, call every shelter or humane organization in your area (and surrounding cities if need be) until you find a no-kill facility that has room for him. If Prince is a purebred and you must get rid of him right away, see "Emergency Placement" later in this chapter.

ASKING QUESTIONS THAT COUNT

No matter where you search for superowner, your initial contact will probably be by telephone. After the introductions, work some of these questions into your conversation. They will help you learn about the prospective owner's attitude toward dogs in general, and Prince's breed in particular:

1. Have you ever had a dog(s) before? How many? What happened to it (them)? Who is your veterinarian?

    People who have had a dog before know what they are getting into. But beware if they appear to have had too many dogs in a relatively short period of time. Did the dogs get run over because this person's idea of exercising a dog is opening the door and allowing it to roam? Did the dogs die of diseases that should have been prevented through annual vaccinations? Do the prospective owners know their veterinarian's name? If not, and they had a dog recently, doesn't that strike you as odd?

    If Prince's potential new owners never had a dog before, that certainly shouldn't disqualify them. After all, didn't you prepare Prince for life as a house dog? He may be the best thing that could possibly happen to a novice dog owner, and the new owner may be thoroughly captivated by him.

2. Why do you want a dog of Prince's breed? Is there something you especially like about the breed? Will Prince have a special

job? If so, what will it be? Have you ever had a Rottweiler (or whatever breed Prince is) before? What did you and that dog enjoy doing together? What other pets do you have now?

These questions will help you decide if the prospective owner wants a dog like Prince for the right reasons, and if their concept of his canine career is humane and compatible with his abilities. Look for people who like Prince's personality traits, not just his looks. For example, if Prince is a Poodle, and someone says they want him because they fell in love with the Poodle they saw on a televised dog show, they should be told that few pet Poodles have show coats because maintaining such a coat demands skill and a major investment of time. Or, if Prince is a Rottweiler, and someone says they like the breed because it's tough enough to stop the scum that steals from their junkyard, look further for a new owner. If Prince is starting to slow down, and the prospective owner wants to train him for Agility competition, the match already has a strike against it. But if Prince loves to hunt, and the prospective owner is a hunter, this match may have a lot going for it.

If the person had a dog of Prince's breed before, that's good. If they have trouble remembering what activities they enjoyed with their dog (cuddling and petting counts as an activity), that's bad, and sad.

If the family has other pets, let them know how Prince will probably react to them. If he chases cats, hunts rabbits, or goes berserk at the sight of a bird, tell them. That doesn't mean the adoption is off, but it does mean that adjustments will have to be made at first or the consequences could be tragic.

3. Where will you keep Prince during the day? Where will he sleep at night? How many hours a day will he usually be home alone?

Chained to a tree, or confined to the yard twenty-four hours a day, is not the royal retirement you want for your Prince. But there's nothing wrong with putting him outside for part of the day provided he has a fenced yard, shade, water, and shelter. If Prince stays in the house (or his crate) all day,

will someone be home at reasonable intervals to take him outside to relieve himself? Who gets home first, the children or
the parents? If it's the kids, are they mature enough to handle
Prince and can they be counted on to take him for a walk right
away—before heading for the telephone, television, computer, or
refrigerator?

4. Do you have children? How old are they? Do they want a dog?
What kind of dog do they want? Who will be responsible for
Prince's daily care?

If Prince loves children, then a family with kids could be ideal.
But sometimes kids are at odds with their parents or with each
other about what kind of dog to get. If Bobby wants a Boxer and
Kathy wants a Dachshund and the family adopts a Dachshund,
it's possible that Bobby will never learn to like the dog and might
even take out his frustration on it. Children don't hide their con-
tempt well, so if there's a problem you will see it when the entire
family comes to meet Prince.

Some parents believe that having a dog will teach their children
responsibility. If you hear that the children will be in charge of
Prince's daily care, educate the parents. They need to know that
most children can't wait to do dog chores when the dog is new,
but begin making excuses in just a few weeks. There are exceptions, of course. Kids who belong to 4-H, for example, are often
more responsible and knowledgeable about animal husbandry
than their parents are. But no matter how dedicated the child, a
family should get a dog only if one parent is willing to assume
overall responsibility. Certainly dog chores can be shared, but if
an adult fails to act as overseer, it's often the dog that suffers.
And while you're on the subject, tell the family how important it
is that Prince be allowed to relieve himself on schedule. If they
forget when he needs to be walked, he'll soon forget about being
housebroken.

5. Have you ever trained a dog? Would you be willing to learn
training skills by attending obedience classes? Do you have a
fenced yard? How do you plan to housebreak Prince (or maintain his good house manners)? If Prince made a mistake by

going potty in the house, what would you do? How will Prince get his exercise, and where will he be expected to go potty?

Successfully training a previous dog or planning to attend obedience classes are real plusses. So is having a fenced yard. Use the other questions to make sure the prospective owners understand the basics of crate training and how it aids housebreaking. These questions also give you an opportunity to discuss the importance of schedules and make sure the prospective owners won't overreact to a mistake or use cruel or unsuitable methods of correction.

6. Who will do major grooming, such as bathing and clipping (if applicable)?

Does Prince need to be professionally groomed every six weeks or so? The prospective owners need to know that. This question can also lead into a discussion of coat care. If Prince is a profusely-coated dog, explain the importance of combing or brushing him thoroughly from the skin out. This isn't child's play, but 4-H trained kids may handle it beautifully.

Besides these general questions, add your own breed-specific ones. For example, if Prince is a breed that needs more exercise than most, or can't handle much heat, or might drown in a swimming pool, use questions to start a discussion that educates potential owners about his idiosyncrasies.

MEETING IN PERSON

If the conversation goes well, and you believe the person or family may be just what you wanted for Prince, invite them over to meet him.

One negative family member can sabotage a successful adoption, so when placing Prince, make sure every member of the new family meets him and likes him. At the same time, watch Prince's reaction to them. Chemistry counts in successful matchmaking. If your instincts say something is wrong, believe them, and look for a different placement for Prince. You may want to visit the prospective owner's home before placing Prince. If it will reassure you, do it. And if you are the type of person who has a hard time saying "No," keep everything tentative, from the phone interview to the visits.

EMERGENCY PLACEMENT

Maybe you wish you could network and hand-pick Prince's new home, but if placing him is an emergency and time's running out you may not have such a luxury. Is there anyone who cares enough to network for you and locate the kind of home Prince deserves? Yes, there is.

BREED RESCUE

If Prince is a purebred, there is probably a rescue organization set up for his breed. The American Kennel Club (see Appendix) will tell you how to locate your breed's national rescue headquarters, where you will be put in touch with the rescue volunteer closest to you. If an emergency such as death in the family, serious illness, divorce, sudden move, or severe financial setback makes it impossible for you to keep Prince, breed rescue will help you. Its purpose is to give good guys like your Prince a second start when they need one. Prince is a good guy, isn't he? Rescue volunteers won't foster or place dogs that are aggressive toward people. They also won't place pets suffering from a terminal illness, or find homes for puppies when an irresponsible owner is stuck with an unsold litter.

What breed rescue will do is give Prince foster care in a family home; evaluate his temperament around adults, children, and other pets; make sure he is socialized, crate-trained, and housebroken; and assess his activity level, previous training, trainability, and instinctive abilities. That helps them find the right owner for him and make a successful match. But there's more. Breed rescue will have your dog spayed or neutered and allow sufficient recovery time before making a placement. Then, after Prince is placed in a permanent home, the new owners will be encouraged to ask the foster care-giver for advice whenever they have a question or a problem. And if for any reason they cannot keep Prince, he will be returned to breed rescue and the process of placing him will begin again.

How can you help the rescue volunteer find a suitable home for your dog? Help by having Prince or Princess neutered or spayed before turning him/her over to breed rescue. Or, if there isn't time, help defray the expenses if you are financially capable of paying for the minor surgery. Help by having Prince checked for parasites, making sure his vaccinations up to date, and giving his health record to the rescue volunteer. Help by telling the rescuer everything you can think of concerning Prince's personality and health. Does he like adults and children of all ages? Does he try to chase cats? Does he get along with other dogs? Does he get scared and nervous when you leave him alone in the house? Is he trained to obey some simple commands? Does he eat prescription dog food or take daily medication? Can he do a trick or two? Knowing everything about Prince, the good and the bad, will help the volunteer find Prince what he needs most in your absence— a permanent person of his own.

BREAKING THE TIE THAT BINDS

Send Prince off to his new owners with his health records, favorite toys, and enough of his regular brand of dog food for the first few days. If you aren't planning on getting another dog, you might want to make them an offer on the crate, grooming equipment, lead, and collar. Prince will adjust to new surroundings more quickly if a few familiar objects go with him. Give the new owners a written copy of his daily routine, including his feeding, exercise, potty, and grooming schedule. It will come in handy even though they will probably change the hours to suit their lifestyle.

Letting Go Graciously

Chances are you'll miss Prince after he moves into his new home and wish you could visit him. Resist the temptation, at least for the first few months. Prince may miss you terribly at first, and seeing you even briefly before he has adjusted to his new family could set back the bonding process and make the transition tougher for him. Instead, help Prince and his new family adjust to each other by being supportive to the new owners. Let them know they are welcome to call you if they have any questions, and just in case they are shy about bothering you, give them a call to find out how everything is going after Prince has lived with them for a couple of weeks.

JAKE SPREADS JOY

Dave Wedum, a Golden Retriever breeder and obedience trainer from Whitefish, Montana, agreed to board a Golden Retriever until a fellow's divorce was settled. The man never returned. When it was clear that gentle Jake no longer had an owner, Dave had him neutered, trained him, and tried to find him a new home since he already had a houseful of dogs.

Dave Wedum trained Jake and would have kept him, but giving all his Golden Retrievers enough attention was already a challenge. So he presented Jake to a nearby nursing home, making Jake the only dog for all the loving his new family had to give.

One day the administrator of a nearby nursing home called. She knew a friendly dog would boost morale among the residents, and wanted to purchase one of Dave's Golden Retriever puppies to live at the facility. Dave said a well-mannered adult dog would be more suitable and offered to donate Jake. The administrator accepted.

Jake fit in immediately. He learned which residents eagerly await his daily visits and distributes his love without letting any of them down. His house manners are impeccable and he understands that the kitchen and dining rooms are off limits. "He's a wonderful dog and a real diplomat," according to the administrator.

The day you hear Prince has adjusted beautifully and behaves as if he had lived with his new owners forever may be one of mixed emotions for you. Let happiness win out. Perhaps one day the timing will be right for you to have another dog. In the meantime, you deserve a pat on the back. You made such a fine dog out of Prince that he adjusted well and brought joy to others when you couldn't keep him any longer.

APPENDIX

ORGANIZATIONS

American Kennel Club (AKC)

51 Madison Ave.
New York, NY 10010
and
5580 Centerview Dr., Suite 200
Raleigh, NC 27606
(919) 233-9780
World Wide Web Home Page: http://www.akc.org/akc/
E-Mail address: info@akc.org

Free information and rule books available on dog shows, Junior Showmanship, Obedience, Canine Good Citizen, Tracking, Agility, Lure Coursing, Hunting Tests, Earthdog Tests, Herding, Beagle Field Trials, Basset Hound Field Trials, and Coonhound events. Also available are geographical lists of dog shows and Obedience clubs, geographical lists of hunting test and field trial clubs, and Canine Good Citizen information packets.

Use the North Carolina address to request written material. For information on purebred rescue organizations by breed, call *AKC Gazette* at (212) 696-8321.

United Kennel Club (UKC)

100 East Kilgore Rd.
Kalamazoo, MI 49001
(616) 343-9020

Information on dog shows, Junior Showmanship, Obedience, Agility, Hunting Retriever program, and Coonhound events. Mixed-bred dogs may compete in obedience and Agility through affiliations with AMBOR (American Mixed Breed Obedience Registry).

American Mixed Breed Obedience Registry (AMBOR)

205 1st St. S.W.
New Prague, MN 56071
(612) 758-4598

Information on Obedience, Tracking, Junior Showmanship, Agility, Canine Good Citizen, Carting, Herding Instinct, Frisbee, Versatility, Water Trials, and Rescue.

4-H

National 4-H Council
7100 Connecticut Ave.
Chevy Chase, MD 20815-4999

To locate clubs in your area, call your state Extension Service, listed under "County Government Offices" in your phone book.

ACTIVITIES

Canine Good Citizen Program (CGC)

For written material, contact AKC.

Questions answered by:
Dr. Mary Burch, AKC Field Representative for the CGC Program
(904) 877-2901

Obedience

For written material, contact AKC, UKC, and AMBOR.

Write to the Superintendents (later in this Appendix) to get on their mailing lists.

Animal-Assisted Therapy Volunteers

Delta Society
Pet Partners Program
P.O. Box 1080
Renton, WA 98057
(206) 226-7357

Therapy Dogs International
6 Hilltop Rd.
Mendham, NJ 07945
(908) 429-0670

Therapy Dogs Incorporated
P.O. Box 2786
Cheyenne, WY 82003
(307) 638-3223

Agility

United States Dog Agility Association (USDAA)
P.O. Box 850955
Richardson, TX 75085-0955
(214) 231-9700

National Club of Dog Agility (NCDA)
401 Bluemont Circle,
Manhattan, KS 66502
(913) 537-7022

For written material, contact AKC, UKC, and AMBOR.

Tracking

For written material, contact AKC and AMBOR.

Dog Showing

For written material, contact AKC and UKC.

Write to the Superintendents (later in this Appendix) to get on their mailing lists.

Hunting Tests

For written material, contact AKC and UKC.

North American Hunting Retriever Association (NAHRA)
P.O. Box 1590
Stafford, VA 22555

Lure Coursing

For written material, contact AKC.

To answer questions:
Dean Wright, AKC Coursing Field Director
(717) 637-3011 or (717) 632-6806

American Sighthound Field Association (ASFA)
Kathy Budney
1098 New Britain Ave.
Rocky Hill, CT 06067

Herding

For written material, contact AKC.

Earthdog Events

For written material, contact AKC.

American Working Terrier Association (AWTA)
Louise Thomas
2580 Town Line Rd.
Nunda, NY 14517

Information on Adopting a Racing Greyhound

Greyhound Pets of America
(31 chapters)
Gloria Sanders, President
800-FON 1 GPA

Calls will be forwarded to the nearest chapter.

Greyhound Rescue League of Tallahassee, Inc.
Dr. Cynda Crawford, Director
P.O. Box 13314
Tallahassee, FL 32317
(904) 878-1204

National Greyhound Adoption Program
David Wolfe
8301 Torresdale Ave.
Philadelphia, PA 19136
(800) 348-2517

National Greyhound Network
(415) 851-7812

Represents independent groups. Your call will be referred to the adoption
group nearest you.

Good Reading (and Places Where Good Breeders Advertise Their Dogs)

AKC Gazette—available on newsstands and by subscription
5580 Centerview Dr.
Raleigh, NC 27606

For information on purebred rescue, call (212) 696-8321.

Dog Fancy—available on newstands and by subscription
P.O. Box 6050
Mission Viejo, CA 92690

Dog World—available on newstands and by subscription
300 West Adams St.
Chicago, IL 60606

Gun Dog—available by subscription
P.O. Box 343
Mt. Morris, IL 61054-0343

The Pointing Dog Journal—available by subscription
P.O. Box 11395
Des Moines, IA 50340

The Retriever Journal—available by subscription
P.O. Box 11395
Des Moines, IA 50340

Spaniels in the Field—available by subscription
10714 Escondido Dr.
Cincinnati, Ohio 45247

AKC Hunting Test Herald—available by subscription
5580 Centerview Dr.
Raleigh, NC 27606

LICENSED SUPERINTENDENTS

When you're ready to enter Obedience Trials, Agility Trials, or dog shows, send a postcard with your name and address to any of the superintendents listed in the *AKC Gazette* and ask to be put on their mailing list to receive premium lists.